Manchester Medieval Sources Series

series advisers Rosemary Horrox and Simon M

This series aims to meet a growing need amongst students and teachers of medieval history for translations of key sources that are directly usable in students' own work. It provides texts central to medieval studies courses and focuses upon the diverse cultural and social as well as political conditions that affected the functioning of all levels of medieval society. The basic premise of the new series is that translations must be accompanied by sufficient introductory and explanatory material and each volume therefore includes a comprehensive guide to the sources' interpretation, including discussion of critical linguistic problems and an assessment of the most recent research on the topics being covered.

also available in the series

John H. Arnold and Pete Biller *Heresy and inquisition in France, 1200–1300*

Andrew Brown and Graeme Small *Court and civic society in the Burgundian Low Countries c. 1420–1520*

Martin Heale *Monasticism in late medieval England, c.1300–1535*

David Jones *Friars' Tales: Thirteenth-century exempla from the British Isles*

Graham Loud *Roger II and the making of the Kingdom of Sicily*

T.J.H. McCarthy *Chronicles of the Investiture Contest: Frutolf of Michelsberg and his continuators*

A.K. McHardy *The reign of Richard II*

Simon MacLean *History and politics in late Carolingian and Ottonian Europe: The Chronicle of Regino of Prüm and Adalbert of Magdeburg*

Anthony Musson and Edward Powell *Crime, law and society in the later middle ages*

Andrew Rabin *The political writings of Archbishop Wulfstan of York*

I. S. Robinson *Eleventh-century Germany: The Swabian Chronicles*

I. S. Robinson *The Annals of Lampert of Hersfeld*

Rachel Stone and Charles West *Hincmar of Rheims: On the divorce of King Lothar and Queen Theutberga*

Craig Taylor *Joan of Arc: La Pucelle*

Diana Webb *Saints and cities in medieval Italy*

HERMITS AND ANCHORITES IN ENGLAND, 1200–1550

Manchester University Press

Medieval Sources*online*

Complementing the printed editions of the Medieval Sources series, Manchester University Press has developed a web-based learning resource which is now available on a yearly subscription basis.

Medieval Sources*online* brings quality history source material to the desktops of students and teachers and allows them open and unrestricted access throughout the entire college or university campus. Designed to be fully integrated with academic courses, this is a one-stop answer for many medieval history students, academics and researchers keeping thousands of pages of source material 'in print' over the Internet for research and teaching.

titles available now at Medieval Sources*online include*

Trevor Dean *The towns of Italy in the later Middle Ages*

John Edwards *The Jews in Western Europe, 1400–1600*

Paul Fouracre and Richard A. Gerberding *Late Merovingian France: History and hagiography 640–720*

Chris Given-Wilson *Chronicles of the Revolution 1397–1400: The reign of Richard II*

P. J. P. Goldberg *Women in England, c. 1275–1525*

Janet Hamilton and Bernard Hamilton *Christian dualist heresies in the Byzantine world, c. 650–c. 1450*

Rosemary Horrox *The Black Death*

David Jones *Friars' Tales: Thirteenth-century exempla from the British Isles*

Graham A. Loud and Thomas Wiedemann *The history of the tyrants of Sicily by 'Hugo Falcandus', 1153–69*

A. K. McHardy *The reign of Richard II: From minority to tyranny 1377-97*

Simon MacLean *History and politics in late Carolingian and Ottonian Europe: The* Chronicle *of Regino of Prüm and Adalbert of Magdeburg*

Anthony Musson and Edward Powell *Crime, law and society in the later Middle Ages*

Janet L. Nelson *The Annals of St-Bertin: Ninth-century histories, volume I*

Timothy Reuter *The Annals of Fulda: Ninth-century histories, volume II*

R. N. Swanson *Catholic England: Faith, religion and observance before the Reformation*

Elisabeth van Houts *The Normans in Europe*

Jennifer Ward *Women of the English nobility and gentry 1066–1500*

HERMITS AND ANCHORITES IN ENGLAND, 1200-1550

selected sources translated and annotated

by E.A. Jones

Manchester University Press

Published by Manchester University Press
Altrincham Street, Manchester M1 7JA
www.manchesteruniversitypress.co.uk

British Library Cataloguing-in-Publication Data is available

ISBN 978 1 5261 2721 1 hardback
ISBN 978 1 5261 2723 5 paperback

First published 2019

Typeset by Servis Filmsetting Ltd, Stockport, Cheshire

CONTENTS

ABBREVIATIONS

Aelred, trans. Macpherson	Aelred of Rievaulx. 'Rule of Life for a Recluse.' Translated by Mary Paul Macpherson. In *Treatises and Pastoral Prayer*, edited by David Knowles, pp. 41–102. Kalamazoo: Cistercian Publications, 1971.
Ancrene Wisse, trans. Millett	Millett, Bella, trans. *Ancrene Wisse. A guide for anchoresses: a translation based on Cambridge, Corpus Christi College, MS 402.* Exeter: University of Exeter Press, 2009.
Cal. Pat. Rolls	*Calendar of Patent Rolls.* 53 vols. London: HMSO, 1891–1916.
Clay, *Hermits and Anchorites*	Rotha Mary Clay. *The Hermits and Anchorites of England.* London: Methuen & Co. Ltd, 1914.
Letters & Papers, Henry VIII	*Letters and Papers, Foreign and Domestic, of the Reign of Henry VIII: Preserved in the Public Record Office, the British Museum, and elsewhere in England*, edited by J.S. Brewer, James Gairdner, R.S. Brodie. 21 vols, London: HMSO, 1862–1932.
ODNB	*Oxford Dictionary of National Biography.* Online edition. Oxford University Press. www.oxforddnb.com.
OED	*Oxford English Dictionary Online.* Oxford University Press. www.oed.com.
PL	*Patrologia Latina cursus completus*, ed. J.-P. Migne, 221 vols. Paris, 1844–65.
TNA	The National Archives
Warren, *Anchorites and Their Patrons*	Ann K. Warren. *Anchorites and Their Patrons in Medieval England.* Berkeley: University of California Press, 1985.

INTRODUCTION

Solitude, or at least some form of significant separation from the rest of society, carries symbolic power – often with religious connotations – in most, if not all, cultures. But the particular forms that solitariness and withdrawal take vary from culture to culture, and are sensitive to changes in place and time.[1] This book is concerned with the principal forms of solitary religious life in England between the thirteenth and the sixteenth centuries: with anchorites, who lived a life of strict bodily enclosure in a 'cell', usually attached to a parish church; and hermits, whose vocation was less clearly defined and subject to fewer constraints. It represents the first comprehensive look at the two vocations in late medieval England in more than a century.[2]

The solitary lives in the West before 1200

Medieval solitaries could look to biblical models: Elijah, who made the lonely journey of forty days and forty nights to Mount Horeb, to hear God's voice not in the wind, earthquake or fire, but in a 'still small voice' (see 1 Kings 19); John the Baptist, the 'voice crying in the wilderness' (Matt. 3:3), who, clad in skins and surviving on locusts and wild honey, preached repentance and prophesied Christ's coming; or Jesus himself, who was led by the spirit into the desert there to be tempted by the devil before he embarked on his ministry (Matt. 4:1–11).

Even more than to the biblical examples, however, medieval solitaries turned for their inspiration to Egypt in the third and fourth centuries, and those Christians who retreated from the rich lands and populous villages of the Nile valley to the surrounding deserts, and who

1 Two wide-ranging and appealing introductions to the history of the solitary life in the Christian West are Peter F. Anson, *The Call of the Desert: The solitary life in the Christian church* (London: SPCK, 1964), and Isabel Colegate's *A Pelican in the Wilderness: Hermits, solitaries and recluses* (London: HarperCollins, 2002).

2 Its predecessor in this respect is Clay, *Hermits and Anchorites*.

are known collectively as the Desert Fathers.[3] (Modern scholarship has pointed out that there were Desert Mothers, too, but the Middle Ages do not emphasise the role of women in the early eremitic movement.) With the end of the persecutions of Diocletian and the outbreak of religious tolerance in the Roman Empire under Constantine (emperor 306–337), Christianity had lost its dangerous, 'edgy' status as a countercultural movement (it would become the official religion of the Empire in 380). Now that the martyr's crown was no longer readily available, devout Christians could aspire instead to seek so-called 'white' martyrdom (white as opposed to red, because it was achieved without the shedding of blood), by denying and overcoming the body and its desires and appetites. For this programme of disciplining and defining the self early Christian writers borrowed the Greek term *askesis*, originally used for the training undergone by athletes in preparation for a contest. And the prime location for such Christian ascetic practices was the pared-down, 'bare life' afforded by the desert.

The best-known of the desert solitaries, though not the first, was St Anthony of Egypt, also known as Anthony the Great (c. 251–356). Details of his life and horrifying diabolical temptations were brought to the West by Athanasius, bishop of Alexandria. Soon after, St Jerome wrote his Life of St Paul the First Hermit, Anthony's alleged (and probably apocryphal) predecessor in desert solitude. The desert, it seems, quickly filled up with hermits, whose feats of endurance and self-denial, and gems of wisdom, were recorded for posterity in the collections that came to be known as the *Vitas Patrum* ('The Lives of the Fathers'). Sources such as these emphasise the exceptional individuals (one thinks most obviously of Simeon Stylites, immortalised as an example of religious extremism by Tennyson's poem), but the reality of early eremitic practice was more diverse, ranging from pure solitude, through small groupings of solitaries who would come together periodically for shared worship (such a grouping was known as a *lavra* or 'skete'), to more formally organised groups, living out their solitary vocation together in a community or *coenobium* (from the Greek *koinos*, common, and *bios*, life). They were identified by a range of terms, three of which would be important in the subsequent history of the solitary vocations. Because they lived alone, they were called *monks* (Greek *monachoi*, from *monos*, alone); from their dwelling-place they were

3 For an excellent introductory survey see William Harmless, *Desert Christians: An introduction to the literature of early monasticism* (Oxford: Oxford University Press, 2004).

known as *hermits* (from *eremos*: desert, wilderness), and their retreat from normal human society was signified in *anchorites* (from the verb *anachorein*, to withdraw, though the verb was not originally confined to withdrawal for religious reasons). The three terms seem to have been used interchangeably in these early sources.

It was only later, therefore, and only in the West, that the monastic life came to be regarded as distinct from the solitary life of the hermit. The split was given decisive expression in *The Rule of St Benedict*, composed in the sixth century by Benedict of Nursia. Though Benedict himself had lived as a hermit in caves around Subiaco, in the mountains to the west of Rome, before he went on to found several monasteries in the region, his rule does not reflect his own life history. It sees the solitary life not as preparatory, but as supplementary to the life in common – a more challenging vocation to which only exceptional monks would graduate. He speaks of

> the anchorites or hermits, who have come through the test of living in a monastery for a long time, and have passed beyond the first fervor of monastic life. Thanks to the help and guidance of many, they are now trained to fight against the devil. They have built up their strength and go from the battle line in the ranks of their brothers to the single combat of the desert. Self-reliant now, without the support of another, they are ready with God's help to grapple single-handed with the vices of body and mind.[4]

Thus, whilst Benedict continues to recognise the hermit's life as an ideal, he denies its practice to all but a few of his monks. At the same time, Benedictine sources present their brand of monasticism as the fulfilment and completion of the desert project.[5] The life in common, in these sources, is a natural evolution from, and replacement for, the unregulated existence of the first hermits.

The Benedictine model largely holds sway in the West for the remainder of the first millennium, monasteries of the order increasing in number and – especially in the wake of the reforms instituted at Cluny (founded 910) – in wealth and complexity of liturgical observance. To some, they had become victims of their own success, and the reaction, when it came, took the form of an explicit attempt to reconnect

4 *The Rule of Saint Benedict in Latin and in English with Notes*, edited and translated by Timothy Fry OSB (Collegeville: The Liturgical Press, 1981), 1.3–5.

5 See, for example, Jean-Marie Sansterre, 'Le monachisme bénédictin d'Italie et les bénédictins italiens en France face au renouveau de l'érémitisme à la fin du Xe et au XIe siècle', in *Ermites de France et d'Italie (XIe–XVe siècle)*, edited by André Vauchez (Rome: École française de Rome, 2003), pp. 29–46.

monasticism with its desert origins, to recapture the purity and simplicity that had inspired Benedict in the first place.[6] Across much of Europe during the eleventh and twelfth centuries, monks left their monasteries to live alone or in small groups as hermits. Many would attract disciples, and some would end up founding a monastery – or even a whole religious order – of their own. The movement's first important figure was the Italian Romuald of Ravenna (c. 950–1027). Having left his monastery to live as a hermit, he went on to found monasteries at Fonte Avellana and Camaldoli in which monks lived alone in separate cells, coming together only for recitation of the divine office. Camaldoli in due course became the mother house of the Camaldolese order. Later in the century, in France, the founders of the Cistercians likewise cast their reforms as a return to the values of the desert. These same impulses gave rise to the Carthusian and Premonstratensian orders, as well as a number of smaller and shorter-lived congregations.

Such was the strength of the eremitic revival that, by the mid-twelfth century, Geoffrey Grossus, monk of the reformed house of Tiron, could describe his region of Maine and Brittany in northern France as 'almost like a Second Egypt' for its 'multitude of hermits'.[7] The phrase is testament both to the renewed visibility of the vocation and to the value attached to a direct connection with its desert origins. In England, prominent monasteries including Fountains, Kirkstall and the refounded Whitby Abbey (N. Yorks.), Jarrow (Northumb.), Bordesley (Worcs.) and Kirkstead (Lincs.) all owed their beginnings to this movement. Elsewhere, some groups of hermits crystallised into small priories, typically of the Augustinian order. This period of innovation and experimentation was, however, brought to an end in 1215, when the Fourth Lateran Council decreed that henceforward no new religious orders would receive papal approval.

In the meantime, the vocation of anchorite had been becoming more clearly defined. Benedict, as we have seen, uses the terms *hermit* and *anchorite* as synonyms, in contradistinction to the coenobitic *monk*. Now 'anchorite' begins to be reserved (alongside other terms, including – in English usage – 'recluse' or the Latin *inclusus*) for enclosed solitaries. Strict bodily enclosure is recorded occasionally for the desert

6 For the hermit-inspired monastic renewal of the eleventh and twelfth centuries, see Henrietta Leyser, *Hermits and the New Monasticism* (London: Macmillan Press, 1984).

7 Geoffrey Grossus, *The Life of Blessed Bernard of Tiron*, trans. Ruth Harwood Cline (Washington, DC: The Catholic University of America Press, 2009), p. 27.

period (the former harlot Thaïs was a celebrated example) and sporadically during ensuing centuries, but the practice does not seem to have become widespread or regularised in northern Europe until the late ninth century. Initially it was regarded as a special form of the monastic life (of the kind that Benedict might have envisaged), but in this period of increasing popularity the majority of anchorites were secular priests or laywomen, and they tended more often to be enclosed at parish churches. In some parts of Europe, though apparently never in England, the vocation seems to have been associated more or less exclusively with women. Anchorites appear first in English sources during the eleventh century, and quickly come to prominence during the twelfth.[8]

At the point at which this book begins, then, the age of the reforming hermit-monk was past, and the solitary religious life had established itself into two distinct vocations. The distinction was summed up in 1215 by the Latin scholar Gerald of Wales, who stated, 'Hermits wander about alone, while anchorites are strictly enclosed'.[9] It is put more colourfully, if less pithily, in the fifteenth-century English *Friar Daw's Reply*:

> Some flee from the world and shut themselves within walls,
> Enclose themselves in stone, and speak but little,
> To avoid those sins that human weakness is prey to,
> And these we call *ankers* in the common speech.
> And there are many others seeking contemplation
> Who withdraw to the desert and endure much pain,
> Live on herbs, roots and fruit, all for the love of God:
> And people like this are known as *hermits*.[10]

Hermits and anchorites in late medieval England

In the late Middle Ages, it could be argued, the solitary lives are best understood not so much in the context of monastic institutions but as

8 The solitaries of this period, including the emergence of enclosed anchorites as a distinct group, have been expertly covered by Tom Licence in his *Hermits & Recluses in English Society 950–1200* (Oxford: Oxford University Press, 2011).

9 *Heremitae solivagi aut Anachoritae conclusi.* Cited by Francis D. Darwin, *The English Mediaeval Recluse* (London: SPCK, 1944), p. 4.

10 In James M. Dean, ed., *Six Ecclesiastical Satires* (Kalamazoo: Medieval Institute Publications, 1991), lines 290–7, my translation.

part of the range of semi-religious or non-regular vocations.[11] Reflecting a growth in levels of literacy, devotional competence and spiritual ambition among the laity, these forms of living increasingly colonised the 'grey areas' in and around established ecclesiastical structures. Such people were not in – or, at any rate, they did not consider themselves to be entirely *of* – the secular world, but nor did they join a religious order; they aspired to a spiritual life more developed than was normal, and normally considered appropriate, for the laity, but were not clerics. Many were women. They pursued a life that claimed a degree of separation and regularity that in the past would have been reserved to the religious orders, but without either the constraint or the security offered by a canonically recognised and approved rule. Alongside hermits and anchorites, the category could be taken to include beguines and tertiaries (though these never took root in England), as well as (especially later in the period) vowesses – women, usually widows, vowed to a life of chastity and withdrawal from the world – and those who sought a 'mixed life' of piety and contemplation combined with a continued engagement with secular affairs.[12] In most cases, compared with the established orders, the lives were unstructured, their boundaries fluid, and their relation to the ecclesiastical authorities *ad hoc*. In late medieval England the question of regularity, and the presence or absence of mechanisms associated with canonicity or orderliness (such as vows, rules, registration), are a recurrent feature in the history of the solitary vocations. For anchorites, such procedures were securely in place by the point that this book begins, and examples are given in Chapter I. For hermits, by contrast, these were active and increasingly urgent questions during the period covered here, and the materials included in Chapter VI give some idea of how the problem was (at least partly) resolved.

The sources collected in this book fall in general into two classes. Either they are concerned with individual hermits or anchorites in their particular circumstances, or they come from theoretical or pre-

11 For a window on this range of possibilities, see John Van Engen, 'Multiple Options: The world of the fifteenth-century church', *Church History* 77 (2008): 257–84. An overview of the solitary lives across western Europe in this period (with a particular focus on enclosed anchorites) is provided by the essays collected in *Anchoritic Traditions of Medieval Europe* edited by Liz Herbert McAvoy (Woodbridge: The Boydell Press, 2010).

12 On these phenomena, see P.H. Cullum, 'Vowesses and Female Lay Piety in the Province of York, 1300–1530', *Northern History* 32 (1996): 21–41; and Nicole Rice, *Lay Piety and Religious Discipline in Middle English Literature* (Cambridge: Cambridge University Press, 2008).

scriptive texts such as rules or liturgy whose relation to the lived experience of real solitaries it is usually impossible to recover.[13] It falls to this Introduction, then, to try and give a sense of the overall picture of numbers and distribution: how widely were the solitary vocations practised in late medieval England, and by whom? In fact, the question is far from straightforward to answer. Whereas for the clergy we have ordination lists, and for monks and nuns we have annals, visitation records and sometimes extensive administrative documentation, the solitary lives were not subject to any consistent system of registration, and often what we know about a particular individual we owe to serendipity. The last concerted attempt to record all medieval English solitaries was made a century ago, by Rotha Clay.[14] Working almost entirely from such sources as were then available in print, she found in excess of a thousand individuals at more than 750 sites. The true figure must be substantially higher. Where further research has been done on a particular locality or region, Clay's totals have been exceeded by at least fifty per cent. For her 1985 study of anchorites in England, Ann Warren identifed 780 enclosed solitaries at 601 sites between 1100 and the end of the Middle Ages, again mostly from printed sources.[15] Comparable research on unenclosed hermits is still to be done, but there is no reason to doubt that it would yield similar numbers. And then there must be many more of both kinds of solitary in unpublished sources, not to mention those who left no trace in the record.

So we are still some way from a complete picture of the hermits and anchorites of late medieval England. Instead, we can glance through a few snapshots. In London, for example, there were anchorites attached to the churches of St Peter Cornhill, St Benet Fink, St Clement Danes, and the Dominicans' church of Blackfriars [**6b**]; hermits in the parishes of St Clement's, St Lawrence Jewry and Charing Cross, and solitaries dwelling in or near the city wall at Aldgate, Bishopsgate, Cripplegate [**40**], [**62**], All Hallows in the Wall [**6a**], [**35b**], and at the Tower of London.[16] In Norwich between Julian of Norwich at the

13 On this, see Mari Hughes-Edwards, *Reading Medieval Anchoritism: Ideology and spiritual practices* (Cardiff: University of Wales Press, 2012).

14 Clay, *Hermits and Anchorites*. I have a long-term project to revise Clay's study. Records of individual solitaries will be found in the database *Hermits & Anchorites of England* at http://hermits.ex.ac.uk.

15 See Warren, *Anchorites and Their Patrons*.

16 William Page, *The Victoria History of the County of London: Vol. One: Including London within the Bars, Westminster and Southwark* (London: The University of London, 1909), pp. 585–8.

end of the fourteenth century and the dissolution of the monasteries in the sixteenth, at least 35 and perhaps as many as 47 solitaries appear in the record. Norman Tanner estimates that 'From the 1420s to the 1470s there were probably at least eight hermits and anchorites living in the city at any given time'.[17] In 1271, the Oxford merchant Nicholas de Weston left money to nine anchorites in and around that city. When Henry Lord Scrope made his will in 1415 (he was about to be executed for treason), he included a very substantial bequest of 100s to John, the anchorite of Westminster, 40s to Robert, recluse of Beverley, 13s 4d to John the hermit outside Pontefract, plus the same amount to anchorites at Stafford, Kirby Wiske, and Peasholme near York, to the male recluses at Kexby and the Dominicans of Newcastle, to anchorites at Wighton, Chester, Thorganby, Leake by Upsall, Gainsborough, Kneesall by Southwell, Stamford, Dartford, and at the Dominicans of Shrewsbury, the same to Elizabeth the former servant of the anchorite at Hampole, 20s to the anchorite at Wath, and 6s 8d to each anchorite and recluse in London and its suburbs, and in York and its suburbs, and to each anchorite and anchoress who should come to his executors' attention within three months of his decease.[18] Whenever Margery Kempe visits a new place, one of the first things she does is to look up the local anchorite. Household accounts often include small gifts to hermits who appear at the castle door, or who are encountered on the way, apparently as a matter of routine [**44**]. Literary texts from Langland to Malory introduce hermits or anchorites casually, without seeming to feel the need to explain to their readers what they are. Solitaries were, in short, a familiar feature of the late medieval English landscape.

Almost without exception, all hermits were men. (An Alice Hermit is recorded in Norwich in the early fifteenth century. Assuming that 'Hermit' is a description, and not a surname, she is our only example so far discovered of a female hermit.)[19] Given medieval anxieties about unenclosed women's bodies, this should probably not surprise us. By the same token, it is perhaps as to be expected that more women than men

17 Norman P. Tanner, *The Church in Late Medieval Norwich: 1370–1532* (Toronto: Pontifical Institute of Mediaeval Studies, 1984), p. 58.

18 Thomas Rymer, *Foedera* (10 vols, The Hague: Joannes Neulme, 1739–45), vol. 4, part 2, p. 132. Several of these solitaries appear in this volume: for Westminster, see [**28**], [**15b**]; for Newcastle, [**23**]; for Kneesall (an earlier occupant), [**3a**]; for Stamford, [**15**]. The convent at Hampole was connected with Richard Rolle [**21**], [**47**].

19 Tanner, *Church in Late Medieval Norwich*, p. 202.

chose the stricter vocation and became anchorites, though other factors may have included the more limited range of opportunities for women to express a religious calling compared with men, and, more positively, the evidence (especially from continental sources, but perhaps relevant to England too) for anchoritism as a distinctively female, or feminine, vocation. Statistical analysis done by Ann Warren in the 1980s showed that female anchorites outnumbered male throughout the period, by a ratio of at least 3:2, and in the thirteenth century by more than 3:1.[20] Most male anchorites were priests; some had previously been monks or friars, though they were a minority compared with the secular priests. Similarly, only a few women came to the anchoritic vocation having previously been nuns. (See [**31**] for an example of a woman who tried and failed to make this transition.) (The old theory that Julian of Norwich had previously been a Benedictine nun at Carrow Priory in Norwich has no solid evidence behind it.) With very few exceptions, hermits were laymen. Most supported themselves by manual work and begging, and they could be difficult to distinguish from other members of the labouring class from which many of them originated. (See [**36**] for William Langland's satirical take on contemporary hermits' social origins.) Anchorites had to be of sufficient independent means to guarantee their support during a lifetime of enclosure [**2**], [**3**], [**6**]. A few candidates may have been of relatively humble origin, and a few were noble, such as the well-known sisters Loretta and Annora de Braose, enclosed in the thirteenth century at Hackington (Kent) and Iffley (Oxon.) respectively,[21] but (like the majority of late medieval monks and nuns) most belonged to the burgess and gentry classes.

Solitaries seem to have enjoyed support from all levels of society. Ann Warren's systematic study of anchoritic patronage showed that recluses benefited from endowments, bequests, and customary and occasional gifts, from everyone from the king and his barons down to relatively humble individuals (see [**13**]–[**17**]). Hermitages were rarely endowed (but see Cripplegate in London [**40**] for an exception). More often, hermits were the beneficiaries of casual gifts, though such charity could be given official encouragement by licences to beg [**37**] or indulgences [**38**], [**39**]. Unlike some earlier periods, there are no significant signs of tension between solitaries and the secular or regular clergy.

20 Warren, *Anchorites and Their Patrons*, pp. 18–29.

21 On Loretta and Annora, see Catherine Innes-Parker, 'Medieval Widowhood and Textual Guidance: The Corpus revisions of *Ancrene Wisse* and the de Braose anchoresses', *Florilegium* 28 (2011): 95–124.

The motives of patrons and donors, in so far as we can recover them, were often conventional: in return for alms, the solitary would pray for the donor's soul. But there are signs, too, that individual patrons placed particular value on a direct personal connection with a holy man or woman. On the night his father died, the future Henry V prepared for his coronation by visiting the anchorite at Westminster Abbey, and making his confession to him. He made a further gift to the anchorite on the occasion of his queen's coronation in 1421, and remembered him in his will the following year.[22] One of Henry's foremost knights, Richard Beauchamp, earl of Warwick, consulted Emma Rawghton, anchoress at All Saints North Street in York, on several occasions. She was known for her visions of Our Lady and for her gift of prophecy, and correctly predicted both his role as guardian of the young Henry VI and the birth of his own son, Henry, in 1425 [**26**]. Medieval England's most famous visionary, Julian of Norwich, was an anchorite too, of course. Today, thanks to her *Revelations*, we know rather more about her inner life than the circumstances of her enclosure at Conisford in the south of the city. During her lifetime, however, she was better known as a spiritual adviser than a writer, as her visit from Margery Kempe bears witness. The first of the 'Middle English Mystics', Richard Rolle, was likewise sought out as a spiritual director, and after his death was revered as a saint. Much of his writing touches (sometimes quite defensively) on his life as a hermit: his improvised entry into the vocation is [**47**] (and see [**21**] for an excerpt from his writings). And Walter Hilton (whose advice to recluses lies behind [**25**]) spent time as a solitary himself before settling down as a canon of the Augustinian order.

Changes within the vocations, 1215–1550

The outline and character of the anchoritic life were more or less established by the point at which this book begins. Enclosure was by now expected to be strict and irrevocable. The role of the bishop in approving and supervising the vocation had been asserted and passed into usual practice, and was underlined by the prominent part he took in the process of enclosure [**2**]–[**5**]. Aelred of Rievaulx had written his 'rule' for anchorites, *De Institutione inclusarum* (or 'Rule of Life for a Recluse'). Composed by the Cistercian abbot for his sister in the early

22 See my 'O Sely Ankir' in *Medieval Anchorites in Their Communities* edited by Cate Gunn and Liz Herbert McAvoy (Cambridge: D.S. Brewer, 2017), pp. 13–34.

1160s, it served as a model and a source for many later works of guidance for both anchorites and hermits [**18**], [**19**], [**54**]. Most importantly, it provides a framework and a significant amount of material for the early Middle English *Ancrene Wisse* ('Guide for Anchoresses'), written in the 1220s, and the most complete and enduring of English anchoritic rules. It is divided between an 'outer rule', which focuses on prayers and other observances and the practicalities of daily life, and an 'inner rule' that addresses the anchorite's moral and spiritual life, including discussions of sin, temptations, penance and love for God. The proportions of the work, however, give much greater weight to the inner life of the spirit than to the externals that are the main focus of the texts collected in this volume. *Ancrene Wisse* continued to be read throughout the Middle Ages, and it would make an ideal comparative volume to this one.

The principal evolution in the character of the anchoritic life during this period is really no more than a footnote to the biggest change affecting society as a whole: the growth of towns and an urban economy, and the migration of a significant proportion of the population from country to city. It is possible to overstate the case: the anchoritic life was popular across the country throughout the period, and anchorites could be found in rural parishes as well as urban centres, but, as in demographics more generally, there was a steady drift towards the towns as the Middle Ages went on, and by the sixteenth century urban anchorites were in the majority. As a case in point, medieval England's most celebrated anchorite, Julian of Norwich, comes across in her writings as the most serenely other-worldly of English mystics. It can be a surprise, then, to learn that her cell was located in Norwich's bustling quarter of Conisford, among the merchants' warehouses near the wharf on the River Wensum, in one of late medieval England's biggest and busiest cities.[23]

Demographic changes are also an important factor in the development of the hermit's vocation during the late Middle Ages. The differences between a typical twelfth-century hermit and his fifteenth-century counterpart are more striking than the corresponding differences between central and late medieval anchorites. In the twelfth century, hermits frequently had monastic connections, and were generally to be found in rural locations, often involved in clearing marginal land

23 Felicity Riddy, 'Julian of Norwich and Self-textualization' in *Editing Women* edited by Ann M. Hutchison (Cardiff: University of Wales Press, 1998), pp. 101–24.

(such as marsh or forest) for cultivation. There were hermit saints (such as Godric of Finchale or Robert of Knaresborough), while other prominent hermits were involved in the monastic reform movement described above. In the period covered by this book, however, hermits were humbler in origin and ambition. Most were involved in what we would think of as public works, especially in connection with the emerging world of mobility and communication, and often around the urban fringes: building roads, maintaining causeways, keeping bridges. In the first half of our period they seem to have enjoyed popular and official patronage and support, but things changed markedly after the Black Death of 1348–9. The labour shortages and social upheaval that were the legacy of the plague led to considerable tensions around labour, begging, and social and geographical mobility, and hermits found themselves caught up in an increasingly strident discourse of vagrancy and 'sturdy beggars' [**36**]. This is the context for a suite of measures that seem to have been designed to put the hermit vocation on a secure canonical foundation, to match that already in place for anchorites. The examination of candidates and testing of their vocations, profession ceremonies, and rules or guides for living – all of which already existed for anchorites in 1215 – started to be provided for hermits around the beginning of the fifteenth century. (For more on this, see Chapter VI.)

And so to the events of the 1530s. There is no evidence of a decline in vocations to the solitary life, nor of a falling away of patronage and support, in the years preceding the break with Rome. How hermits and anchorites fit into the process of the dissolution of the monasteries and chantries has yet to be determined by modern scholarship, and indeed the issue seems to have been uncertain for contemporaries [**67a**]. The material collected in this section suggests that there is a question to be addressed, and that there may be a degree of nuance in the answer. But quite clearly the vocations were out of tune with Protestant belief and practice and, though a few individuals continued some form of solitary life beyond 1540, by the reign of Queen Mary (if John Foxe is to be believed) only the unfortunate Thomas Parkinson remained [**74**], the last solitary of medieval England.

The texts and translations

The volume comprises 76 entries, some of them subdivided. They are distributed among eight chapters: Chapters I to IV focus on anchorites, Chapters V to VII on hermits (with an exception for the Lollard anchoress Amy Palmer [**61**] who belongs logically with the hermit William Swinderby [**60**]), before the final chapter brings the vocations together again for a discussion of the Dissolution and the end of the solitary lives in England. A few entries are divided into two or more closely related sub-entries, and these are distinguished by lower-case letters (a) (b), etc. Where an entry or sub-entry comprises a sequence of similar excerpts or references that all refer to the same heading or sub-heading, these are numbered in roman (i) (ii), etc.

Almost all the translations are my own, and in most cases this is the first published translation of the source. More than twenty entries or sub-entries are translated from sources that have never before been available in print. The texts are drawn from a wide range of sources: administrative records, wills, liturgy, rules or guidance texts, literary works. The original language is in most cases Latin, though a number of the later texts are in English, and there are a few examples in French. The language of the original document is indicated in the headnote. I have varied the idiom of the translations according to that of the originals. Thus a legal treatise [**2**] will be rendered in language more formal than is usual for the guidance texts, and liturgy [**5**], [**49**] will be more rigid and archaic than a meditation [**30**]. In the case of fifteenth- and sixteenth-century English sources, I have wherever possible chosen simply to modernise the language, since this gives a better feel for the original language than a full translation.

A few decisions require further comment. The Latin honorific *Dom* (for *Dominus*), which sometimes appears in English sources as *Dan*, usually designates a priest. I have followed the customary practice of rendering it as 'Sir'. In lists (for example, of the bequests in a will) the Latin *Item* is used as a preface for each new clause. Rather than translating it as 'Again', or merely substituting perhaps the nearest modern equivalent, a bullet-point, I have left it as *Item*. More consequentially, there was some fluidity in the medieval English terminology for the solitary vocations. My 'hermit' invariably represents Latin *heremita* or *eremita*, or Middle English *heremyte* or similar, in the original. The lexis of enclosure is less straightforward. I have generally used the gender-neutral term *anchorite*, reflecting the Latin *anchorita* or *anachorita*.

Latin sources also use *inclusus* (masculine) or *inclusa* (feminine), or (less commonly) *reclusus/-a*, 'enclosed person', apparently without any distinction in meaning. French records tend to use *recluse*, which is also borrowed by Middle English for use alongside the native pair *ancer* or *anker* (for men) and *ancress* or *ankress* for women. The modern English *anchoress* derives from this last. There are arguments against this term, both linguistic (it is a back-formation from *anchorite*, rather than a genuine Middle English word) and political (like 'authoress' it marks the female as a deviation from a male norm), but it is in common parlance, and I have occasionally made use of it.

A few entries are quoted from previously printed sources, and formal acknowledgements for these are given *in situ*. More generally, I am grateful to all those librarians and archivists who have assisted me in finding and obtaining source material for the book. They are too numerous to list here, but appreciated none the less. I should also like to thank Joel T. Rosenthal for some very useful discussions about the design and scope of the volume in its early stages of development; James Downs for his assistance with the bibliography, and any number of colleagues and friends for their help and advice with individual entries, of whom the two that I have probably badgered the most have been James Clark and Nicholas Orme.

I: BECOMING AN ANCHORITE

Introduction

The life of an anchorite was not to be entered into unadvisedly or lightly. The aspirant would assuredly want to spend some time pondering his or her vocation; seeking the views of friends, family and spiritual advisers; and ensuring that all material arrangements had been put in place, before making the momentous entry into a life of strict and irrevocable enclosure. Over time, it came also to be expected that formal permission would be sought and obtained from the bishop of the diocese, and by the second half of the twelfth century it could seem surprising if an anchorite had been enclosed without his involvement.[1] By the point at which this book begins, therefore, these mechanisms and procedures were already well established, and the purpose of this section is to illustrate them in practice.

The first excerpt is taken from perhaps the latest of English anchoritic 'rules' or guidance texts, though the only one to give detailed attention to this earliest phase of the process of becoming an anchorite. In the first part of the early fifteenth-century *Speculum Inclusorum*, the author considers why people choose the anchoritic life [1]. The first reason he suggests is one that might never have occurred to a modern reader: because being an anchorite is easier and more comfortable than ordinary life in the world. Then come two motives that are essentially negative, and perhaps more predictable: to do penance for sins committed in the past, and to avoid as many occasions of sin as possible in the future. Last and best is the desire to give up all worldly occupation in order to dedicate oneself entirely to contemplation and the praise of God. The excerpts include a discussion of how a prospective anchorite should examine his vocation; a clear and sympathetic account of the system of probation; a candid enumeration of the sins and temptations that the anchorite could not escape, including the dangers of masturbation; and a strong defence of the 'holy idleness' that is the prerequisite for contemplation.

1 *Wulfric of Haselbury [by] John, Abbot of Ford* edited by Maurice Bell, Somerset Record Society 47 (1933), p. 15; and see my 'Rites of Enclosure: The English *Ordines* for the enclosing of anchorites, s. xii–s.xvi', *Traditio* 67 (2012): 145–234, pp. 158–9.

The other sources are written from the side of the authorities. Any bishop presented with an intending anchorite would want to satisfy himself of the character and spiritual preparedness of the candidate, the suitability of the proposed place of enclosure, and that sufficient provision had been made to guarantee the candidate's material needs once enclosed – not least because canon law made any inadequately supported anchorites the financial responsibility of the bishop himself [**2**]. On this last point he would want to ensure that all interested parties had been consulted, and in particular the rector of the church to which the reclusory would be annexed [**3e**]. Though an anchorite of good repute might be an asset to any church (both increasing its spiritual merit and, through the visitors and pilgrims he or she might attract, benefiting it materially as well), proprietors might equally have been anxious that a resident solitary could become a nuisance, a distraction or a financial burden [**6b**]. On the moral and spiritual questions, our sources are generally quieter, though a tempting hypothesis suggests that Julian of Norwich may have prepared the Short Text of her *Revelations* in connection with such an enquiry into her suitability for the anchoritic life. In some cases the bishop would supervise the process himself, but he often entrusted it to a deputy: sometimes a suffragan bishop, sometimes one or two senior churchmen of the diocese commissioned for the purpose. The letters of appointment addressed to such deputies [**3a–f**] are valuable because they spell out a procedure that, were the bishop performing the task himself, would normally go unrecorded. These commissions often include details of the enquiries that were to precede an enclosure; sometimes a period of probation is mentioned [**3b**]; sometimes there can be more precise information than we generally have about the location and design of the intended cell; and the preamble to the bishop's letter – though formal, conventional and often rather flowery – can give us an idea of the values that contemporaries might attach to the anchoritic life.[2]

Once the bishop (or his deputy) was satisfied, he would enclose the new anchorite in his or her cell, in a ritual that seems to have been first developed during the twelfth century [**5**]. The ceremony was a powerful piece of liturgical theatre. The first part of the rite, conducted in the church, emphasised the candidate's change of life, by recalling

2 For some more examples of such commissions, and brief discussion, see Clay, *Hermits and Anchorites*, pp. 90–2; Francis D. Darwin, *The English Mediaeval Recluse* (London: SPCK, 1944), pp. 45–52; P.J.P. Goldberg, ed., *Women in England c. 1275–1525: Documentary sources* (Manchester: Manchester University Press, 1995), p. 278.

other services of initiation (baptism, ordination, monastic profession), whilst the second half underscored the idea that anchorites were dead to the world by numerous striking echoes of the medieval liturgy of death and burial: from the procession through the cemetery to reach the cell, to the psalms and antiphons chosen, the performance of the 'last rites', the open grave and the sprinkling of dust upon the recluse.[3] The verbatim recording of an anchorite's profession [**6**] is a late development, and perhaps connected with a general move to 'tighten up' the regulation and registration of the solitary vocations during the last century or so of the Middle Ages.[4]

1. Four reasons that people choose to become anchorites, from the *Speculum Inclusorum*

The *Speculum Inclusorum* is a guide for male anchorites probably written at the beginning of the fifteenth century. Its title means 'mirror for recluses', although, in the many medieval works in which it is used, the title *speculum* is often best translated as something like 'encyclopaedia'. The treatise has a number of associations with the Carthusian order, and may have been connected with the reclusory at Sheen Charterhouse, Surrey, founded in 1417. A Middle English translation of the *Speculum* was made around the middle of the fifteenth century, and was intended primarily for female anchorites.[5] The treatise is presented as a commentary on 1 Corinthians 1:26, *Videte vocationem vestram*: literally 'See your vocation', though in context *videte* is usually better translated as 'look at' or 'observe'. In Part One, from which these excerpts are taken, the author considers the four motives that can lead people to choose the anchoritic life. Parts Two and Three proceed to expand on the life of the anchorite with its concentration on prayer, meditation and reading, whilst the final part looks forward

3 For a commentary on the rite translated here, see my 'Ceremonies of Enclosure: Rite, rhetoric and reality', in *Rhetoric of the Anchorhold: Space, place and body within the discourses of enclosure* edited by Liz Herbert McAvoy (Cardiff: University of Wales Press, 2008), pp. 34–49, and for the enclosure rite in general, my 'Rites of Enclosure'.

4 See my *Speculum Inclusorum / A Mirror for Recluses: A late-medieval guide for anchorites and its Middle English translation* (Liverpool: Liverpool University Press, 2013), pp. lxv–lxviii, and below, Chapter VI. The episcopal authorities also started noting, and often recording, the professions of hermits during this same period [**52**].

5 See my edition, supplemented by '*A Mirror for Recluses*: A new manuscript, new information and some new hypotheses', *The Library* 7/15 (2014): 424–31.

to the ecstasies of the love of God and contemplation that offer a foretaste of the joys of heaven.[6]

Excerpts translated from the Latin in my edition: *Speculum Inclusorum / A Mirror for Recluses: A late-medieval guide for anchorites and its Middle English translation* (Liverpool: Liverpool University Press, 2013), pp. 9–37. Reproduced with permission of Liverpool University Press through PLSclear.

Chapter 2

It happens that some people … are led to the solitary life by a spirit of error, with the intention to receive by the devotion of faithful Christians more of what they can live on or spend than they would likely have had in another kind of living; and so that in vigils, fasts, prayers and other occupations they might dispose themselves according to their will, fleeing, out of a certain voluptuous slothfulness, as far as possible, the yoke of obedience and bodily labours and the difficulties of this life; as certain members of religious orders in modern times strive to do who, for as long as they are in any way restrained by the sacred observances of their order from their pleasures in food, clothing, occupations unsuitable for them and excessive recreation, in all ways and means possible to them struggle, grumble and resist, deeming their superiors ill-intentioned or undiscriminating, and unless they are permitted to live in a certain way according to the dictate of their will, they abandon their order, just like the sons of perdition, or without a scruple of conscience they procure some exemption, as for example that they are the Pope's chaplains or 'bishops of nowhere',[7] and thus they can freely have leisure for their dangerous pleasures and as a consequence be entangled in the devil's snares, with no-one to stop them.

Are these not just like those people who desire the solitary life not first and foremost for the love of God, but to lead their life according to the dictate of their will? Truly I believe that it is so. But it cannot easily be known for certain who such people are. Let each investigate his own conscience without feigning, from what motive above all he chose the solitary life and what was the principal intention moving him. If the first and greatest motivation was quiet or some worldly comfort, the freedom to have his own will, the support of relatives and friends or the crafty acquisition of worldly goods, let him fear, let him

6 For a further excerpt from the *Speculum*, see [**22**].

7 This is a scathing reference to the practice of appointing clerics to bishoprics (mostly in the Middle East) which were in fact no longer under Christian control. Such titular bishops generally worked in diocesan administration; many were friars.

repent, and finally let him establish his intention henceforth principally in the love of God and his service, having put behind him all inordinate affections whatsoever. …

It also happens that recluses who are less well ordered and not circumspect are in many ways contaminated and their conduct made worse by an abundance of worldly things and a throng of people of diverse conditions visiting them. Those things are evident in some recluses in our day, [who dwell] not in the desert but in the city, where they may receive generous alms with which they can maintain a great household, relatives and friends – more than they were able to do in their other estate – help and advance them, and in almost all things enjoy a more luxurious way of life than they would have been able to do in the secular estate. People of either sex and of diverse condition frequently visit these [recluses], pouring into their ears and showing before their eyes sensual delights and slanders, and curious and harmful things as well, and all kinds of rumours or happenings in the neighbourhood; the traces of which remaining in the memory, although they do not impel them to external acts of deadly sin, nevertheless vex and distress the mind inwardly in various fantasies, so that their reading is made insipid, their prayer impious, and all their meditation full of vice.

Oh noble knights of Jesus Christ, oh students of perfection, oh privy chamberlains of your God! In accordance with the counsel of John in his first epistle,[8] in its only chapter, 'Look to yourselves, so that you do not lose what you have made' [2 John 8]. It does not pertain to your estate to live pleasurably, to receive guests, the poor or pilgrims, to maintain a household, to educate the young, to be troubled about the upkeep of relatives or friends, nor to be occupied with unprofitable or vain conversations. But since you have food and something with which to cover yourselves if the occasion demands, be content with these, in accordance with the counsel of the Apostle [1 Tim. 6:8], so as to be totally free for those things which pertain to the salvation of your souls – and do not let anger impede you from continuing such virtuous works, nor sloth (which is an immeasurable bodily temptation for the unoccupied) hold you back. …

Chapter 3

Recluses' second motive or principal intention may be a fervent desire to do penance for their sins for the whole term of this life. And, if they

8 In fact, the quotation is from John's second epistle.

persevere in their purpose, we believe such people to be called by the Holy Spirit, in accordance with the words of Jesus Christ, saying in Luke 5: 'I have not come to call the righteous, but sinners, to repentance' [Luke 5:32]. But nevertheless a very cautious prudence is necessary in those choosing a solitary life in this way, so that the austerities of such a life are not chosen out of a sudden levity of soul or unexpectedly, [and] either strengthened in purpose, or promised as it were in an absolute vow, by the intervention of the angel Satan, who often transfigures himself into an angel of light,[9] so that by first raising someone's unstable soul the higher under the likeness of holiness, he may afterwards make it fall the worse and more dangerously into the depths, as I know to have happened to some people, to their everlasting grief. This life is holiest and most perfect in those people who, having fought for a long time against temptations through an abundance of divine grace, have utterly conquered all passions and (as far as is possible to a soul still on its journey through this life) extinguished totally all inordinate affections, and are now able to fight against all temptations alone, and possess and have acquired by grace such sweetness of divine love and contemplation that for them earthly things have no savour, but they delight in heavenly things alone. Such people have no need of human instruction, and I do not write for such people, but only to the imperfect who aspire to the greatest degree of perfection, for to such people the solitary life is very dangerous – which is no wonder when someone has set out to fight continually until death against all possible temptations and the terrifying army of wicked spirits. And therefore this life requires and demands someone perfect, concerning which the Wise Man says: 'I found one man among a thousand' [Eccles. 7:29 (AV 7:28)].

Therefore if anyone desires the solitary life with the impulse to do penance, I neither wholly counsel him against such a purpose, nor will I advise it, because I do not know what spirit moves him, but I give advice according to this kind of counsel: that is that he should at once reveal his holy purpose to two or three men of discretion and of praiseworthy life, who may diligently examine his intention with everything appertaining to it. Next with their advice and assent he should put himself on probation for a whole year together, living in all respects in a similar manner or more strictly than a recluse is obliged to do. In the mean time, however, he shall not bind his will to this or make a vow.

9 See also [**3e**]. For more on such temptations, see Chapter III.

When this whole year has passed, let him pray with daily entreaties to the Father of mercy that he will see fit to inspire him concerning his purpose, as to what is better for the salvation of his soul and in what way he will ultimately please God the more. Then, if the longing described above remains as before, and the counsel of men of discretion, having had mature deliberation on this matter in advance, is in agreement, let him make firm his resolve in this respect; let him confirm his purpose and take on that life or make a vow, confident of the grace and mercy of his God. In no other way than this, or in an equivalent way, do I advise anyone to choose or vow the life of recluses. Yet, after an absolute vow has been made, or this kind of life taken on with deliberation, it must of necessity be observed until the end, on pain of eternal damnation. Wherefore to all those professing this life the exhortation of the Apostle (Ephesians 4) is lovingly to be made known, where he says: 'I beseech that you walk worthily in the vocation to which you are called' [Eph. 4:1]. …

I also desire you carefully to keep watch against the temptations of the devil, so that nothing may relax too greatly the austerity of your life under the disguise of false necessity, nor anything increase it beyond your strength, but in accordance with the dictate of discretion you should chastise and nourish your body by turns, so that it may be both subjected to the authority of your spirit and able to perform the work required of it. And so in great debility or infirmity you should provide the refreshment necessary for your body and, when your body's strength has returned, take up the arms of spiritual warfare more bravely, knowing that you will be continuing in your meritorious labours not only for yourself, but also for all the souls suffering in purgatory and for all Christians to whom you are bound by the law of charity. …

Chapter 4

Recluses' third motive or principal intention may be the intention of avoiding the opportunities or occasions which tend to lead to mortal sin. Now the five bodily senses, like less than prudent messengers of the human heart, tend always and everywhere to repeat whatever things they receive, however vain or unprofitable or hurtful they might be, or however much they tend to sin. For this reason it sometimes happens that unsophisticated people[10] and those fearful of stumbling into mortal

10 The Latin word is *simplices*, whose meanings include 'naive' and 'foolish', as well as 'simple'.

sin – when they consider their frailty and the innumerable impending dangers of committing sins, which arise from the five senses wandering in the world without hindrance, without restraint – for the safer avoidance of all these kinds of dangers, ⌜and⌝ stimulated by a certain prudent fervour or fervent prudence, desire to be enclosed, in accordance with the advice of Solomon (Proverbs 7), saying thus: 'Make prudence your friend' ⌜Prov. 7:1⌝, that is the guardian of your soul. …

⌜*Warnings are given against the sins associated with the senses of sight and hearing.*⌝

And moreover such people are kept very safely from the dangers of the sense of touch, through which occur a multitude of sexual pleasures, both natural and against nature, which disqualify a person from all good, and make him abominable to the angels, hateful to God, and estranged from any grace. The recluse is secluded far away from all varieties of lechery of this kind, unless perhaps from the pleasurable delight of the mind in an unlawful thought, which if it is lingering and gives rise to consent to such taking of delight, without a doubt it leads to mortal sin. And if someone continues such delectation while he is awake until the sensual pollution of the body follows, then a certain type of lechery against nature occurs, which is called by the Apostle *mollicies*, where he says that 'neither those who practise *mollicies*, nor those who sleep with men, shall possess the kingdom of God' ⌜1 Cor. 6:10 (AV 6:9)⌝.[11] And let it not displease anyone here that in my writing I bring such shameful things before pure and perfect people, for where there is the possibility of temptation, there a prudent explanation of how to resist it is necessary. For a true story bears witness that a certain hermit, reputed as most holy, while he was afflicted with the vice of *mollicies*, and did not do penance as if he considered it a sin, suddenly disappeared, ravished by demons. And doubtless this was revealed by God to other people for their instruction, so that they should always resist voluptuous delight of this kind with all their strength, and never consent to it. And if (God forbid!) they were ever to fall, they should do appropriate penance, and so receive the crown for victory in the severest spiritual battle.

Chapter 5

Recluses' fourth motive or principal intention may be the desire more freely to have leisure for the contemplation and praises of God, in

11 The word is traditionally interpreted as a reference to masturbation, and in context this is clearly what is meant. The author of the Middle English version of the *Speculum* leaves it untranslated.

accordance with the counsel of the prophet David, where he says: 'Be still and see that the Lord is good'.[12] They desire this vocation who by experience feel God's grace in themselves so much that, for as long as they are free from worldly occupations, they will be able fully, fervently and devoutly to contemplate God, and to give him heartfelt thanks for all his gifts. And so it is no wonder if above all they desire to avoid worldly anxieties. For this good emptiness, this holy idleness, this profitable rest tends to be hindered by mental anxiety, by occupation of the senses, and by bodily labour in the cares of this world. ...

For this reason, anyone who, when he chooses the solitary life, feels within himself the Holy Spirit through grace and mercy lighting and maintaining the fire of devotion, ought firmly to believe that he is called to that estate by the Holy Spirit. And thus, you recluses, by the grace of God and his mercy shown to you, 'Look to your vocation'.

2. Enclosure: a legal view, from Lyndwood's *Provinciale*

William Lyndwood (c. 1375–1446) was the leading ecclesiastical lawyer in England in the first half of the fifteenth century. His *Provinciale* (completed by 1434) was an attempt to gather into a single volume all the important statements of canon law that had emanated from the archbishops of Canterbury over the previous two centuries, and to provide them with an interpretative commentary. It held its field throughout the rest of the Middle Ages, and was still in regular use in ecclesiastical cases into the seventeenth century.[13] Lyndwood included one piece of legislation on the enclosure of anchorites. He ascribes it to 'Edmund', by which he must mean St Edmund Rich, archbishop of Canterbury 1234–40. The statute itself, modern scholarship has determined, is not genuine, though Lyndwood probably did not know this.[14] It none the less gives a clear and (from what other sources tell us) accurate statement of bishops' legal responsibilities with respect to any anchorites in their diocese at this period; and Lyndwood's glosses give detailed insight into the kinds of questions that a fifteenth-century

12 Ps. 45:11 (AV 46:10) apparently conflated with Ps. 33:9 (AV 34:8).

13 See the entry by R.H. Helmholz in *ODNB*.

14 F.M. Powicke and C.R. Cheney, eds, *Councils and Synods with Other Documents Relating to the English Church* (2 vols, Oxford: Clarendon Press, 1964), vol. 1, pp. 65–7.

bishop would expect to ask himself before agreeing to a prospective anchorite's enclosure.[15]

Translated from the Latin of the standard printed edition: *Provinciale, seu Constitutiones Angliae* (Oxford: H. Hall, 1679), pp. 214–15. In the original, the work is presented as a text with gloss – that is, the authoritative texts appear, in a larger script, in the centre of each page, while Lyndwood's commentary, keyed to particular words within the texts, is written all around them in a smaller and (in manuscript copies) less formal script. In the translation presented here, the text is given first in italic, and the gloss following it; the keywords are preceded by an asterisk. The commentary is somewhat abridged, particularly in passages where Lyndwood's exposition goes into legal technicalities.

No one should be made an anchorite without the specific approval of the bishop; and those who are made anchorites should not offer hospitality to secular persons without good reason.

Edmund: … Moreover we very strictly forbid that male or female *recluses should be established anywhere without the specific licence of the local *diocesan bishop, he to consider the *location, the *character and status of the *people, and how they will be *maintained. And in no circumstances are *secular persons to be entertained in their houses without good and clear reason.

[*Glosses*]

*Recluses
Understand this as those enclosed individually, as anchorites are with us; this should not be understood as those enclosed as a community, as all nuns are (or should be).

*Diocesan bishop
And so someone lower than the rank of bishop cannot give this licence. It follows that an abbot cannot license one of his monks to be enclosed because, although canon law states that monks can transfer to a solitary and eremitical life by licence of their abbot, they cannot do so in order to be enclosed alone; this is not what it means, but it refers to those who want to live in the wilderness with their companions.

15 For a further discussion see my 'Hermits and Anchorites in Historical Context' in *Teaching Anchorites and Mystics* edited by Roger Ellis, Dee Dyas and Valerie Edden (Cambridge: D.S. Brewer, 2005), pp. 3–18, at pp. 9–11.

*Location
[...] The bishop must consider whether the place where someone wants to be enclosed is close to a church, or a long way from one. Also whether it is in a town or in the country, since a recluse's needs can more easily be looked after in a town, where there are lots of people, than in the country, where there are few, and the greater part of them poor people who are unable to help them. It should also be considered whether the place is near some monastery, by whose alms a recluse might be maintained, or far from one.

*Character
That is, whether the person is notoriously vicious, or virtuous. Also whether they are steadfast or easily changeable, for it is necessary for everyone who desires to live devoutly in Christ to be steadfast in adversity. Also whether they are perfect in the Active Life, and established in virtue, because someone less than perfect, or otherwise unsuited to the perfection of the Active Life, will not readily bring profit to himself or to others in the Contemplative Life. And so the Active Life is preparatory to the Contemplative Life; as Isidore says, 'The person who initially succeeds in the Active Life ascends from it to contemplation'.[16] Therefore, so long as a man has not reached perfection in the Active Life, there can be within him nothing more than as it were the beginning of the Contemplative Life.

*People
That is, whether they are religious or secular, cleric or layperson, man or woman, someone who has prior experience of austerity of living or someone without that experience, young or old, and so on.

*Maintained
For instance, because they have enough of their own to live on. For recluses, if they are not members of one of the approved religious orders and bound by their profession, are able to have personal property, in the same way as hermits are. But if, on the other hand, they do not have enough of their own to live on, they should not lightly be enclosed, unless they are able at least to be maintained in common with others – for example, if the intending recluse is a religious and able to live on the property of his monastery. For it does not seem secure for a recluse to live by begging, unless he is a member of one of the

16 *PL* 83, 689.

mendicant orders, in which case he can be supplied with his needs by those other members of his order who are not enclosed, in accordance with the practice of their order. The arrangements in this case I believe do not fall within the remit of the bishop, because mendicants of this kind are generally exempt from episcopal jurisdiction. But those others who are subject to his jurisdiction, the bishop is obliged to consider, and to see that they are not forced to seek their maintenance in uncertain circumstances. Therefore, if the person who wishes to be enclosed is a cleric who owes obedience to the bishop, the latter can justly and reasonably refuse to allow his enclosure if he would not have enough, either personally or as part of a community, to support himself. The reason is that clerics' begging is a source of shame to bishops. For in this case not only would it be said 'the wretched cleric begs in the street',[17] but 'the wretched enclosed cleric bewails his need to beg in his cell', and there is no one to see his misery and poverty, and with no one to come to his aid he will likely die of starvation and want. A bishop must be careful, therefore, that he does not enclose anyone other than the kind of people who are described in this chapter above; and only those of whose future maintenance he is certain – otherwise (as it seems reasonable to me) he will be obliged to provide for those who have been enclosed by him from his own resources, just as he is obliged to provide for a cleric that he advances to holy orders without a title.[18]

Furthermore you should also know, concerning this topic, that, although the solitary life may suit a contemplative person who has already attained to perfection (which may happen in two ways: one by the gift of God, as in the case of John the Baptist; the second, by practising virtuous behaviour), nevertheless a man can profit from the society of others, in two ways. First, as regards his understanding, in that he may receive instruction in the proper objects of contemplation – as Jerome[19] in his letter to the monk Rusticus says, 'It is good that you have the fellowship of holy people, and do not teach yourself'. Secondly, as regards his practice, in that the harmful desires characteristic of humankind may be checked by example, or by other people's correction. As the same author says to the same man: 'In solitude, pride

17 An allusion to Gratian's *Decretum*.

18 A man was not supposed to be ordained priest unless he held a title to a benefice – in other words, unless he had been nominated for a position that carried a guaranteed income.

19 The 1679 edition reads *Henri*, an error for *Hieron[ymus]*. The reference is to Jerome's Epistle 125 (see *PL* 22, 1077).

creeps up quickly, it sleeps when it wishes, does what it wants, etc.' To the person who lives in a community he says, 'You shall not do what you want, you shall eat what you are given, you shall be subject to desires not your own, you shall serve your brethren, you shall fear the superior of the monastery, as you love God or your father, etc.'

*Secular persons
You can understand this to mean both secular priests and laypeople. For secular priests should not be entertained in cells of the kind described here, while they are engaged in secular life. I would judge otherwise if they intended to give themselves to contemplation and prayer in one of these places, having withdrawn completely from worldly affairs. And I should perhaps say the same about a layperson who turned entirely to contemplation and prayer, albeit without having been enclosed, for people like this should not be called mere seculars, but religious.[20]

3. The examination and enclosure of an anchorite

The documents selected here, ranging from the thirteenth to the fifteenth century, are consistent in their focus on the essential questions around enclosure: as the canonist Lyndwood put it, the prospective anchorite's location, character and maintenance [**2**]. Alongside these typical elements, they also illustrate some unusual cases.

3a. Commission to enclose Isolda de Kneesall, 1340

The anchoress at Kneesall was among the solitaries remembered in the will of Henry Lord Scrope of Masham in 1415 (see the Introduction, p. 8), though presumably she was a later occupant of the cell referred to here. This typical document combines a consideration of the candidate's personal suitability for the solitary life with practical questions around the material arrangements for her enclosure. No trace of the cell now remains at the church of St Bartholomew, Kneesall.

Translated from the Latin in R. Brocklesbury, ed., *The Register of William Melton, Archbishop of York, 1317–1340*, Vol. 4, Canterbury & York Society 85 (1997), p. 213.

20 This kind of 'mixed life' was popular among spiritually ambitious laypeople in the late Middle Ages.

William etc. to our beloved sons … the Abbot of Rufford in our diocese and our dean of Newark, ⌜wishing you⌝ health ⌜etc.⌝.[21]

Fully confident in your faithfulness and careful diligence, we commission you jointly and severally by these present letters, reinforced by the addition of our seal, to enclose on our behalf Isolda of Kneesall, whose character and life, merits and honest conversation ⌜*behaviour*⌝ have been established before us by trustworthy testimony, in a place appropriate and available; that is in a house adjoining the wall of the parish church of Kneesall in our diocese, newly built for this purpose, by the will and consent of the patron and rector of the said church and of all others whom it concerns, and where the same Isolda desires to serve the Lord continually through leading a solitary life.

Farewell. ⌜Cawood,[22] 18 March 1340⌝

3b. Commission to enclose Cecily Moys, 1403

Marhamchurch is a few miles inland from the north Cornish coast, near Bude: it is not difficult to see why the bishop of Exeter might have entrusted the enclosure of an anchorite in this remote corner of his diocese to a pair of local deputies. The document is of particular interest for the stipulation of a period of probation: though often mentioned in theory (see ⌜**1**⌝), this requirement was rarely recorded in practice. A licence to choose her own confessor issued to *Lucie* Moyes, anchorite at Marhamchurch, in 1405 may refer (by clerical error) to the same woman.[23] There is no anchorhold standing at the church of St Marwenne, Marhamchurch, but a small stone window found in the rectory garden at the time of the church restoration is thought to have been part of the anchorite's cell. It is now mounted in a niche high in the west wall of the north aisle.

Translated from the Latin in 'Register of Stafford vol. 1': Devon Record Office, Exeter diocesan records, Chanter Catalogue 8, fols 64r–v.

Edmund, by divine condescension bishop of Exeter, to our beloved sons in Christ Philip, abbot of the monastery of Hartland, and Master

21 William Melton, archbishop of York 1317–40. The registered copy omits the usual enumeration of the bishop's titles. The dean of Newark was the bishop's agent in Nottinghamshire, whilst Rufford is about 3 miles from Kneesall.

22 The archbishop's palace of Cawood Castle, Cawood (N. Yorks.).

23 For discussion of Cecily/Lucie, see my 'A Mystic by Any Other Name: Julian(?) of Norwich', *Mystics Quarterly* 33/3–4 (2007), 1–17.

Walter Dollebeare, rector of the parish church of South Hill, in our diocese: [wishing you] health, grace and blessing.[24]

We have recently heard by trustworthy report that a certain Cecily [*Cecilia*] Moys of our aforesaid diocese, [a woman] of good life and reputable manners, desires and aspires to pursue the contemplative or anchoritic life in a certain house newly built in the cemetery of the parish church of Marhamchurch in our said diocese, and dwelling there to serve her Lord in virtues perpetually. Although this praiseworthy intention of hers is rightly to be commended, because we are attentive to the fact that the ancient enemy with his cunning leads some astray (even those who according to human judgement are highly deserving), and so that such a misfortune should not befall in this case – especially since the frail sex is concerned; wishing to proceed properly in this matter, we commission and mandate you jointly and severally that, by our authority as ordinary, when you are asked on her behalf, you place and enclose her in the aforesaid house there to dwell as mentioned before, following the [liturgical] form that we are sending you along with these present letters;[25] assigning to the same Cecily the time from this enclosure and placing until the feast of Christmas next following as a time of probation to consider whether she wishes and is able to continue to lead this aforesaid life as described above.

In witness to which my seal is appended to the present letters. Given in our manor of Clyst [St Mary, nr Exeter], the 4th day of May, AD 1403, and the eighth [year] since our consecration.

3c. Licence to William de Pershore, 1278

In the majority of cases, those enquiries and enclosures that are recorded in bishops' registers concern female candidates for the anchoritic life. This could be because (as outlined in the Introduction) there were more women than men who took up the vocation; but it is also possible that, as Bishop Stafford's anxieties in [**3b**] suggest, the authorities were extra-careful where 'the frail sex' was concerned, both to conduct a full enquiry and to make sure that it was recorded. In almost all cases, the men who became anchorites had already been ordained as priests,

24 Edmund Stafford, bishop of Exeter 1395–1419. The Augustinian abbey of Hartland was situated a little less than 20 miles north of Marhamchurch on the North Devon coast, while South Hill was near Callington in Cornwall.

25 Presumably the commission was accompanied by a text of the enclosure rite, similar to [**5**].

and so many of the candidate's personal qualities could perhaps have been taken as read. But questions of material support and the consent of those likely to be affected by an enclosure still needed to be checked, as in this example. The church of Holy Trinity, Wickwar, was extensively altered in the fourteenth and fifteenth centuries, and no trace of the cell that William built remains.

Translated from the Latin in 'Register of Godfrey Giffard': Worcestershire Record Office, x716.093/BA2648/Parcel 1(i), fol. 79d.

G[odfrey] by divine permission, etc.[26] to our beloved son William de Pershore, priest, [wishing you] health, grace and blessing.

Whereas, as you have humbly beseeched us, you intend to build a little house suitable for yourself in the parish of Wickwar, enclosed in which you desire to practise the solitary life, and therein to serve the lord Jesus Christ in perpetuity; and you have (as you assert) the consent of the patron and rector of the church of that place; and, moreover, you have provided yourself with what you need to survive; having bowed to your entreaties that, if we do so, you will strengthen the purpose to fulfil this worthy intention, we grant permission by the terms of these present letters.

Given at Henbury in the Saltmarsh[27] 4 kal. September [29 Aug. 1278].

3d. Commission to enclose Margaret Lakenby with Emmota Sherman, 1402

There had been a reclusory in the chapel of St Helen in Pontefract since at least the middle of the thirteenth century. It was in the patronage of the lords of Pontefract and adjoined the castle there. It later passed to the Duchy of Lancaster and then to the Crown, securing its future into the 16th century. There are suggestions in some of the records that the site was able to accommodate two anchoresses, so it was probably here that Margaret Lakenby joined Emmota Sherman in reclusion.[28] The need for the consent of the prioress of Arthington suggests that Lakenby had previously been a nun of that Cluniac house; the prior of Pontefract to whom the case was entrusted was a member of

26 Godfrey Giffard, bishop of Worcester 1268–1302.

27 Henbury near Westbury on Trym (Glos.), where the bishop had one of his palaces.

28 Anchorholds in multiple occupancy are discussed by Warren, *Anchorites and Their Patrons*, pp. 33–6.

the same order. Emmota Sherman (or Scherman) had recently moved from another cell in the town [**11**].

Translated from the Latin entry in the register of Archbishop Richard Scrope, York Abp Reg 16, fol. 35r.[29]

Richard etc.[30] to his beloved son the prior of the priory of St John Baptist of Pontefract, greetings, grace and blessing.

Given that we are obliged by right to accede to those who come to us with just requests, and chiefly those who strive to devote themselves to the fruit of a better life, and those whose frailty of sex is more inclined, through worldly concerns and the common intercourse of mankind, to be snatched away to evil by the promptings of nature;

So it is that, whereas our beloved daughter Margaret Lakenby, that she may more particularly dedicate herself to God, desires to be enclosed with the anchoress Emmota Sherman, also enclosed in Pontefract, by the present letters we commit to you, in whose fidelity and industry in this regard we have full faith, full power to enclose the said Margaret, provided that the consent of the Prioress of Arthington and of the said Emmota and of other people who might be affected is forthcoming.

We wish, moreover, that you should inform yourself fully concerning the express desire, the personal suitability and the sufficiency of maintenance after her enclosure of the said Margaret, so that she may not be forced (God forbid!) to return to the world by reason of penury.

Given in our manor of Rest [Rest Park, nr Sherburn in Elmet], the 11th day of the month of July, AD 1402, and the fifth since our translation.

3e. Commission to enclose Christine Holby, 1447

The longest of the documents in this section, and the most involved enquiry, was prompted by an unusual case. When Christine Holby, a refugee from the priory of Kildare in war-torn Ireland, turned up in Exeter declaring her intention to become an anchorite, the bishop, Edmund Lacy, had more than the usual range of questions to consider. As well as satisfying himself as to her personal and spiritual suitability for the life, he had to be sure that she had received the proper licence

29 Calendared by R.N. Swanson, *A Calendar of the Register of Richard Scrope, Archbishop of York, 1398–1405*, Part 1, Borthwick Texts and Calendars 8 (York: Borthwick Institute of Historical Research, 1981), p. 34.

30 Richard Scrope, archbishop of York 1398–1405.

from her spiritual superiors in Kildare, so that there would be no impediment to her taking her new vows. And, since one of her express reasons for leaving Ireland was extreme poverty, he would want to be absolutely certain that she had sufficient backing to guarantee her material support throughout the time that she was enclosed. For an earlier anchorite at the church of St Leonard in Exeter see [**16**]. The medieval church is no longer standing, the present St Leonard's dating from 1876.

Translated from the Latin in G.R. Dunstan, ed., *The Register of Edmund Lacy, Bishop of Exeter, 1420–1455: Registrum Commune*, Vol. 5, Canterbury & York Society 66 (1971), pp. 394–6.

Edmund by divine authority bishop of Exeter to our beloved son in Christ Master Walter Collys, precentor of our cathedral church of Exeter:[31] [wishing you] health, grace and blessing.

A humble request has been made to us on behalf of Christine Holby, a religious woman and nun of the priory of Kildare, near St Patrick's Purgatory in Ireland,[32] of the Order of St Augustine, that she who, as she has declared to us, has been serving God continually together with her sisters in religion in the said priory of Kildare of the aforementioned order, where she is fully professed, has been reduced to poverty through the misfortunes of war and by the wild Irish,[33] which have caused the destruction and devastation of the aforesaid priory and region of Kildare, so that she does not have the means to live unless supported by the faithful, and on account of this poverty and with the consent of her prioress she has travelled to these parts, just as the rest of the sisters of that priory have in a similar fate ended up scattered in various parts of the world, as will it seems to us be more fully apparent from certain letters shown to us on behalf of the aforesaid Christine, a faithful copy of which is annexed to the present letters; she, intending as she declares to serve God more devoutly and to lead the stricter life of an anchorite in a house situated in the churchyard of the parish church of St Leonard outside the south gate of our city of Exeter, desires to have our consent.

31 Edmund Lacy, bishop of Exeter 1420–1455. The precentor was the cathedral choir-master, though by the late Middle Ages it was more of an honorary appointment.

32 The cave through which St Patrick was said to have entered the underworld is in fact located on an island in Lough Derg, Co. Donegal, and some distance from Kildare.

33 *Hibernie silvestri* – a derogatory term frequently used in English sources of the time.

Although this laudable intention of hers deserves to be commended, we none the less, perceiving keenly in our mind's eye that Satan often transforms himself into an angel of light, and conscious of the words of the apostle where he asserts that the laying on of hands should not be done hastily,[34] commission and instruct you diligently and faithfully to analyse and examine the said Christine's letters of permission, by which alone she has been granted licence to journey to the realm of England in relief of her poverty and distress, and by which she might be able to be received by the faithful and cherished in a loving embrace, to determine whether her letters or licence expressly sought from her prioress are sufficient in law for her to take on the life of an anchorite by means of a solemn and perpetual vow, and thus ⌜by extension⌝ to migrate to other vows. And if so, and furthermore once you have summoned all those who ought by right to be summoned in this case, and specifically and in particular the rector of the said church of St Leonard, together with all and anyone who might have a right or interest in this case, you are diligently and faithfully to find out the truth as to whether she can be enclosed in the aforesaid place without prejudice to the rights of anyone else; and also concerning her life and character; her suitable, secure and guaranteed sustenance, and who will endow and maintain her there until the end of her life; and how much, where, and what things this perpetual endowment or support of hers should securely consist of, so that neither we nor our successors should in any way be burdened in this regard by this enclosure; and other points and all considerations touching this business of enclosure.

And if, through this enquiry, investigation and examination you find no legal obstacle against this, we commission you (in whose care and attention we place our trust) by the terms of these present letters on our behalf to enclose or reclude the same ⌜Christine⌝ in the little house prepared for her in the churchyard of the aforesaid church of St Leonard, with the solemn ritual necessary in such cases, and also solemnly to receive her vow in our place and name and with our authority in this case; and once she is enclosed to close, lock and if necessary block up the door, and to do and expedite each and everything else that might be necessary or suitable in these matters; provided always, for the security of ourselves and our cathedral church of Exeter, that suitable and reliable provision is made for the same Christine, before her enclosure or reclusion, for the sustaining of her life and her sufficient

34 1 Tim. 5:22: 'Impose not hands lightly upon any man', understood as an injunction not to ordain anyone to the ministry without due process and diligence.

endowment, lest, to the shame of this holy work that she has begun, she should end up unfortunately being forced to break her solemn vow because of a lack of suitable support.

And once you have completed the foregoing task, you should be sure to give us an account of what you have done and what discovered in these matters, together with the responses given and made to you by those with an interest in this case, and the whole process that you have carried out in this case, duly according to the terms of these present letters. Given etc. [at Radeway,[35] 14 Sept. 1447].

3f. Record of enclosure of Emma Sprenghose, 1311

This last example is not a commission to enclose, but the letter of a bishop certifying that he himself has conducted an enquiry and enclosure, perhaps sought by the newly made anchorite as a written guarantee that her admission to the solitary life had followed due procedure.

Translated from the Latin in *The Register of Walter Langton, Bishop of Coventry and Lichfield 1296–1321*, Vol. 2, edited by J.B. Hughes, Canterbury & York Society 97 (2007), p. 202.

Walter etc.[36] to our beloved daughter Emma Sprenghose of our diocese [wishing you] health, grace and blessing.

Conscious of your devout and pious intention that, inspired by the divine spirit of God Almighty, you have desired since your childhood to serve God continually in the solitary life of an anchorite, and desire it still in the present, we nevertheless still wanted to understand as far as possible the truth of your life and your manner of living, and we made diligent enquiries into your suitability through appropriate men who had knowledge of your manner of living in the present time and in the past; through which we find you to be suitable for this solitary life as regards your character and other things touching the aforesaid life; and accordingly by these present letters we admit you as an anchorite, to serve God in the houses in the churchyard of St George's chapel, Shrewsbury.

In witness of which, etc. Given at Eccleshall,[37] 16 kal. February in the aforementioned year of our Lord [17 Jan. 1311].

35 Bishopsteignton (S. Devon) where, as the name suggests, the bishops of Exeter held the manor and had a residence.

36 Walter Langton, bishop of Coventry and Lichfield 1296–1321.

37 Eccleshall Castle, residence of the bishops of Coventry and Lichfield.

4. Enclosure of an anchorite, from the Clifford Pontifical

Corpus Christi College Cambridge MS 79 is a fine example of a late medieval Pontifical, a one-volume collection of all the liturgical offices that were reserved to a bishop. The book takes its popular name from one of its owners, Richard Clifford, bishop of Worcester 1402–7 and of London 1407–21. Though originally begun for another bishop, it was completed and provided with illustrations during Clifford's time in London.[38] The illustrations are positioned at the start of each text, and provide a handy key to the book's contents for anyone leafing through in search of a particular office. With that in mind, it is

38 Kathleen L. Scott, *A Survey of Manuscripts Illuminated in the British Isles: Vol. 6: Later Gothic Manuscripts 1390–1490* (2 vols, London: Harvey Miller, 1996), no. 18, Vol. 2, pp. 80–1.

interesting that, although in its text of the rite for enclosure of anchorites [**5**] the Clifford Pontifical uses generic masculine forms throughout, in the illustration that precedes the text the anchorite in process of being enclosed is female.[39]

Reproduced from Corpus Christi College, Cambridge, MS 79, fol. 72r, by permission of the Master and Fellows of Corpus Christi College, Cambridge.

5. Rite for the enclosing of an anchorite

The version of the *ordo*, or liturgical rite, for enclosing an anchorite translated here dates from the mid-12th century, and is the earliest known. There are some dozen other copies of the rite from medieval England, and many of them follow the text reproduced here closely; it was still being used at the end of the fifteenth century. In some later examples the rite becomes longer and more complex, but its essential features are already present here.[40]

Translated from the Latin printed as an appendix to H.A. Wilson, *The Pontifical of Magdalen College, with an appendix of extracts from other English Mss. of the twelfth century*, Henry Bradshaw Society 39 (1910), pp. 243–4. Rubrics (written in red in the manuscript) are here printed as italics.

If [the candidate] is female, she should initially lie in the western part of the church where it is usual for women to be accommodated. If [the candidate] is male and a member of the laity, he should lie at the entrance to the choir. If he is a clerk or a priest, he should lie prostrate and barefoot, praying, in the middle of the choir.

Then two clerks standing before the altar step should sing a full litany for all to hear, with the choir responding to each [invocation] saying Pray for him.[41] *When they come to the patron saint of the church they should name him or her three times, with bowing of their heads.*

Once the litany is complete, the bishop (if he is present), dressed in priestly vestments but without chasuble, together with the deacon and subdeacon, should come to the candidate still lying prostrate, with a cross placed before him and with holy water and a thurible. And he should first walk around him three

39 For further discussion of this manuscript, see my 'Ceremonies of Enclosure'.

40 For a full study of the rite, see my 'Rites of Enclosure'.

41 Though recognising that the rite may be used for both genders, the text in the manuscript uses masculine forms throughout.

times sprinkling holy water, and then do the same with the censer.[42] *If the bishop is not present, this should be done by a priest.*

Then two older men, who should be priests, and anyone they ask to help them, should raise the candidate up, and put two burning wax tapers into his hands, to show that he should burn with love for God and for his neighbour. Holding one of these in each of his hands, the candidate should listen attentively while the subdeacon reads this lesson:

> [Isaiah 26:20–27:4] Go, my people, enter into thy chamber, shut thy doors upon thee, hide thyself a little for a moment, until the indignation pass away. For behold the Lord will come out of his place, to visit the iniquity of the inhabitant of the earth against him: and the earth shall disclose her blood, and shall cover her slain no more. In that day the Lord with his hard, and great, and strong sword shall visit Leviathan the bar serpent, and Leviathan the crooked serpent,[43] and shall slay the whale that is in the sea. In that day there shall be singing to the vineyard of pure wine. I am the Lord that keep it, I will suddenly give it drink: lest any hurt come to it, I keep it night and day. There is no indignation in me.
>
> So says the Lord Almighty.

After this the gospel according to Luke should be read:

> [Luke 10:38–42] He entered into a certain town: and a certain woman named Martha received him into her house. And she had a sister called Mary, who, sitting also at the Lord's feet, heard his word. But Martha was busy about much serving. Who stood and said: Lord, hast thou no care that my sister hath left me alone to serve? Speak to her therefore, that she help me. And the Lord answering, said to her: Martha, Martha, thou art careful and art troubled about many things: But one thing is necessary. Mary hath chosen the best part, which shall not be taken away from her.

When this is finished the cantor should begin Come creator spirit *for all to hear, and the chorus should duly sing the rest of it. The aforesaid older men, one on each side of the one-to-be-enclosed, should lead him to the altar while the choir sings the hymn as they do on feast days.*

42 The chasuble is the cloak-like outer garment worn on top of the other vestments. A thurible or censer is used for burning incense.

43 (Douai translation.) The precise meaning of these phrases is unclear. The New International Version has 'Leviathan the gliding serpent, Leviathan the coiling serpent'.

When that is complete, the one-to-be-enclosed should genuflect three times, whilst saying this verse three times: Receive me Lord according to thy word, and I shall live: and let me not be confounded in my expectation.[44] *When this has been said three times he should offer his tapers at the candelabra on the altar, and then again sit in silence or lie prostrate.*

The priest or another person should expound the lesson and gospel to the people, and commend the one-to-be-enclosed to the people, requesting that they should pray for him. Then the priest – or the one-to-be-enclosed, if he is a priest – should say a Mass of the Holy Spirit.

Once this is finished, the aforementioned older men should take the one-to-be-enclosed, one on each side, and lead him to his reclusory. As they go, they should begin this antiphon

> May angels lead you into paradise; upon your arrival, may the martyrs receive you and lead you to the holy city of Jerusalem. May the ranks of angels receive you, and with Lazarus, the poor man, may you have eternal rest.

and the choir should sing the psalm Give thanks to the Lord[45] *accompanied by the same antiphon. When they reach the door, the one-to-be-enclosed should himself begin the antiphon* I shall go over into the place of the wonderful tabernacle, even to the house of God *and the choir should sing the psalm* As the hart panteth,[46] *and with that they should enter the little house, with the cross and thurible and the water blessed by the bishop. Then the priest should sprinkle the whole house with holy water, and then cense it, and then perform the whole office of Anointing the Sick, beginning the antiphon:*

> The archangel Raphael went in and greeted Tobias and said, 'Joy be to thee always'. And Tobias said, 'What manner of joy shall be to me, who sit in darkness, and see not the light of heaven?' And the angel said to him, 'Be of good courage, thy desire from God is at hand'. [Cf. Tobias 5:11–13]

And the priest should begin all the antiphons, with the choir outside continuing to sing the psalms together with the same antiphons.

44 Cf. Psalm 118:116. The verse is similarly repeated three times when a Benedictine monk makes his profession.

45 Psalm 117, used, with the foregoing antiphon, in the burial service at the opening of the grave.

46 Psalm 41, used, with the antiphon, in the burial service at the moment when the body is placed into the grave.

In the same way the priest should recite Commendations of the Soul,[47] *up to the point where the deceased is placed upon the bier, so that the recluse will not miss out on this holy service by the intervention of death. When, with great devotion, these have been completed, the grave should be opened. And then, getting into it, the one-to-be-enclosed himself should begin the antiphon* Here shall be my repose for ever and ever; here shall I dwell for I have chosen it, *the choir outside singing the psalm* O Lord, remember David *together with the same antiphon.*[48] *Then, casting a little dust onto him, the priest should begin the antiphon* From the earth you formed me, My Lord and Redeemer, raise me up on the last day, *the choir then singing the psalm* Lord, thou hast proved me [Psalm 138] *and repeating the antiphon.*

After this, everyone should go out, though the priest should remain for a little while, enjoining the recluse that he should obediently rise up [from his grave] and in obedience see out the remainder of his life. And with that the door of the house should be blocked up. And, once the psalm with its antiphon, and the prayers – that is It is indeed audacious *and* O God, giver of life[49] – *are finished, all should depart quietly.*

6. Two anchorites' professions from sixteenth-century London

The vows of these two sixteenth-century anchorites were recorded in the register of the bishop of London, Richard FitzJames (bishop 1506–22). A formal vow of this kind was sometimes included in later versions of the enclosure rite (though it is absent from [**5**]), doubtless by analogy with monastic profession. Following the reading of the gospel, candidates were required to approach the altar and, standing before the altar step, to read their profession aloud (or, if illiterate, to have it read for them), before signing it and laying it upon the altar.[50]

47 A series of prayers associated with the Office of the Dead, in which the soul is commended to the protection of God and various saints, for its safe reception into heaven.

48 Psalm 131. This psalm and antiphon are also found in the Burial of the Dead, just after the grave has been closed.

49 Both prayers come towards the end of the Burial of the Dead.

50 For a version of the enclosure rite that includes the reading of a vow, see Clay, *Hermits and Anchorites*, p. 195. The form of words used is very similar to that recorded here.

6a. Simon Appulby

Simon Appulby was the last of the anchorites enclosed at All Hallows, London Wall.[51] The church abutted the city wall, and Appulby's cell, on the north side of the church, may have been part of the defensive structure itself. There had been anchorites at All Hallows since at least the beginning of the fifteenth century, and there are more or less continuous records of occupation from the middle of the century until Appulby's time. He remained an anchorite at All Hallows for the next quarter century: for his will, dated 1537, see [**35b**].

Translated from the Latin printed by R.M. Clay, 'Further Studies on Medieval Recluses', *The Journal of the British Archaeological Association* 3rd series 16 (1953): 74–86, at p. 86.

Profession of Sir Simon Appulby, anchorite

I, Simon Appulby, priest, offer and give myself to the mercy of God to serve in the order of an anchorite; and, according to the rule of that order, I promise to continue in the service of God from this time forward, by the grace of God and with the guidance of the Church, and to show obedience according to the law to my spiritual fathers.

This profession and promise of submission and obedience was read before the reverend father Sir Richard FitzJames, bishop of London, in the monastery of Holy Trinity in London, on Sunday 26th June, AD [1513].

6b. Margery Elyote

Simon Appulby's profession (so far as we know) went off without a hitch, but Margery Elyote had to contend with a last-minute objection. The Black Friars, or Dominicans, occupied a large site in the south-western corner of the city, just inside the wall, which still bears their name. Margery Elyote's cell adjoined the north-west porch of the church. It was still described as 'a messuage called the Ancres Lodgyng' in 1544, when it was granted to a layman, Thomas Godwyne, and the name 'Ancres howse' was remembered as late as 1570.[52] Though physically

51 For more on Appulby, see Mary C. Erler, *Reading and Writing During the Dissolution: Monks, Friars, and Nuns 1530–1558* (Cambridge: Cambridge University Press, 2013), pp. 14–37 and 144–7; and Clare M. Dowding, '"Item receyvyd of ye Anker": The relationships between a parish and its anchorites as seen through the churchwardens' accounts' in *Anchorites in Their Communities* edited by Cate Gunn and Liz Herbert McAvoy (Cambridge: D.S. Brewer, 2017), pp. 117–30.

52 For more on Elyote, see R.M. Clay, 'Some Northern Anchorites', *Archaeologica Aeliana* 4th series, 33 (1955): 202–17, at pp. 213–14. For her cell, see Nick Holder, *The Friaries of Medieval London: From foundation to dissolution* (Woodbridge: Boydell Press, 2017), p. 40.

attached to the church of the friars' convent, the cell was not dependent on it, as their Prior was keen to establish.

(i) is modernised from the English in 'Repertories of the Aldermen of the City of London, Repertory 5': London Metropolitan Archives COL/CA/01/01/005, fol. 228r; (ii) is from a seventeenth-century transcript excerpted from the vicar general's register, Bodleian Library, Oxford, MS Tanner 176, fol. 132v; the vow is originally in English and the date clause in Latin.

(i) 25 Sept. 1521
At the court of Aldermen came a woman which on Sunday next should be professed an anchoress in a new house made at the Blackfriars adjoining to the church there, and also as she said she is professed in the order of Black Friars, and further said that the Prior of the said friars will not suffer her to be professed nor to be enclosed in the said house unless that she would find sufficient collateral surety to discharge his house for any meat [*food*], drink or clothing, or any other charge, that she should hereafter claim or ask of the said house.

Whereupon the said Prior, now sent for, at his coming he said in like wise as the said recluse had said and, after long consideration had, the said Prior in response to the entreaties of this court, agreed that she should be professed here and have all her petition, provided that she would here make faithful promise to this court that hereafter she will never claim or ask any such thing as is mentioned before.

To the which she made full and faithful promise so to do, and never to claim as of right any meat, drink or any other obligation whatsoever in the future from the said house.

(ii) I, Sister Margery Elyote, offer and give myself to the mercy of God in the order of an anchoress, to live in his service after the rule of an anchoress, and here in the presence of you, worshipful father in God Thomas, bishop of Lydence,[53] I make my obedience to the worshipful father in God, Lord Richard FitzJames, bishop of London, and to his successors.

On the 29th day of September, AD 1521, in the conventual church of the Friars Preachers of London, she made her vow and was solemnly professed.

53 Thomas Bale, titular bishop of Lydda in the Holy Land, and a suffragan of the bishop of London. His pontifical survives, and its version of the rite for a hermit's profession is translated in Clay, *Hermits and Anchorites*, appendix B.

II: A CELL OF ONE'S OWN[1]

Introduction

We do not have much information about the size and design of anchorholds or reclusories: the documents rarely give details, and standing remains or archaeological evidence are both rare and rarely straightforward to interpret.[2] Though a priest-anchorite could, in theory, be spiritually self-sufficient, cells were almost invariably attached to a larger religious establishment, where the anchorite could participate – albeit from a distance – in the worship and spiritual life of a wider community. The host institution might be a monastery, or a hospital, or under civic control, like a gatehouse chapel; or a cell could be in royal or aristocratic patronage, as the chapels in the Tower of London and a range of other royal and baronial castles.[3] But the great majority of anchorholds were attached to one of the external walls of a parish church, 'under the eaves of the church', as *Ancrene Wisse* puts it.[4]

The foundations of a stone-built anchorhold at Leatherhead (Surrey) indicate a building 2.43 m square. The plan of the reclusory at Compton in the same county [**8**] was even smaller, but it had two storeys, as

1 The reminiscence of Virginia Woolf is borrowed from Elizabeth Robertson, 'An Anchorhold of Her Own: Female anchoritic literature in thirteenth century England' in *Equally in God's Image: Women in the Middle Ages* edited by Julia Bolton Holloway, Constance S. Wright and Joan Bechtold (New York: P. Lang, 1990), pp. 170–83. For the Desert Fathers, too, the cell was central to anchoritic identity: 'Go, stay inside your cell, and your cell will teach you all things': quoted from the *Apophthegmata Patrum* by William Harmless, *Desert Christians: An introduction to the literature of early monasticism* (Oxford: Oxford University Press, 2004), p. 228.

2 For more on the design of cells, see Roberta Gilchrist, *Contemplation and Action* (London: Leicester University Press, 1995), pp. 185–93. For discussion of a recently-investigated example, see Cate Gunn, 'Was There an Anchoress at Colne Priory?', *Transactions of the Essex Society for Archaeology and History* 4/2 (2011–13): 117–23. See also Jeremy Lander, 'The Sacristy, the Church of St. Mary & All Saints, Willingham, Cambridgeshire: The case for an anchorhold' (2005), www.oldwillingham.com/History/SMAS/Lander/Lander.htm.

3 For these, see my 'O Sely Ankir' in *Medieval Anchorites in Their Communities* edited by Cate Gunn and Liz Herbert McAvoy (Cambridge: D.S. Brewer, 2017), pp. 13–34.

4 Trans. Millett, p. 56. In the sixteenth century, Thomas Parkinson lived in a room above the church porch in Thirsk (N. Yorks.) [**74**].

did the no-longer-extant cell occupied by John Lacy in Newcastle-upon-Tyne [**23**]. (See also the plan of the cell at Lewes, [**29**].) Stone buildings are found only infrequently, however; most cells were probably built of wood on minimal foundations, and the nature of their construction, together with the frequent extension and rebuilding to which most parish churches have been subject, has generally left few architectural traces (for an exception, see [**9**]).

With respect to the foregoing examples, the site granted in [**7**] is comparatively generous, at a little over 6 m square. It compares with the plot given in 1402 to William Bolle (or Bull), who resigned as rector of Aldrington (Sussex) in order to live as an anchorite, and was assigned a piece of land adjoining Chichester Cathedral measuring 7.3 by 8.8 m.[5] A dwelling of such dimensions would not be unheard-of: the cells occupied by individual Carthusian monks are of very similar size. But it is possible that the land granted in these cases was intended not only for the anchorite's dwelling-house but for a small courtyard or garden as well [**11**]. The provision of some outside space seems not to have been particularly unusual: in 1256 Juliana, anchoress at St Nicholas's Worcester, was permitted to widen the courtyard adjoining her cell by up to seven feet in each direction, and the anchorhold attached to the Carthusian priory at Sheen (Surrey) had a garden added to it some time after its foundation in 1417.[6] The cells of Carthusian monks each had a small private garden, and the restored cell at Mount Grace Priory (N. Yorks.) gives an idea of what such a garden might have looked like. Such evidence for attention to an anchorite's physical health and well-being provides a pleasant counter-balance to Roberta Gilchrist's rather grim finding that the majority of anchorite's cells were positioned on the north side of the church, whose shadow would have kept them cold and dark.[7] So too the efforts made by the parishioners of Rye (Sussex) on behalf of their anchorite, for whom they installed heating in the sixteenth century [**10**].

The rite for enclosing an anchorite [**5**] ends with the door to the cell being blocked up, and in some cases the solitary really was walled into his or her cell (see [**34**] for an example of this), or at least securely

5 Edward Turner, 'Domus Anachoritae, Aldrington,' *Sussex Archaeological Collections* 12 (1860): 117–39, pp. 135–6.

6 See my, 'Hermits and Anchorites in Historical Context' in *Teaching Anchorites and Mystics* edited by Roger Ellis, Dee Dyas and Valerie Edden (Cambridge: D.S. Brewer, 2005), pp. 3–18, at pp. 12–13.

7 Roberta Gilchrist, *Contemplation and Action*, pp. 187–90.

locked in.[8] Even the late and humane *Speculum Inclusorum* [**1**] speaks of the solitary's cell as a 'perpetual prison'. The furnishings mentioned in the sources are sparse: a bed, though not a comfortable one [**27**]; if a male anchorite is a priest, an altar; and, most strikingly, an open grave [**29**], [**30**]. *Ancrene Wisse* envisages three windows: one opening into the church, for worship; one into the servants' quarters, through which food could be passed in and waste passed out; and a third into the parlour, where guests might be received. (There is no mention in this text at least of a window opening to the outside.) The window into the church would usually be a 'squint': a widely splayed opening narrowing to a vertical slit that was designed to afford a view into the church of the high altar, and not much else [**8**].[9] Windows should be obscured by a curtain, or fitted with a shutter [**29**].

It seems to have been expected that anchorites would have servants, usually accommodated on site. Aelred advised his sister to limit their number to two, an older woman of proven character to manage the household and regulate access to the solitary, and a younger one to do the manual work [**12a**]. *Ancrene Wisse* likewise recommends two serving women, one of whom will not normally leave the enclosure of the reclusory. They are to follow some religious observances as well as catering to the material needs of the anchorite, and she is to act as their religious superior as well as the head of their household.[10] Indeed, we know of a number of instances when anchorites succeeded their master or mistress after their death [**35a**]. The anchorites of Whalley were expected to keep two female servants [**13**], and in the sixteenth century the anchoress at Faversham (Kent) likewise had two serving women. Since one received a substantially greater legacy than the other, we may assume a situation similar to that envisaged by Aelred [**12b**]. Another notable instance is Julian of Norwich. Four fifteenth-century wills contain bequests to Julian (either by name or beyond reasonable doubt); two of those mention her servant: in 1404 Thomas Emund left 12d to Julian, anchorite at the church of St Julian,

8 For a discussion of the evidence for and against the blocking up of the cell door, see my 'Ceremonies of Enclosure: Rite, rhetoric and reality' in *Rhetoric of the Anchorhold: Space, place and body within the discourses of enclosure* edited by Liz Herbert McAvoy (Cardiff: University of Wales Press, 2008), pp. 34–49.

9 A photograph of the view through the squint at Chester-le-Street (Durham) features on the cover of my *Speculum Inclusorum / A Mirror for Recluses: A late-medieval guide for anchorites and its Middle English translation* (Liverpool: Liverpool University Press, 2013).

10 Millett, *Ancrene Wisse*, pp. 161–4.

and 8d to Sarah who lives with her, and in 1415 John Plumpton left 40d to the anchorite at St Julian's, 12d to her maidservant, and 12d to her former maid, Alice.[11]

As we saw in Chapter I, an anchorite could not be enclosed without proof of financial security [**2**], [**6b**]. The best way to ensure the steady income that would guarantee a recluse's maintenance was an endowment with land. Such an arrangement, however, was relatively uncommon, even before the Statute of Mortmain (1279) made it harder to alienate land to religious bodies. An individual could be endowed for life [**17**] or, even more rarely, an anchorhold could be endowed in perpetuity [**13**]. Even in cases such as these, however, a donor's best intentions could be disrupted by unforeseen circumstances [**17**], [**32**].[12] More common was a 'fixed alms' or recurrent gift taken out of the patron's income [**14**]. The Crown supported a number of anchorites in this way, and the regular payments are recorded on the pipe rolls.[13] At Frodsham in the thirteenth century [**14**] the king took over a fixed alms originally granted by the earl of Chester, continuing the annual payment of 30s 5d, or 365 pence. Such an income would have provided an ample level of maintenance in the thirteenth century. Anchorites supported directly by the king himself could have expected to receive 1d a day as standard in the twelfth century, rising towards 1½d in the thirteenth.[14] Even in the fourteenth century an income of 30s per annum, or just under a penny a day [**17**], would have been a modest but adequate living: it was about the same as the usual wages for an unskilled labourer. Only very rarely do our sources allow us to see beyond the financial commitments to glimpse a genuine warmth and friendship between anchorite and patron [**15**].

Anchorites would undoubtedly have topped up their core income with occasional gifts from visitors. William Langland is scathing in his criticism of 'ancres there a box hangeth' – that is, whose cells feature

11 The wills containing bequests to Julian of Norwich are translated in Nicholas Watson and Jacqueline Jenkins, eds, *The Writings of Julian of Norwich: A vision showed to a devout woman and a revelation of love* (Turnhout: Brepols, 2006), pp. 431–5.

12 For other cases illustrating the precariousness of anchorites' incomes, see Warren, *Anchorites and Their Patrons*, pp. 44–8.

13 These were studied in detail by Warren in *Anchorites and Their Patrons*, though she restricted her analysis to the published rolls, which end in 1224. (The series continues into the 19th century: see TNA E 372.)

14 For rates of royal and baronial support, see Warren, *Anchorites and Their Patrons*, esp. pp. 134 and 157.

a prominently displayed collection box.[15] The household accounts of nobles and gentry often include small donations made on visits to a recluse. Anchorites could also be singled out for legacies when people came to make their wills. We noted in the Introduction the bequests made by Henry Lord Scrope to seventeen specified recluses, plus all the anchorites in and around London and York. Scrope was exceptional, of course. Among ordinary testators, gifts to the parish church and its charities, and local orders of monks, nuns and friars, were likely to be remembered before anchorites. A bequest to a solitary might be a mark of particular devotion to the host church, or perhaps a way for the testator to identify themselves, at least in intention, with the highest spiritual ideals. The sequence of bequests to the anchoress at St Leonard's in Exeter [**16**], for example, indicates the esteem in which anchorites were held, and the value placed upon their prayers for the testators' souls.

7. A site for an anchorhold in Smithfield

Katherine Hardel was a well-connected Londoner. Her husband William had been mayor between 1215 and 1217,[16] while she was the daughter of Robert de Basing, another mayoral family. She made several substantial grants to St Bartholomew's Hospital, Smithfield, in 1227–8, and it seems reasonable to associate these with the arrangements for her enclosure there. Some time afterwards, William Hardel confirmed to St Bartholomew's the grant to the Hospital of land and houses in London made by his late wife Katherine. So it appears either that she entered reclusion during her husband's lifetime (this was permitted, provided he gave his consent), or perhaps that she put everything in place for her retirement while both she and William were living, but in the event she predeceased him.[17] The hospital and adjacent priory of St Bartholomew were founded in the twelfth century on a site in Smithfield, outside the city walls, where the present St Bartholomew's Hospital ('Barts') still stands.

15 *Piers Plowman* (B-Text), XV.214: William Langland, *The Vision of Piers Plowman* edited by A.V.C. Schmidt (London: J.M. Dent, 1995).

16 Caroline M. Barron, *London in the Later Middle Ages: Government and people 1200–1500* (Oxford: Oxford University Press, 2010), p. 312.

17 See *Cartulary of St. Bartholomew's Hospital, founded 1123: A calendar*, edited by Nellie J.M. Kerling (London: St Bartholomew's Hospital, 1973), nos 868, 1036, app. I no. 267; no. 713. My thanks to Caroline Barron and Euan Roger for their help with this entry.

Translated from the Latin entry in *Rotuli litterarum clausarum in Turri londinensi asservati*, edited by T.D. Hardy (2 vols, London: Eyre & Spottiswoode, 1833, 1844), Vol. 2, p. 181.

The lord King granted to Katherine, wife of William Hardel, a piece of land twenty feet in length and the same in breadth in Smithfield, next to the chapel of the hospital of St Bartholomew, London, to construct a reclusory for herself. And the mayor and sheriffs are instructed that the said twenty feet of land should be assigned to the aforementioned Katherine as detailed above.

Witnessed as above [10 April 1227].

8. The anchorhold at Compton church

The church of St Nicholas at Compton near Guildford (Surrey) is part Anglo-Saxon. A squint (identified as a lychnoscope or 'low-side window' in (i) below) near the east end of the south aisle is thought to be associated with an early anchorite's cell at the church. More survives of the second anchorhold, a two-storey structure measuring only 2.04 by 1.31 m. It was investigated during the restoration of the church in 1906, and soon afterwards a description was included in the *Victoria County History*:

> The anchorite's cell, or watching-place, whichever it be, on the south side of the chancel has several interesting features: a tiny round-headed window apparently of 12th-century date; a door opening outwards suggesting that there was a porch or out-building of timber attached to the southern side; and a squint with a peculiar cross-shaped opening to the chancel. This squint, which would command a view of the altar, is high enough for a person to kneel within it on the cell side, and the oak board on its sill shows a depression worn by constant use. The squint also looks towards a nameless tomb, quatrefoil panelled, of 15th-century date, beneath a window of the same period in the north wall of the sanctuary, which probably served as an Easter Sepulchre. In the recent underpinning of the chancel walls several male skeletons (one having abundant bright red hair on the skull), buried one above another, were found beneath this tomb, and it has been suggested that these were successive occupants of the anchorite's cell.[18]

18 H.E. Malden, 'Parishes: Compton' in *The Victoria History of the County of Surrey: Vol. 3* (London: Constable and Company Limited, 1911), p. 23.

(i) from J. Lewis André, 'Compton Church', *Surrey Archaeological Collections* 12 (1895): 1–19, facing p. 1. (ii) from Mari Hughes-Edwards, 'Solitude and Sociability: The world of the medieval anchorite', *Historic Churches* (2012). Reproduced by kind permission of the publishers, Cathedral Communications Limited, Tisbury, Wiltshire. See: www.buildingconservation.com/articles/anchorites/anchorites.htm.

(i) Plan of St Nicholas, Compton

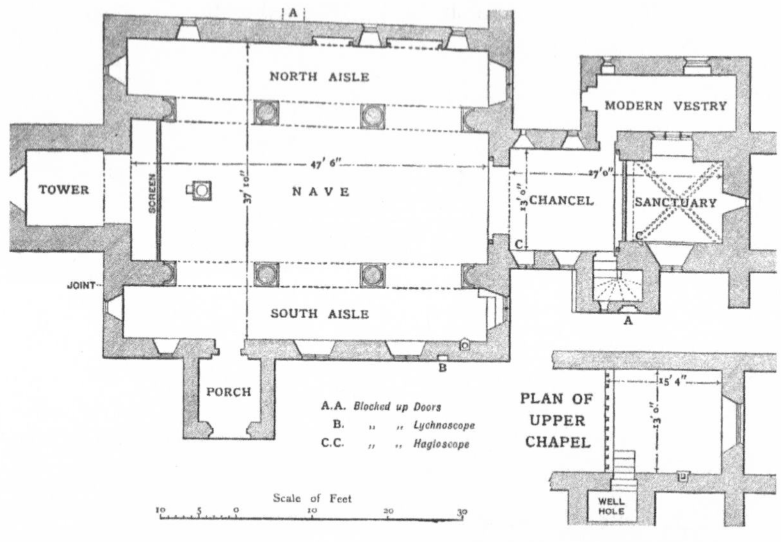

(ii) Squint, looking into the church

9. Traces of an anchorite's cell at Kingston Buci

There is no documentary record of an anchorite at the church of St Julian, Kingston Buci, in Shoreham-by-Sea in West Sussex, but there are architectural traces on the north side of the chancel that seem most likely to be associated with an anchorite's cell. They were uncovered in the 1920s,[19] and include the small window through which the kneeling anchorite could look towards the high altar and receive communion, and the line of the cell roof, clearly visible in the buttress on the right of the photograph. The cell must have fallen out of use and been demolished by the time the priest's door and large window were inserted in the chancel wall in the fourteenth century.

Photograph by the author.

10. A new roof and chimney for the anchorite at Rye

The magnificent church of St Mary dominates the prosperous Sussex town of Rye, one of the Cinque Ports confederation of south-coast towns that led English trade with the continent throughout the Middle Ages. There is no record of an anchorite here before the sixteenth

19 There is a brief account of the cell's discovery by Ray Silver, 'The Anchorite's Cell at Kingston Buci,' *Sussex County Magazine* 1 (1927), 144.

century.[20] The first reference comes in 1513, when the churchwardens paid for a key to the anchorite's door, and this might indicate the enclosure of a new recluse.[21] Five years later, the churchwardens went to no little expense to ensure the comfort of their anchorite. The chimney alone cost them over £1 2s, a sum more than one-eighth of their total expenses for that year.

Modernised from the English text of the accounts of the churchwardens of Rye: East Sussex Record Office, RYE/147/1, fol. 23v.

1518

Item paid for 5000 bricks for a chimney in the anker-house	8s 9d
Item paid for carrying the said bricks from the wharf to the church	12d
Item paid for water for making the same chimney	5½d
Item paid for 6 loads of sand for the same chimney	12d
Item paid to a mason for making the same chimney	11s
. . .	
Item paid for the tiling of the anker-house (workmanship only)	10d
Item paid for meat [*food*] and drink for the tiler	4d
Item paid for laths	½d
Item paid for sprigs [*roofing nails*]	½d
Item paid for one hundred tiles for the same house, and two ridging tiles	8d
Item paid for one load [of] sand for the same tiling	2d
Item paid for 2 baskets to carry hooks (?) and sand	2½d

11. A reclusory garden

As already noted, anchorites in the later Middle Ages were most frequently sited in towns (compare [**7**]), and in some cases it must have been a challenge to maintain a contemplative vocation in the midst of the urban bustle. Soon after she moved cell, Emma (or Emmota) was joined by a second anchoress, Margaret Lakenby [**3d**]. An indult is a licence or permission issued by the pope which grants some special privilege that the Church would not normally allow.

Translation of the Latin original quoted from *Calendar of Papal Registers*

20 For a hermit at Rye later in the century, see [**45**].

21 Rye: East Sussex Record Office, RYE/147/1, fols 4r, 5r. The extant accounts only begin in 1513, so earlier references could be lost.

Relating to Great Britain and Ireland, vol. 5: 1398–1404, edited by W.H. Bliss and J.A. Twemlow (London: HMSO, 1904), p. 471, with slight modifications.[22]

St Peter's, Rome, 16 Nov. 1401.

To Emma Scherman, of the diocese of York.

Indult to her – who formerly took a vow of a recluse, and has had herself for many years enclosed in a cell in the place of Pontefract, with a little garden contiguous thereto for the sake of taking fresh air, – on account of the tumults and clamours of the people in the said place, to transfer herself to a more suitable place, to have there another cell with a like garden, and to leave her cell yearly for the purpose of visiting churches and other pious places, and of gaining the indulgences granted there, without requiring licence of the diocesan or other.

12. Anchorites and their servants

These two selections represent a statement of theory, written originally in the late 12th century, and some evidence for practice, from the early 16th.

12a. Aelred's Rule of Life for a Recluse

Aelred of Rievaulx's short but comprehensive rule written in Latin for his enclosed sister was one of the most popular and enduringly influential works of guidance for English anchorites. Two separate translations into Middle English survive, though only one of them is complete. This excerpt is from the longer version which was made around the middle of the fifteenth century in the south of England, with the title 'A Treatise that is a rule and a form of living pertaining to a recluse'.

Translated from the Middle English, chapter 3 of MS Bodley 423 in *Aelred of Rievaulx's De Institutione Inclusarum*, edited by John Ayto and Alexandra Barratt, Early English Text Society o.s., 287 (1984), pp. 3–4.[23]

See now the kind of household you should maintain. First choose an old woman of virtuous living – no chatterbox or gadabout, not a scold or

22 Also quoted in Warren, *Anchorites and Their Patrons*, pp. 77–8.

23 The corresponding passage of Aelred's original is in his chapter 4 (trans. Macpherson, p. 49).

a gossip, but someone virtuous, who can provide evidence of her good character. Her duties shall be to look after your household supplies and provisions, to secure your doors, and to admit what needs to be admitted, and keep out what needs to be kept out. Under her authority she should have a woman of younger age to take on the heavier work, such as fetching of wood and water, and boiling and preparing of food and drink. And see that she is supervised under strict discipline, lest through her wantonness and dissolution your holy temple should be defiled and laid open to slander. Be careful, also, that you are not occupied with the teaching of children. For there are some recluses who, by the teaching of children, turn their cell into a school-house: do not do this but, in terms of company and of service, be satisfied with these two women aforesaid.

12b. The anchoress of Faversham and her servants

A household similar to that envisaged by Aelred seems to have existed at Faversham (Kent), about 10 miles from Canterbury on the London road, in the early sixteenth century.[24] In his last will and testament, Robert Billesdon of Faversham makes a number of pious bequests to local religious houses as well as to the anchorite there. She received a substantial bequest of half a mark, the same as several high-ranking monastic officers. Her 'woman' evidently also held a position of some worth: she received the same as a monk of Faversham, and twice as much as an ordinary nun at Davington or Sheppey. The duties of the servant who received 10d were probably purely menial, though Billesdon expects her too to pray for his soul.[25]

Modernised text from Billesdon's will, written in English, proved in the Archdeaconry Court of Canterbury; now at Maidstone, Centre for Kentish Studies, PRC 17/9/150.

In the name of the Father and of the Son and of the Holy Spirit, amen.

I, Robert Billesdon of Faversham, calling to my remembrance the natural, the uncertain and inevitable course of death, being of sound mind

24 See also Anon., 'Anchorites in Faversham Churchyard', *Archaeologia Cantiana* 11 (1877), 24–39. A cruciform opening in the north transept may be associated with this cell.

25 The Faversham anchoress and her women occur also in a will of 1496, and there is a bequest to the anchoress and her servant in 1511. See Leland L. Duncan, ed., *Testamenta Cantiana* (London: Mitchell Hughes and Clarke, 1906), pp. 128–9. Billesdon's will is also listed here, although the date given is wrong. See also [**15b**].

and in health of body, the 12th day of June the year of our lord God 1503, make my testament in form following.

...

Item I will that the prioress in Sheppey shall have after my decease 10s and each of her sisters 20d; the prioress of Davington, 6s 8d and each sister 20d, to pray for me and my wife. Also my lord abbot in Faversham shall have 10s, the prior 6s 8d, and each of his brethren 3s 4d for the service of my burying and month's mind. ... *Item* to the monks of the charterhouse in London, 40s (not into one man's hand but one portion to each man) and [they should be sent] my letter of confraternity[26] with them, for them to pray for me and my wife. And to the anchoress in Faversham 6s 8d, to her woman 3s 4d, and to her servant 10d for the same intent.

13. Arrangements for the material support of the anchorites of Whalley

Henry of Grosmont, first duke of Lancaster (c. 1310–61), was one of the foremost soldiers of his day, a leading politician and diplomat, and grandfather of King Henry IV. He was also a man of piety, as revealed in his penitential, semi-autobiographical treatise *Livre de seyntz medicines* ('Book of Holy Medicine').[27] He supported a number of hermits and anchorites, besides founding this reclusory at Whalley in Lancashire. Whilst most of the records that have come down to us deal with the support of an individual solitary, this document sees Henry endowing an anchorite's cell in perpetuity. Fundamental to his plans were the Cistercian monks of Whalley Abbey: the abbey gatehouse (now the Visitor Centre) is a short walk from the parish church, where the reclusory was founded. There is some evidence of difficulties in the relationship between the monks and the anchorites, however, and in 1443 the abbot of Whalley took the opportunity to have the foundation dissolved [**32**].

26 Letters of confraternity offered laypeople a share in the devotions of a religious community during life, and prayers for their souls after death. They were often sold as a straightforward fund-raising venture, though the Carthusians were more restrained in this respect than some of the other orders.

27 For Henry's life, see the entry by W.M. Ormrod in *ODNB*. An excerpt from the *Livre de seyntz medicines* is translated by M. Teresa Tavormina in *Cultures of Piety: Medieval English devotional literature in translation* edited by Anne Clark Bartlett and Thomas H. Bestul (Ithaca: Cornell University Press, 1999), pp. 19–40.

Translated from the French in William Dugdale et al., *Monasticon Anglicanum* (6 vols in 8, London: Longman, Hurst, Rees, Orme & Brown, 1817–30), Vol. 5, pp. 645–6, corrected against the manuscripts.[28]

This indenture made at Whalley on the 16th of December in the 34th year of the third King Edward since the Conquest [1360] between Henry duke of Lancaster, earl of Derby, Lincoln and Leicester and Steward of England on one side, and the abbot and convent of Whalley on the other side, witnesses that

the said duke, by special licence received of our lord the king for this purpose, has given and granted, and by this present document confirmed, to the said abbot and convent and their successors for all time two cottages, seven acres of land, 193 acres of pasture and 200 acres of wood with appurtenances called Rommesgrene in his chase [*hunting ground*] beside Blackburn; and also that the said duke by the same licence has granted two messuages, 126 acres of land, 26 acres of meadow and 130 acres of pasture with appurtenances called Standen, Hulcroft and Grenelathe in the townships of Pendleton and Clitheroe together with the sheepfold of Standen and the faldage of the same sheepfold[29] with all the profits, income and benefits associated with the said sheepfold by ancient custom, which messuages, land, meadow and pasture, sheepfold and faldage with appurtenances and profits aforesaid, William de Ynes holds for life by lease and grant of the said duke and which will revert to the said duke and his heirs on the death of this same William, wholly remaining to the said abbot and convent and their successors for all time after the death of the said William;

the said abbot and convent to have and to hold the aforesaid messuages, cottages, lands, meadows, pastures, woods, sheepfold and faldage with all their easements, liberties, severalties, commons, and with all other profits and appurtenances, of the said duke and his heirs for all time, as wholly, freely, fully, quit and peacefully in all points and all profits as the said duke and his ancestors have had or held them in former times, by the following services:

28 TNA DL 27/119, and Northallerton: North Yorkshire County Record Office, ZDV I 80. For another translation of this document, with brief contextual discussion, see Alexandra Barratt, 'Creating an Anchorhold' in *Medieval Christianity in Practice* edited by Miri Rubin (Princeton: Princeton University Press, 2009), pp. 311–17.

29 Faldage is a feudal privilege that obliged tenants to pen their sheep on the lord of the manor's fields when required, so as to manure his land.

That is to say, to find sufficient and appropriate maintenance for one recluse dwelling in a place in the cemetery of the parish church of Whalley, and her successors as recluse dwelling in the same place for all time, and for two women chosen as servants by the said recluses, and for each of those that there shall be at any time, praying perpetually for the said duke, his ancestors and heirs. That is, in the said abbey to pay to the said recluses and their successors as recluses in the same place for all time each week, from year to year and every year, 17 conventual loaves (each loaf of the weight of 50 shillings sterling), 7 loaves of the second quality of the same weight, 8 gallons of the better conventual beer, and 3d for accompaniments;[30] and to find and pay, each year in perpetuity, at the feast of All Saints [1 Nov.] in the said abbey to the same recluses and their successors in that place 10 hard fish called stockfish made from larger ling, one bushel of meal for their pottage and one bushel of rye, two gallons of oil for lighting their lamps, one stone of tallow for candles, and also six cartloads of turves and a cartload of logs for fuel, to be carried by the said abbot and his successors to the recluses' place; and also for coverer [*roofing*], repairing and maintaining all the houses and enclosures that will be built in that place as dwellings for the said recluses and their successors and rethatching them when necessary in a manner appropriate for the status of the said recluses for all time, in the condition that they are built at present, at the cost of the said abbot and convent and their successors. And to find a monk chaplain of the same abbey of a sound manner of living, and a clerk to serve him at mass, to sing mass each day in perpetuity in the chapel of the said recluse and her successors as recluse there for the said duke, his ancestors and his heirs for all time, provided that the said monk shall be ruled in the choice of the offices for the mass and the time of their singing according to the preference of the said recluse and to each of her successors as recluse there for the time being.

And in times when one of the recluses has left a vacancy, whether by the death of the recluse or if for any other reason there is no recluse there, the said abbot and convent shall accept and receive without contradiction or demur another woman to live there as recluse according to the nomination, commandment or order of the said duke or his heirs, and she shall take, receive and have all those things listed above. And the said monk shall sing mass in the said chapel as described above on

30 The word here is *compaignage* – food (such as butter, cheese, fish) that is eaten along with bread as an accompaniment or relish. Cf. *OED* 'companage'.

each day of the vacancy. And the same abbot and convent and their successors will provide vestments, chalice, bread, wine, lights and other ornaments necessary for the said masses in perpetuity.

And in addition to this they will pay to the said duke and his heirs an annual rent for the aforementioned lands and tenements, that is one rose yearly on the feast of the Nativity of St John the Baptist [24 June, Midsummer's Day] during the life of the said William de Ynes, and after the death of the said William 66s 8d annually for all time at two terms of the year, that is at the said Nativity [of St John] and the feast of St Martin in winter [11 Nov.], by equal portions. [... *There follow various penalty, warranty and witness clauses.* ...]

Given at Whalley, the 2nd of January in the tenth year since the said duke's succession [1361].

14. A penny a day for the anchorite at Frodsham – enclosed for fifty years

The town of Frodsham, situated at the confluence of the Rivers Weaver and Mersey, was an important port in the Middle Ages, a centre for the export of Cheshire salt. It belonged to the earls of Chester. Some time before his death in 1232, Ranulf III, the sixth earl, made arrangements for the support of a woman named Wymark (or Wimark) to live as an anchorite, probably at the parish church of St Laurence, though none of the records states this explicitly. Ranulf's biographer notes the low number and value of the earl's gifts to religious bodies, in a chapter entitled 'A pinchpenny patron'; Wymark, he says, 'may have been the earl's most expensive single benefaction'.[31] Nothing is known of her background, but the name is an unusual one, and it is attractive to speculate that she might have been descended from the Wymark who was nurse to Ranulf in his infancy (he was born in 1170).[32] After Ranulf's death, the earldom passed to his nephew John, but when he died in 1237 Chester was taken into possession by the Crown. Wymark's maintenance was vulnerable to changes of lordship because it was provided not by an endowment of land but by a 'fixed

31 James W. Alexander, *Ranulf of Chester, a Relic of the Conquest* (Athens: University of Georgia Press, 1983), p. 44. See also the entry by Richard Eales in *ODNB*.

32 J. Phillip Dodd, 'The Anchoress of Frodsham 1240–1280', *Cheshire History* 8 (1981): 30–51, is an essay for the general reader, containing some speculations on the identity of Wymark and the location of her cell.

alms' or recurrent charitable payment. The first record in this series comes from early in that period and represents royal confirmation of the earl's original commitment. Although there is a substantial gap in the record, the order of 1275 shows that Wymark had remained as anchorite throughout this period. When she died in 1278 she had been enclosed for somewhere in the region of fifty years.

The summary in (i) is quoted from *Calendar of Liberate Rolls: Henry III, 1226–1272* (6 vols, London, 1916–64), Vol. ii, p, 70; (ii)–(iii) (v)–(viii) are excerpted and translated from the Latin in R. Stewart-Brown, *Cheshire in the Pipe Rolls, 1158–1301*, Lancashire and Cheshire Record Society 92 (1938), pp. 67, 71, 113, 118, 123, 135; (iv) is *Calendar of Close Rolls, 1272–1279*, p. 209; (ix) is quoted from John Brownbill, *The Ledger Book of Vale Royal Abbey*, Lancashire and Cheshire Record Society 68 (1914), p. 231.

(i) 4 Sept. 1241
Copy of writ sent to the justice of Chester to cause the recluse of Frodsham to have 1d daily for her maintenance till further instruction.

(ii) Year to Dec. 1241
... And in fixed alms and tithes granted by charters of the earl of Chester in Cheshire, £35 1d, according to a royal writ in which it is contained that 'you should render the aforesaid alms and tithes for as long as the county remains in the hands of the king'.

... and to the recluse of Frodsham from the 4th day of September to Christmas, 9s 4d, according to a writ in which it is contained that she should receive 1d each day for her maintenance until other instruction is received.

(iii) Year to Dec. 1242
... and to the recluse of Frodsham 30s 5d as is contained in the same place [*sc.* in the preceding roll].

(iv) Aug. 26 [1275]
Order to Guncelin de Badelesmere, justice of Chester,[33] to pay 1d daily to Wimark, the anchorite of Frodsham, together with the arrears thereof for the justice's time, as Ranulph, sometime earl of Chester, granted that sum to Wimark, to be received at the exchequer of Chester for her life; and she received that sum until the coming of the said justice, and the king long ago accepted the grant, and wills that it shall be continued.

33 Guncelin had been appointed in 1274.

(v) Year to Sept. 1275
... and to Wymark the anchorite of Frodsham, as part of the same [*sc.* fixed] alms during the same period, 30s 4d[34] according to the same [*sc.* royal] writ.

(vi) Year to Sept. 1276
... and to Wymark the anchorite of Frodsham, as part of the same alms during the same period, 30s 4d according to the same writ.

(vii) Year to Sept. 1277
... and to Wymark the anchorite of Frodsham, as part of the same alms during the same period, 30s 4d according to the same writ.

(viii) 1277–80 [year to Sept. 1278][35]
... and to the recluse of Frodsham for the sixth year, for that penny a day that she used to receive at the exchequer of Chester in fixed alms, 13s 4d according to the same writ.

(ix) Account for 1278–81 [1278]
Next, paid to the recluse of Frodsham, as an alms of 1d a day, 1 mark, and not more, because she died.[36]

15. Lady Margaret Beaufort and the anchoresses of Stamford

Margaret Beaufort (1443–1509), countess of Richmond and Derby and mother of King Henry VII, was the most powerful woman in late medieval England.[37] She was a significant patron of learning, founding Christ's College and (by provision of her will) St John's College, Cambridge, having endowed chairs in divinity at both Oxford and Cambridge. She was also noted for her piety: her daily routine included the hearing of four masses besides numerous other devotions, and she

34 30s 4d is of course 364 pence, not 365, which perhaps suggests that Wymark's alms was paid out, or at least calculated, weekly (52 x 7 = 364).

35 The accounts for this period (the sixth, seventh and eighth years of Edward's reign) are less orderly, and were submitted together in 1280.

36 A mark was equivalent to two-thirds of a pound, or 13s 4d, so this is the same payment as that accounted for in the preceding entry.

37 See her life by Michael K. Jones in *ODNB*, and further Michael K. Jones and Malcolm G. Underwood, *The King's Mother* (Cambridge: Cambridge University Press, 1992).

was instrumental in the printing of a number of religious works. She had a special papal dispensation to enter houses of enclosed religious women, including the Bridgettine nuns of Syon Abbey, where chambers were maintained for her. Her principal residence was her palace at Collyweston (Northants.), a few miles from the important town of Stamford (Lincs.). Here she maintained close relations with the town's two anchoresses. In 1504, she arranged for a door to be made through the town wall and into the back of the anchorhold at the church of St Paul, to allow her more easily to visit the anchoress, Agnes Leche. Later that year she visited, bringing a gift of apples and wine.[38] She was involved from the first with Stamford's other anchoress, Margaret White, who was enclosed at the priory of St Michael.

15a. Excerpts from household accounts

Modernised from English documents in the archives of St John's College, Cambridge. (i) is from the account of the clerk of the works at Collyweston for 1505, SJCA/D91/13, p. 89; (ii)–(iv) are from the account of the cofferer (or treasurer) for 1505, SJCA/D91/20, pp. 156, 179, 183, 184; (v) is from the account of the same for 1506, SJCA/D91/21, p. 30.

(i) Payments made the Saturday the 12 day of October [1505] toward the making of the foresaid new house [Collyweston], and also toward the making of 4 little chambers for the anchoress at the nunnery in Stamford as it doth appear there more at large, with making of 'sweeps' [*hanging rails?*] for the copes in the vestry and also for the making of a frame of timber for the making of carpets[39] and for cushions etc.

[*payments to a range of carpenters, joiners and sawyers for all the above work*]

(ii) *Item* paid unto Oliver Holland the 11 day of November [1505] for a sparver [*canopy*] to a bed for the anchoress 4d

Item for 4 stained [*dyed*] cloths for her chamber 4s 8d

...

Item paid unto Mr Dean for money given to the anchoress at the nuns of Stamford towards her finding [*financial support*] 10s

38 St John's College Cambridge, SJCA/D91/13, p. 98; SJCA/D91/20, p. 156. For the identification of the anchoress, see my 'A New Look into the *Speculum Inclusorum*' in *The Medieval Mystical Tradition: England, Ireland and Wales*, edited by Marion Glasscoe, Exeter Symposium VI (Cambridge: D.S. Brewer, 1999), pp. 123–45, p. 143.

39 The word in Middle English refers to any thick cloth, not only that used for floor-covering.

(iii) *Item* the 7th day of December [1505] given unto the prioress of the nuns of Stamford at the profession of the anchoress there 20s[40]

(iv) *Item* the 9th day of December [1505] delivered unto my lady's grace for money given unto the anchoress at the nuns of Stamford 10s

(v) *Item* delivered unto Mr Grendell the 21 day of June [1506] for a quarter wages for the anchoress of Stamford from Our Lady Day [25 March] unto Midsummer 26s 8d

15b. Excerpts from her will

Beaufort's lengthy will, begun 6 June 1508 and proved 22 Oct. 1512, included brief remembrances of the two Stamford anchoresses alongside several similar bequests.[41] More detailed provision was made for her protegée Margaret White.

Excerpts modernised from the English, printed *Collegium divi Johannis Evangelistae 1511–1911* (Cambridge: Cambridge University Press, 1911), pp. 103, 115–16, 121.

In the name of Almighty God amen.

We, Margaret, countess of Richmond and Derby, mother to the most excellent prince King Henry the 7th, by the grace of God king of England and of France and lord of Ireland, our most dear son, have called to our remembrance the unstableness of this transitory world and that every creature here living is mortal, and the time and place of death to every creature uncertain; and also calling to our remembrance the great reward of eternal life that every Christian creature in steadfast faith of Holy Church shall have for their good deeds done by them in their present life; We therefore being of whole and good mind etc. the 6th day of June the year of our Lord one thousand five hundred and eight, and in the 23rd year of the reign of our said most dear son the king, make ordain and declare our testament and last will in manner and form following:

...

And whereas we the said princess by our deed bearing the date the first day of April last past, the 20th year of the reign of our said most

40 Beaufort also arranged and paid for the anchoress's sister to come from the Isle of Sheppey (Kent) for the occasion: see SJCA/D91/20, p. 184.

41 For discussion of Beaufort's will and legacy, see Jones and Underwood, *The King's Mother*, pp. 232–50.

dear son King Henry the 7th have enfeoffed the right reverend father in God John [Fisher], bishop of Rochester, Hugh [Oldham] bishop of Exeter and others, of and in our manors of Maxey and Torpell with all our lands and tenements, rents and services in Maxey and Torpell in the county of Northampton, to have to them and their heirs upon confidence thereof to perform our last will. And whereas the said bishops and their co-feoffees sithen that [*subsequently*] at our special request and desire have demised and granted to William Ratcliff, David Cecil and Thomas Williams of Stamford a field and a close with the appurtenance called New Close beside Crakeholme, late in the tenure of James Mandesley, within our lordship of Maxey to have and to hold to them and to their assigns during the life of Margaret White, anchoress in the house of nuns beside Stamford, to the use and intent that the same William Ratcliff, David and Thomas and their assigns shall take and dispose the issues and profits thereof to and for the exhibition and finding [*support and maintenance*] of the said anchoress, and of an honest woman to attend upon her during her life.

...

... *Item* to the nuns of Stamford 20s. *Item* to the 2 anchors of Stamford and of Saint Albans, of Westminster, of Faversham, of London in the Wall,[42] and to each of them then occupying the roomth [*position, office*] 10s.

16. Bequests to Alice Bernard, anchorite at St Leonard's, Exeter

Alice Bernard was enclosed at the church of St Leonard, outside the south gate of the city of Exeter, in 1397. She may have remained there for more than thirty, and perhaps as many as forty years.[43] Over that time she was the recipient of bequests from some of the notable ecclesiastical and secular figures in Exeter and its region. The social status of the benefactors, and the relatively high amounts bequeathed, suggest that Bernard was herself a woman of some status. The different kinds of bequest are also of interest: gifts of money ranging from 40 pence

42 Some of these appear elsewhere in this volume: Faversham [**12b**], London Wall (Simon Appulby at All Hallows) [**6a**], [**35b**]. There was a pair of cells in St Albans, as at Stamford; for an earlier anchorite there see [**35a**].

43 The references in the wills do not always give her name: (vi) and/or (vii), in particular, could refer to a successor.

up to 50 shillings; gifts in kind, to ensure material support (though it is possible that these could have been replaced by a money payment); and the legacy of a book in English. The anchorhold at St Leonard's was vacant by 1447, when Christine Holby petitioned to be allowed to live there [**3e**].

Most of the wills excerpted here were recorded in the registers of the bishops of Exeter. The original language is Latin. (i)–(ii) are from *The Register of Edmund Stafford,1395–1419, an index and abstract of its contents*, edited by F.C. Hingeston-Randolph (London: Bell, 1886), pp. 379–80, 393. (iii)–(iv) are from *The Register of Edmund Lacy, Bishop of Exeter, 1420–1455: Registrum Commune*, vol. 4, edited by G.R. Dunstan, Canterbury & York Society 63 (1971), pp. 4, 7. (v) is from *Somerset medieval wills. Second Series: 1501–1530, with some Somerset wills preserved at Lambeth*, edited by F.W. Weaver, Somerset Record Society 19 (1903), p. 330. (vi)–(vii) are *Register of Edmund Lacy*, pp. 32, 25.

(i) John de Dodyngton, rector of Crewkerne (Somerset), canon of Exeter Cathedral and prebendary of Crediton (Devon), 26 March 1400
To the anchorite of St Leonard's, 40s to pray for his soul.

(ii) Sir William Bonevylle, knight,[44] 13 August 1407
I leave to the woman enclosed at St Leonard's, near to the city of Exeter, 50s.

(iii) Thomas Dunham, rector of Little Torrington (Devon), 18 June 1425
Item I leave to Alice the anchorite at Exeter, 20s and a book of Sunday sermons written in English.

(iv) Roger Bachiler, rector of Churchstow (Devon), 30 August 1427
Item I leave to the anchorite at Exeter 40d.

(v) Reginald Brita, canon of Wells Cathedral (Somerset), 3 October 1430
To Alice recluse at St Leonard next the city of Exeter, 26s 8d.

(vi) William Fylham, canon of Exeter Cathedral, 8 October 1435
Item I leave to the anchorite by the church of St Leonard three canonical loaves in the same way [*sc.* to be delivered each week during the first year after his death].

44 Sir William Bonville was 'among the most prominent west-country gentry in the late fourteenth century'. See the life of his grandson (also William) by Martin Cherry in *ODNB*.

(vii) John Orum, canon and chancellor of Exeter Cathedral, 16 August 1436
Item I leave to the anchorite[45] two loaves per week.

17. When patronage fails: the case of Aline, anchorite of Wigan

Robert Holland (born c. 1283) was a member of the Lancashire gentry, with hereditary estates in Upholland, near Wigan. He became the favourite of Thomas of Lancaster, and profited spectacularly from his patronage, acquiring considerable lands throughout the North and Midlands. He was involved in Lancaster's rebellion against Edward II, though infamously deserted his patron in the run-up to the latter's defeat at the Battle of Boroughbridge in 1322. Despite going over to the king's side, Holland was imprisoned and his lands confiscated. He was finally released and his lands restored in 1327, but he was murdered in murky circumstances (Thomas's brother, Henry of Lancaster, was suspected of involvement) in 1328.[46] This document dates from Holland's period of imprisonment and forfeiture. At Christmas 1317, he had assigned an annual rent of 29s 6d from lands in Wigan and nearby Shevington to Aline the recluse of Wigan for her maintenance.[47] But when Holland's lands were confiscated in 1322 she was left with nothing to live on, and was obliged to go to law. The process was protracted: this document describes how Aline's first attempt to go through the usual channels had been frustrated. The petition is endorsed with a note of its outcome: a second writ was issued to John of Lancaster, reiterating the earlier demand. Eventually in 1325 Aline's endowment was restored, and she received 59s for the two years 1323–25.[48]

Translated from the French, Ancient Petitions TNA SC 8/150/7470.

Aline the poor recluse of Wigan petitions our lord the king that, whereas Sir Robert de Holand sometime gave to the said Aline a rent

45 He does not say 'of Exeter', though all his other bequests are to people and institutions in the city.

46 See the entry by J.R. Maddicott in *ODNB*.

47 See 'Townships: Wigan' in *The Victoria History of the County of Lancaster: Vol. 4*, edited by William Farrer and J. Brownbill (London: Constable and Company Limited, 1911), pp. 76–7.

48 For more on Aline's case, see Warren, *Anchorites and Their Patrons*, pp. 73–4

of 30s per annum in the towns of Wigan and Shevington when she was enclosed, for her support; which rent Sir John Travers, formerly sheriff of Lancashire, took into the hands of our lord the king, amongst the other lands of the said Sir Robert; wherefore the said Aline issued a writ to John de Lancaster, keeper of forfeited lands in the county of Lancashire, to make enquiry; and as a result of that inquest a writ was ordered on behalf of the said Aline to the said John de Lancaster of *oster la main*[49] – in response to which order the said John has done nothing and is not going to do anything; therefore she asks to be given grace and a remedy in God's name for this, since she has nothing else to live on.

49 A writ demanding that lands be *released from the hand* of the king.

III: A DAY IN THE ANCHORITIC LIFE

Introduction

This section is concerned with what *Ancrene Wisse* calls the 'outer rule' that governs 'all outward behaviour, how you should eat, drink, dress, say your prayers, sleep, keep vigil'.[1] The emphasis is on rules or guidance texts composed during the period covered by the volume, though it should be stressed that the twin early classics, Aelred's *De Institutione Inclusarum* and *Ancrene Wisse*, continued to be read, re-copied and adapted for new generations of solitaries throughout the Middle Ages [**12a**].

In Chapter II we considered how and from where anchorites received the material support necessary to sustain their way of life. Returning to one of those documents, the foundation of the reclusory at Whalley [**13**] is a particularly rich source of information about the anchoritic diet and lifestyle. As for most medieval people, the staples were bread and pottage. (Compare also [**18**].) There is no mention of meat, only dried fish; this (if unsupplemented) would be a stricter diet than in most monasteries at this date, where meat-eating was often permitted. On the other hand, the provisions for fuel show some concern for the anchorite's comfort (compare [**10**]). The eight gallons of beer per week are rather striking at first sight, but in fact weak beer was the principal drink of most medieval people (since manufacture included boiling, it was safer to drink than untreated water), and eight pints a day was not an unusual allocation for a monk.

Guidance on clothing is fairly relaxed. Whereas members of a religious order dress alike as a visual reminder that they are all members of a single community, argues *Ancrene Wisse*, anchorites are under no such imperative.[2] For Aelred, the anchorite's clothing should be sufficient to keep out the cold, but no more than that,[3] and the rule known as

1 *Ancrene Wisse*, Preface, trans. Millett, pp. 1–2. For the distinction between inner and outer rules, see the Introduction.

2 Preface, trans. Millett, pp. 4–5. For further guidance on the anchoress's dress, see pp. 158–60.

3 *Rule of Life for a Recluse*, trans. Macpherson, p. 60.

Walter's Rule concurs [**20**]. The blessing of a suitable habit features in longer versions of the enclosure rite, but again details of colour, style and fabric are left unspecified.[4] The newly enclosed anchoress depicted in the Clifford Pontifical [**4**] wears a white veil and wimple, but the rest of her body is invisible – which is, after all, the point. Whereas the lives of earlier anchoritic saints celebrate their endurance of extreme bodily mortification by too little clothing, hairshirts or the penitential wearing of the *lorica* or mailshirt, these later texts are more moderate. *Ancrene Wisse* warns that 'Nobody should wear a belt of any kind next to the skin except with her confessor's permission, or wear anything made of iron or haircloth or hedgehog skins, or beat herself with them, or with a scourge weighted with lead, with holly or with brambles, or draw blood, without her confessor's permission' – though that last condition indicates that such practices were not discouraged altogether.[5] Food asceticism was to be expected [**18**], [**19**], but in their fasting, as in their other penitential practices, anchorites were urged to exercise moderation [**21**]. Evidently those responsible for solitaries' spiritual guidance were worried not that their charges might grow lax but that they might be tempted to take their asceticism too far. St Paul reminded the Corinthians that Satan was able to transform himself into an angel of light in order to deceive the faithful (2 Cor. 11:14). In the Middle Ages, the warning was often applied to those seeking a life of spiritual perfection, whom the devil would attempt to deflect from their course by luring them to take on impossible spiritual challenges, so that, having inevitably failed, they would afterwards fall into the sin of despair [**21**], [**27**]. And solitary anchorites were the most vulnerable of all, since (as 'Walter' says elsewhere in his *Rule*) 'they have to act as their own teachers and guides'.[6]

The biblical injunction to pray without ceasing (1 Thess. 5:17) had been the guiding principle of the Desert Fathers, but the desert texts repeatedly stress that a life of prayer requires structure and discipline. For professed religious in the Middle Ages, of course, such structure was provided by the regular prayers of the divine office: the seven canonical

4 See my 'Rites of Enclosure: The English *Ordines* for the enclosing of anchorites, s. XII – s. XVI', *Traditio* 67 (2012): 145–234, at pp. 192–3

5 Trans. Millett, p. 158. See further Mari Hughes-Edwards, 'Hedgehog Skins and Hairshirts: The changing role of asceticism in the anchoritic ideal', *Mystics Quarterly* 28 (2002): 6–26. The 'Bury Rule' permits use of a hairshirt [**18**].

6 Quoted in my 'Vae Soli! Solitaries and pastoral care' in *Texts and Traditions of Medieval Pastoral Care* edited by Cate Gunn and Catherine Innes-Parker (Woodbridge: York Medieval Press, 2009), pp. 11–28.

hours of the day (lauds, prime, terce, sext, none, vespers, compline), plus the night office of matins. A monastic recluse would continue to structure his day according to his order's *horarium* [**18**], while a priest-anchorite would have his breviary. But the majority of anchorites were neither monks nor priests, though the extant rules none the less take their cues from the divine office. At the most basic level, the *Dublin Rule* [**19**] instructs a lay anchorite to substitute the repetition of a prescribed number of Our Fathers at each of the hours. This recalls a similar suggestion in some manuscripts of *Ancrene Wisse*, which in turn is modelled on the practice of laybrothers in the monastic orders. It will reappear later in this collection, in the rules designed for lay hermits [**53**].

Monks alternated prayer with work (the *ora et labora* of Benedictine tradition), and the Desert Fathers wove baskets or plaited rope to ward off the spiritual lethargy they called *acedia* – put simply, boredom. In an ironic little poem Charles d'Orleans pretends to envy the anchorite, who 'has no more him for to grieve / Than sole alone upon the walls stare'.[7] As St Benedict had pointed out, idleness is the enemy of the soul.[8] To keep their anchorites busy, our texts advocate the traditional monastic occupations of reading, meditation and prayer, to be used in alternation with each other, and with manual labour [**22**]. In the late thirteenth century the anchorite at Blyth had contributed to her support by taking in paid work, until she was overtaken by ill-health [**33**]. *Ancrene Wisse* recommends its anchoresses to practise embroidery and needlework, though 'The plainer the things you make, the better I am pleased'.[9] When Lady Margaret Beaufort was fitting out the accommodation for a new anchoress at Stamford, she included a frame for the working of cloth and making of cushions [**15a**]. Meanwhile, the *Speculum Inclusorum* [**22**] suggests the copying of manuscript books as a suitable occupation,[10] and we still have several volumes written and illustrated by the Newcastle anchorite John Lacy [**23**].

7 'O Sely Ankir', lines 9–10, modernised; original quoted in my 'O Sely Ankir', in *Anchorites in Their Communities*, edited by Cate Gunn and Liz Herbert McAvoy (Cambridge: D.S. Brewer, 2017), pp. 13–34, at p. 13.

8 *Rule of St Benedict*, ch. 48, in *The Rule of Saint Benedict in Latin and in English with Notes*, edited and translated by Timothy Fry OSB (Collegeville: The Liturgical Press, 1981), p. 249.

9 *Ancrene Wisse*, trans. Millett, p. 161.

10 Although the *Speculum* was written for male anchorites, the Middle English translation, which is designed for women, also includes this same recommendation. See my '*A Mirror for Recluses:* A new manuscript, new information and some new hypotheses', *The Library* 7/15 (2014), 424–31, at p. 427.

Maintaining silence was an important – perhaps one of the essential – aspects of the anchoritic life, as of the traditional monastic vocations. As Aelred says, the recluse must 'sit alone, imposing silence on her tongue that her spirit may speak'.[11] All the rules both insist that speech should be limited as much as possible, and specify fixed periods of complete silence, but the practice recommended varies. Aelred (following the *Rule of St Benedict*) identifies certain parts of each day when speech is permitted, while the rest should be spent in silence, and total silence should (if possible) be maintained throughout Lent. *Ancrene Wisse* enjoins complete silence every Friday, more often at some times of the year, up to three days of the week in Lent.[12] The *Dublin Rule* is especially strict on this point, requiring silence on three days of every week in the year [**19**]; even for communication with their servants, anchorites should rely on sign-language [**24**].

Although their conversation might be limited, servants offered companionship. *Ancrene Wisse* also allows a cat,[13] and the visionary anchoress of Winchester has a young girl (presumably a maidservant) who keeps her company when she is unable to sleep [**28**]. Such glimpses offer a touching, and humanising, perspective on a vocation that today can easily seem irreducibly alien. But of course, for that same reason, company is to be treated with caution. Visitors might sometimes be welcome, bringing alms, treats and the warmth of human contact. But they also brought danger, an intrusion of the World into the anchorite's cell, and considerable discernment was required in order to receive them safely [**25**]. Idle chatter was certainly not to be encouraged. Aelred warns his sister against becoming a gossip, enjoying all the latest news and scandals at her parlour window, whilst *Ancrene Wisse* recalls the proverb that says 'News is carried from mill and from market-place, from smithy and from anchor-house'.[14] On the other hand, anchorites could be the sort of independent figures that people would turn to for advice, or merely to share a problem or a confidence.[15] The law of charity required that they should do their best to be good listeners. Julian of Norwich seems to have fallen into this cat-

11 Aelred, trans. Macpherson, p. 50.

12 Aelred, trans. Macpherson, pp. 50–4; *Ancrene Wisse*, trans. Millett, pp. 27–36.

13 *Ancrene Wisse*, trans. Millett, p. 157. In a modern window in Norwich Cathedral, Julian of Norwich is portrayed with a ginger cat at her feet.

14 See Aelred, trans. Macpherson, p. 46, and *Ancrene Wisse*, trans. Millett, p. 36.

15 The classic study of the anchorite as local arbitrator is Henry Mayr-Harting, 'Functions of a Twelfth-century Recluse', *History* 60 (1975), 337–52.

egory. She was visited towards the end of her life, in 1413, by Margery Kempe, who spent 'many days' telling her about her experiences, and in particular her 'many wonderful revelations, which she described to the anchoress to find out if there were any deception in them, for the anchoress was expert in such things and could give good advice'.[16]

As a visionary herself, of course, Julian was especially well placed to advise. Visions required careful discernment, and caution might be the safest policy: *Walter's Rule* counsels that the anchorite 'should pay no attention to dreams, even if a vision seems to be conveying something very holy, and he should rebuke those who do take notice of them' [**27**]. But the warning is further evidence that contemporaries expected anchorites to receive visions. In Arnold Wesker's 1981 play *Caritas* local children repeatedly taunt a recently made recluse (based on the historical anchoress Christine Carpenter): 'Christ-ine! Christ-ine! Had a revelation yet? Had a vision, had a word, had a revelation yet?'[17] This section includes two younger contemporaries of Julian who had revelations that bore on matters both public and private: Emma Rawghton passed on to her noble patron prophecies concerning national policy and his own family fortunes [**26**], while the unnamed anchoress of Winchester [**28**] described the horrifying torments of purgatory undergone by a friend of her former life, at the same time as her account of her vision reflects connections to key figures in the early fifteenth-century reform movement.

18. A rule of life for a monk-anchorite of Bury St Edmunds

In this fourteenth-century document, an unnamed abbot of Bury St Edmunds, one of the richest Benedictine houses in England, grants permission for one of his monks, known only as L., to live as an anchorite, and provides some instructions on how he should order his life.[18] We do not know where he intended to live, but it was evidently in

16 Kempe's visit to Julian is recorded in *The Book of Margery Kempe*, book 1, chapter 18, trans. B.A. Windeatt (Harmondsworth: Penguin, 1985), pp. 77–9

17 *Arnold Wesker's Historical Plays* (London: Oberon Books, 2012), p. 266 and passim. For Carpenter, see below, pp. 91–2.

18 There is a handful of examples of Benedictine solitaries from late medieval England, the best known of whom are the anchorites attached to Westminster Abbey, and the mid-fourteenth century monk of Durham, probably John Whiterig, who left the monastery to live at the hermitage on Farne Island, where he wrote a series of Latin meditations on Christ and the saints.

earshot of the bell that rang to summon the monks to prayer; his cell may have been within the abbey precincts. He was still a Benedictine, and so the obligation to follow the routine of the monastic day, with its seven canonical hours, remained. The abbot includes material from the *Rule of St Benedict* in his instructions, and also draws heavily on Aelred's *De Institutione Inclusarum* (*Rule of Life for a Recluse*).[19]

Translated from the Latin text edited by Antonia Gransden, 'The Reply of a fourteenth-century abbot of Bury St. Edmunds to a man's petition to be a recluse', *English Historical Review* 75 (1960): 464–7.

The response of the lord abbot to the petition of Sir L.

In the first place we grant you that you may live in the manner of an anchorite in the cell assigned to you for ever, never to come out of there or to have communication with anyone either regular or secular, apart from the confessor and servant assigned to you, except with the licence and express wish of the abbot or the prior (or in their absence, the subprior or third prior).

Next, in that cell you shall take care to fulfil, with devotion to God, your duty to keep the hours required by the rule, that is matins, prime,[20] sext, none, vespers and compline, when you hear the signal rung in the choir; and between the hours in place of manual work to dedicate your mind to reading, meditation, and fervent prayer. Between compline and the dawn of the following day you should keep silence. And in the day time, if you wish to give instructions to your servant about daily necessities, you should do so in a few brief words.

Between the Exaltation of the Holy Cross [14 Sept.] and Easter you should take one meal a day, apart from on those solemn feasts and Sundays contained in the privilege granted by our lord Pope Alexander:[21] that is, the Feast of the Relics,[22] All Saints day [1 Nov.], St Edmund's day [16 Nov.], Christmas day with the two days following [25–7 Dec.], the Epiphany [6 Jan.], the Purification of Mary [2 Feb.]. On those days you are allowed, if you wish, to take supper as

19 For a fuller discussion of the *Bury Rule*, see Liz Herbert McAvoy, *Medieval Anchoritisms: Gender, space and the solitary life* (Woodbridge: D.S. Brewer, 2011), pp. 45–56.

20 The office of terce is omitted, presumably in error.

21 The customs of Bury St Edmunds were confirmed by Alexander IV in 1256.

22 The precise date of the Feast of the Relics at Bury has yet to be identified. It must have been celebrated on a date between 19 and 22 October. (Thanks to Nigel Morgan for this information.)

well. But from Easter until the aforesaid feast of the Exaltation of the Holy Cross you should eat twice a day, apart from solemn fasting days, and apart from Wednesdays and Fridays on which, for the whole of the summer, starting at Pentecost, you should fast, as the Rule requires. Moreover during Lent, on Wednesdays, Fridays and Saturdays, you should content yourself with pottage, bread, and ale or (if you wish) water. On other days in Lent, apart from Sundays, pottage and one other dish will be sufficient for your meal. You should always abstain from meat, unless illness or debility prevent you.[23] You should keep silence while you are eating, unless you wish to say something quickly to your servant about taking away or serving things that you need.

When you have had your food and given thanks to God, you should occupy yourself with spiritual exercises until vespers, so that the Devil might not find you idle. Once vespers has been said, and the second meal taken (if it is a day when you have supper), you should read privately some lesson from the lives of the holy fathers, or their 'institutes',[24] or the miracles or passions of the saints, or some other improving reading; so that, your reading having yielded a degree of compunction, you will say your compline (once the bell is rung in the choir, as said before) with some spiritual fervour, and with a heart full of devotion lay your limbs to rest.

But at all times of the year beware that the darkness of night does not obscure the light of day before you go to sleep, and you end up sleeping when you should be awake, for (as St Benedict says), 'Manage the time of your supper so that you can do everything in the light'.[25]

Do not be so bold as to give or receive anything, or to send letters, unless with our licence and the knowledge of the prior, or of your confessor in our absence; and do not keep anything of your own, or any money, with you, or face the penalties imposed on those who hold property by the Lateran Council, in which council it was laid down that such people (whilst alive) should be removed from communion; and if someone is found with private property when he has died, no oblation should be made for him and he should not be buried with his brethren.[26]

23 These stipulations are the same as those followed in the monastery itself. See Antonia Gransden, *A History of the Abbey of Bury St Edmunds, 1257–1301* (Woodbridge: The Boydell Press, 2015), pp. 296–7.

24 Probably the *Institutes* of John Cassian, a staple of monastic reading, are meant.

25 *Rule of St Benedict*, ch. 41 (edited by Fry, p. 241).

26 This is a reference to the Third Lateran Council of 1179 (canon 10).

Also, we desire that the visitors' gifts and such like that you are accustomed to receive for your necessities should henceforth be in the keeping of someone assigned by us, who will provide you with what is necessary and spend the rest (but always with our permission and knowledge).

Beside this, in order to subdue your flesh, and especially when you feel that parts of your body will not follow the direction of your mind, we grant you permission to chastise your flesh with a hairshirt.

We pass on these things concerning the disposition of the outer man, dearest brother, at your request and beseeching, for you to follow, with an eye not to the fervour of ancient times but the tepidity of these modern days.

19. Daily routine, from the *Dublin Rule*

The short thirteenth-century rule for anchorites entitled (by its modern editor) the *Dublin Rule* was in that city by around 1300, though the evidence suggests that it is of English origin. It says it may be used by male and female recluses though, by its composition in Latin, it would have been directly accessible only to men. After a comparatively lengthy prologue that meditates on the love of God, it consists of a series of injunctions on various aspects of the anchoritic life. Most of these are brief, though occasionally a topic receives more extensive treatment: there is, for example, a heartfelt warning in Part II on the intoxicating effects of alcoholic drinks, and the evils that can follow. Most of this passage (including the reference to the *Rule of St Benedict*) is borrowed from Aelred, albeit with some interesting additions.[27]

Translated from the Latin, chapters 19–22, edited by Livarius Oliger, 'Regulae tres reclusorum et eremitarum Angliae saec. XIII–XIV', *Antonianum* 3 (1928): 151–90, 299–320, pp. 181–2.

And from the feast of All Souls [2 Nov.] until Easter you should rise in the middle of the night, in accord with the voice of the Psalmist: 'I rose at midnight to give praise to thee' [Ps. 118:62]. And when you awake you should begin this psalm, 'Save me O God' [Ps. 69:1], and free your mind, as St Benedict teaches in his rule for monks. Then you should

27 For the parallel passage in Aelred, see *Rule of Life for a Recluse*, pp. 55–7. For another excerpt from the *Dublin Rule*, see [**24**].

begin Matins of Our Lady, the nine or three lessons for the day, and say the psalms with great compunction, following the example of Mary Magdalen who wept over the feet of the Lord. And if an anchorite is not educated, he should sing 24 Our Fathers in place of matins, and he should diligently listen to the priest saying his matins. He should say the Office of the Dead every day for the souls of the departed, and he should say the Lord's Prayer seven times for each of the other hours. And at prime and compline he should lie prostrate and say 'I confess to almighty God', who sees into the secret places of our hearts. He should sing as much of the psalter as he can every day.

I know that, following prime, you have certain things that you have to do, or otherwise you sing psalms. You should always keep silence during your meal, as monks do and, after your meal, rise and go before your altar, and there give praise to your Lord God. You should keep silence at all times during Advent and Lent.

And thus every anchorite should live a spiritual life throughout the year, and especially during these times. During Advent and Lent he should live even more strictly. For Moses went without food for 40 days and 40 nights while he was with the Lord, and Jesus in turn completed a similar number of days without food.

All anchorites who live well spend the entire year spiritually in the desert, and avoid drunkenness and gluttony and malicious speech and deadly sins, and live a spiritual life with the Lord.

20. Clothing, from *Walter's Rule*

This excerpt comes from a fascinating and under-studied work of guidance for anchorites known as *Walter's Rule.* It has been dated to the late thirteenth century, though both the date and the ascription to 'Walter' are open to question. During the course of his instructions, the author reveals some interesting details of his own career. At the time of writing he is in his sixties, and has been a recluse himself for approaching ten years. (Note the comment on personal experience in this excerpt.) Prior to that, he spent thirty years living in a monastic community (probably as an Augustinian canon). His rule draws on earlier writings for anchorites, including Aelred's *Rule of Life for a Recluse,* and monastic legislation including the *Rule of St Augustine.* One fifteenth-century manuscript of the *Rule* was owned by John Dygon, an anchorite attached to the Carthusian priory of Sheen.

Translated from the Latin, chapter 18, edited by Livarius Oliger, 'Regula Reclusorum Angliae et Quaestiones tres de Vita solitaria saec. XIII–XIV', *Antonianum* 9 (1934): 37–84; 243–68, pp. 70–1.[28]

He is permitted to have clothes of wool against his flesh, and linen breeches. But if he wants to put anything harsher on his flesh, he should not desire people to know about it in any way. And if he is minded to begin some severe mortification, let him first think about carrying it out. For it is better to be in the middle with the power to increase, than all at once to climb to the top, from where the only way is down.

He should have [his clothes] shaken out as necessary.[29] If he is a secular person, he should wear his canonical [*official*] habit as outer garment; if he is a religious, he should use the same habit as he did before. With regard to his clothes he should consider nothing except how they might protect him from injury by the cold – I don't know what else he should be looking for, whose place it is to sit in sackcloth and ashes! He should beware also that he is not too much weighed down by his clothes, because if he disregards that, he will be sluggish and sleepy. I say this from experience, and experience is worthy of belief. Nor should he afflict himself with too little clothing, except on particular occasions to stimulate his body. He should not have more clothes than he needs, but if he does have any to spare, he should give them to the poor.

21. Richard Rolle on food and drink, from *The Form of Living*

Richard Rolle, Yorkshire hermit and the first of the so-called 'fourteenth-century English mystics', is known for his forthright personality and the overflowing rapture of his mystical writings.[30] Here, however, his topic is more mundane. The *Form of Living* was probably written in the last year of Rolle's life (he died in 1349), and takes the form of an epistle addressed to Margaret Kirkeby. She was a nun of Hampole (a Cistercian nunnery near Doncaster, in Yorkshire) to whom Rolle seems to have acted as a spiritual mentor. She left Hampole to take on the stricter life of an anchorite in 1348. Rolle's letter to her combines characteristically rhapsodic writing on the love of God and

28 There is another excerpt from *Walter's Rule* below, [**27**].

29 I.e. to remove moths, lice etc.

30 See his life by Jonathan Hughes in *ODNB*. For Rolle's life as a hermit, see [**47**].

contemplation with open and engaging advice and encouragement like this, written from one solitary to another, and between friends.

Translated from Rolle's Middle English, 'The Form of Living', i.56–85, 92–107; vii.28–51, in *English Writings of Richard Rolle, Hermit of Hampole*, edited by H.E. Allen (Oxford: Clarendon Press, 1931).

Some are deceived with too much desire and delight in food and drink. They exceed moderation and proceed to excess, and take delight in it. And they believe that it is no sin, and so they do not reform themselves, and thus they destroy the virtues of their soul.

Some [on the other hand] are beguiled with too much abstinence from food and drink and sleep, which comes from the temptation of the Devil, and is designed to make them fall in the middle of their work so that they may not bring it to its conclusion, as they would have done if they had behaved reasonably and maintained discretion; and so they lose all their merit through ill-discipline. Our Enemy lays this trap for us when first we begin to hate wickedness and reorient ourselves towards God. This is when many people begin things that they can never bring to a conclusion; it is when they believe that they can do whatever they set their heart on. But often they fall before they get half way, and something that they thought was for them turns out to be against them. For we have a long way to get to heaven; and every good deed we do, every prayer we make, and every good thought that we think in faith, hope and charity, takes us a step further on our path towards heaven. And so, if we make ourselves so weak and feeble that we cannot work, pray or think as we ought to, are we not greatly to blame, if we break down when above all we need to be strong? And I know for sure it is not God's will that we do this. For the Prophet says, 'Lord, I will keep my strength to thee' [Ps. 58:9], so that he could keep serving God until his dying day, and not waste his strength in a little, short time, and then lie moaning and groaning by the wall. …

There have been many, and there still are, who think they are doing nothing at all, unless they practise such great abstinence and fasting that everyone who knows them talks about it. But it often comes about that, the more joy and marvelling they have outwardly from people praising them, the less joy they have on the inside from the love of God. In my view, they would please Jesus Christ much more if, lovingly thanking and praising him, they took whatever God sent at that time and place, in order to sustain their body in his service and to keep people from talking about them too much, and then dedicated themselves entirely to loving and praising the same lord Jesus Christ – who wants to be loved strongly and served enduringly. And then their holiness would appear more clearly in God's eye than in human eyes. …

And at meal times, always praise God in your thoughts at every mouthful, and in your heart say this:

All praise to you, my king,
All thanks to you, my king,
All blessings to you, my king,
For all your gifts so great.
Jesus, my delight,
Who shed your blood for me
And died upon the cross,
Give me the grace to sing
A fitting song in your praise.

And do not think this only while you are eating, but beforehand and afterwards as well – indeed, at all times, except when you are praying or speaking. Or if you have other thoughts that bring you greater sweetness and devotion than these that I have taught you, you may use those. For I believe that God will put into your heart such thoughts as will please him, and that are appropriate for your station.

When you pray, pay attention not to how much you say, but to how well you say it. The love of your heart should at all times be directed upwards, and your thought focused on what you are saying, as far as is possible. If you spend the whole day in prayers and meditations, I know for sure that you must increase greatly in your love for Jesus Christ, and experience great delight – and in no time at all.

22. On the benefits of reading, and manual labour, from the *Speculum Inclusorum*

The early fifteenth-century guide for male anchorites, the *Speculum Inclusorum*, has already appeared in this collection [1]. Having outlined, in the first of its four parts, the various reasons that people might have for seeking a life of enclosure, it then proceeds, in Parts Two and Three, to a consideration of the practice of that life, which should be based around prayer, meditation and reading. The reading matter recommended is not academically demanding or speculative, but chosen for its exemplary value or affective impact. Although the *Speculum* itself is written in Latin for a priest-anchorite, its author envisages a wider audience that includes those who know only the vernacular, or who are illiterate altogether.

Speculum Inclusorum, part II, chapter iii, from my edition, *Speculum Inclusorum / A Mirror for Recluses: A late-medieval guide for anchorites and its Middle English translation* (Liverpool: Liverpool University Press, 2013), pp. 65–9. Reproduced with permission of Liverpool University Press through PLSclear.

After you have fulfilled the requirements of divine service, which should be performed out loud at the appropriate hours with all the devotion that the Holy Spirit sees fit to inspire, the rest of your time should be spent by turns in prayer, meditation and edifying reading, or in some manual work. And concerning the use of these four things (over and above the requirements of divine service) this law is laid down as being the most expedient: that is that, when your devotion cools or is lessened, or your frail and changeable nature grows weary, in one of these four, you should straight away turn to another, so that variety of occupation may put idleness to flight, drive out lethargy, prolong your devotion and refresh your weary nature.[31] And so, if your taste for prayer or delight in meditation decreases, immediately seek out some edifying reading, the profit of which exceeds all estimation, since it offers a mirror of all vices and virtues, clearing distractions from the mind, attracting and enticing all virtues to the soul, and also sundering it from all vices, by a kind of assault on the reason, and by the urging of fear, as well as of love. …

Therefore (if you are literate) you should gladly read holy literature, saints' lives, the passions of the martyrs, devout meditations; and, from amongst all these, you should read particularly frequently whichever tends in your experience most to increase your devotion. By reading you will certainly see that, ever since the beginning of the world, the proud and impenitent have been cast out by God and finally condemned, the contrite and humble are saved by penitence, the just and those who suffer hardships on God's account have been given eternal reward, the obedient and those who have persevered manfully in the spiritual battle against temptations receive the divine call to an

31 The triad of reading, meditation and prayer is of monastic origin. In the monastic tradition, slow and ruminative reading leads naturally on to meditation, which then transforms itself seamlessly into prayer. The idea that the three activities (and manual labour) may be used in alternation probably originates with Aelred. See further Vincent Gillespie, '*Lukynge in haly bukes*: *Lectio* in some late medieval spiritual miscellanies', *Analecta Cartusiana* 106 (1984), 1–27.

imperishable crown of heavenly glory. From this, however great a sinner you have been before, you should derive consolation and hope of pardon for both your own sins and those of other people for whom you have decided to pray in charity. In accordance with which, the Apostle says, 'What things soever were written were written for our learning: that, through patience and the comfort of the scriptures, we might have hope.' [Rom. 15:4] And so we should contemplate our condition in holy literature, as Christ tells us (Mark 13), saying, 'See yourselves.' [Mark 13:9] …

But if someone does not understand Latin, he should practise devout reading in English or in French, or in his vernacular language, so that he may be similarly edified. And he should read aloud, for when one reads the living voice usually has the greatest effect on the heart. If however someone is completely illiterate, instead of reading he should do some suitable work with his hands, interspersing his work with 'Our Father' and 'Hail Mary', so that his mind should not be distracted into vain, lustful, or illicit thoughts. But let him continue his work in cleanness of heart, in order constantly to drive out idleness, which is (more than you could believe) the enemy of the soul. And don't let anyone claim that he cannot mingle prayer with work, for workmen often as a diversion tell tales of heroes, or sing love-songs with delight. So shouldn't you, God's servant, gladly do for his praise, glory and honour as much as worldly people do so easily for the love of the world and the comfort of their bodies? And further, if you are a layperson, the whole world can be a book for you to read of God's power and goodness, mercy and truth, justice and equity, the punishments of the wicked and the rewards of the good, the joys of eternity and the vanity of the world. What has become now, I ask you, of Samson, the strongest man? Solomon, the wisest? Absolon, the fairest? Alexander, the most powerful? Where are the riches of Croesus? Where are the joys of all those who came before us? Have all these not passed as a shadow? Nor will they be able to remain here any longer, but will be taken from us by the most just and almighty Ruler of the world to the invisible places of eternal punishment or reward, according as they have deserved while in this life to be chosen by God, or cast out. This is exactly why the Apostle says (Romans 1) that 'The invisible things of him, from the creation of the world, are clearly seen, being understood by the things that are made.' [Rom. 1:20]

And so, you recluses, by edifying reading of this kind, 'Look to your vocation.'

23. John Lacy, anchorite

John Lacy was probably born near Newcastle under Lyme (Staffs.), and it was here, at the end of the fourteenth century, that he was ordained priest and joined the convent of Dominican friars. He subsequently moved to the other Newcastle, Newcastle upon Tyne in the north-east of England, and was enclosed as an anchorite at the order's convent

in that town. He is recorded there between 1407 and 1434. He was an accomplished scribe and limner, and copied several books. The most interesting of these is now St John's College Oxford, MS 94, which Lacy worked on between 1420 and 1434. It marries a Latin Book of Hours with catechetical material, some texts on confession and a compilation of a more advanced nature from authors including Walter Hilton. It also has some personal moments, including the appeal 'Prayeth for the soul of friar John Lacy anchor and reclused', and the illustration reproduced here.[32] Lacy depicts himself in his Dominican habit looking out through the grille of his anchorhold, which is a two-storey structure built of stone. He is focused on an image of a crucifix flanked by Mary and St John (though the image has been defaced by the erasure of the crucifix), while the scroll that issues from his mouth to indicate speech implores Christ to have mercy on his soul.

From St John's College Oxford, MS 94, fol. 16v. Reproduced by permission of the President and Fellows of St John's College, Oxford.

24. On speech and silence, from the *Dublin Rule*

The *Dublin Rule* was introduced earlier in this section: see [**19**]. These excerpts are taken from the end of chapter 4, and the beginning of chapter 5.

Translated from the Latin, edited by Oliger, 'Regulae tres', p. 177.

At all times, be afraid to speak; love silence; always say 'Bless me' [*Benedicite*] at the beginning of everything you say. When someone comes to you and knocks at your window, turn to the altar and make a sign of the cross upon your mouth, so that the Enemy might not deceive you. You should respond briefly to your visitor. In every week you should keep silence on three days, that is Monday, Wednesday and Friday. On these days, if it is a major feast or great necessity requires it, listen to what is said and respond with few words. It is proper that every anchorite should rely on hand signals between himself and his servants, as monks and nuns do.

32 For discussion of Lacy and his manuscript, see R.M. Clay, 'Further Studies on Medieval Recluses', *The Journal of the British Archaeological Association* 3rd series, 16 (1953): 74–86, pp. 75–8; Ralph Hanna III, *A Descriptive Catalogue of the Western Medieval Manuscripts of St John's College, Oxford* (Oxford: Oxford University Press, 2002), p. 129, and my 'Vae Soli!'.

No one should hear your voice any distance from your window. Even if someone hears you, they should not see your face. Do not stretch your hand any distance out of your window, unless it is between you and your servants. Do not look for long on another person's face, so you are not disturbed or tempted. It is appropriate for you to speak with great discretion and reverence. Your voice should not be heard coming from your window, nor raised in laughter; rather it is written, 'If anyone speaks, he should do it as one speaking the very words of God' [1 Peter 4:11]. You should not speak or hear lascivious words. Remember that an account will have to be given on the Day of Judgement for every idle word. And so you should not slander or speak ill of people, nor willingly hear people speaking slander. It is not appropriate for you, who are enclosed, withdrawn from people, to get involved in the kinds of things they do; and so we insist that you do not place yourself as a surety or pledge or witness between people, nor swear an oath, since many sins arise from these things. Likewise we forbid any speech between men and women in such a holy place. If it is necessary, and witnesses are present, then speech may be prolonged; if not, it should be curtailed.

25. How an anchoress ought to behave towards those who visit her

This excerpt comes from another of the 'Middle English Mystics'. Book One of Walter Hilton's *Scale of Perfection* is addressed to a woman recluse – though for long stretches of the work it is possible to forget that this is its intended readership. (Indeed, Hilton himself seems at least equally interested in engaging a much wider audience, as he does in Book Two of the *Scale*, or his *Mixed Life*.) This chapter comes from near the end of the book, and offers advice on how the anchoress should manage the demands of visitors coming to her window, so as to strike an appropriate balance between the demands of solitude and of charity. The chapter was also excerpted from the *Scale* for inclusion in a compilation of short texts on the solitary life that is found in several early fifteenth-century manuscripts, and it is from one of these that the text translated here has been taken.[33]

33 See Ralph Hanna, *English Manuscripts of Richard Rolle: A descriptive catalogue* (Exeter: University of Exeter Press, 2010), no. 94 (pp. 174–6). It was originally chapter 83 of Book One of the *Scale of Perfection.*

Translated from the Middle English original in Carl Horstman, *Yorkshire Writers: Richard Rolle of Hampole, an English Father of the Church, and His Followers* (2 vols, London: Swan Sonnenschein & Co., 1895–96), vol. 1, pp. 106–7.

Now you say that you are not able to protect your sense of hearing from vanities, because various people (seculars and others) often come to speak with you and recount things to you, and some of them are idle tales. And to this I say that those visits and interactions with your fellow Christians are not great obstacles to you, but can be a help to you, if you act wisely, for by them you can test the extent of your charity towards your fellow Christians, to see whether it is great or small. You are obliged – as every man and woman is – to love your fellow Christians above all in your heart, and also in your actions, to show them evidence of your love and charity, as far as reason requires, and according to your power and your understanding. Now although it is the case that you are not supposed to go out of your house to look for opportunities to benefit your fellow Christians, because you are enclosed, you are still obliged to love them with all your heart, and faithfully to present evidence of love to those that visit you.

And therefore whenever someone wishes to speak with you, whatever sort of person he is, whatever status he has, even if you do not know what sort of a person he is, nor why he is coming, be ready quickly and with a good grace to find out what it is he wants. Don't be standoffish or make him wait a long time for you, but think how ready and how glad you would be if an angel from heaven wanted to come and speak to you, and be as ready and as obedient in your will to speak to your fellow Christian when he comes to you. For you do not know what sort of person he is, nor why he is coming, nor what need he has of you, nor you of him, until you have found out. And if you are at prayer or at your devotions, so that you are reluctant to break off, for it seems that you should not leave God to speak with any man – not so in this case, in my view. For if you are wise, you will not leave God but you will find him, and have and see him, in your fellow Christian just as well as in your prayer (albeit it will be in a different way that you have him).

If you know properly how to love your fellow Christian, it should be no obstacle to you to speak with him with discretion. You should exercise discernment in this way, as it seems to me. When someone visits you, ask him humbly what he wants. And if he has come to tell you of his troubles and to receive words of comfort from you, hear him gladly and let him say what he wants in order to ease his heart; and when he has finished comfort him if you can gladly and charitably, and then desist. And if after that he falls into idle chatter about worldly nonsense and what other people are up to, give him little answer and do not feed him in his conversation, and he will soon get fed up and take his leave. If someone else comes to instruct you, such as a man of Holy Church, hear him humbly with reverence for his order; and if what he says is a comfort to you, ask him your questions. But do not let yourself instruct him: it is not your place to teach a priest, except in cases of necessity. If what he says is of no comfort to you, give him little answer and he will soon take his leave. If someone else comes to give you his alms or otherwise to hear what you have to say or to be instructed by you, speak virtuously, gladly and humbly to them all. Do not reprove any man for his faults: that is not your place. And to sum up: inasmuch as you believe you can bring profit to your fellow Christian – in particular, spiritual profit – you should say what you can, if he will listen; and in all other cases keep silent as much as you can, and in a short time you will not have much of a crowd to bother you. That is how it seems to me.

26. The visions of Emma Rawghton

Two closely related sources record the visions and prophecies of the York anchoress Emma Rawghton, a contemporary of Margery Kempe and the Winchester visionary who appears below [**28**].[34] Both sources were made in the 1480s, and take the form of pictorial histories promoting the dynasty of the earls of Warwick. They are associated with the scholar and antiquary John Rous (c. 1420–92), who spent his entire working life as chantry chaplain of Guy's Cliffe, near Warwick, under the earls' patronage.[35] The two accounts overlap and must be referring to the same set of prophecies, though they differ in several particulars. Their chronology is also somewhat confused (as one might expect of sources written some fifty to seventy years after the events that they describe). Rawghton's visions are usually dated 1422–3, on the

34 On the strength of the documents printed here she has an entry in *ODNB*, by Jonathan Hughes. The date of her enclosure would rule her out as the anchoress who shuns Margery Kempe on her visit to York in 1417. See *Book of Margery Kempe*, book 1, chapter 50; trans. Windeatt, p. 241.

35 See his life by Nicholas Orme in *ODNB*. For the hermitage at Guy's Cliffe, see [**75**].

basis that Richard Beauchamp, thirteenth earl of Warwick, obtained a licence to found his chantry at Guy's Cliffe in 1423. The public events referred to in the sources, however, belong to the late 1420s,[36] and Warwick provided the anticipated endowment for Guy's Cliffe only in 1430, so they should probably be dated later in the decade.[37] Warwick also consulted Rawghton on his desire for a son and heir (his first wife Elizabeth having given him only three daughters). Henry Beauchamp, the future fourteenth earl, was born on 22 March 1425. Rawghton was enclosed as an anchoress in the parish of All Saints North Street just a couple of weeks later (on 2 April), and it is tempting to speculate that Warwick may have sponsored her enclosure as a thank-offering for his son's safe delivery.[38]

(i) is modernised from the English Rous Roll, no. 50, edited by Charles Ross, *The Rous Roll: with an historical introduction on John Rous and the Warwick Roll by Charles Ross* (Gloucester: A. Sutton, 1980), n. pag.[39] (ii) is modernised from the English of *The Beauchamp Pageant* no. 47, edited by Alexandra Sinclair (Donington: Richard III and Yorkist History Trust in association with Paul Watkins, 2003), p. 144.

(i) Richard Beauchamp, earl of Warwick, a noble knight, as was well proved in his jousting at Mantua in Lombardy, and at the General Council at the city of Constance, where he was for the king and the temporality of England, the royalty of all Christendom there being present, both spiritual and temporal, and after at Guînes, when he was captain of Calais, and in many other lands and in the wars of France. The Emperor called him 'Father of Courtesy' for, and ⌜*if*⌝ all courtesy were lost, he said it might have been found in his person; and the king made him earl of Aumarle.

. . .

36 Though he became a member of Henry VI's minority council within a few months of the king's accession in 1422, Warwick was appointed his tutor or guardian only in 1428. Henry VI was crowned in London in 1429, Warwick holding him in his arms during the ceremony, and in Paris in 1431.

37 W.B. Stephens, ed., *A History of the County of Warwick: Vol 8, The City of Coventry and Borough of Warwick* (London: Oxford University Press for the Institute of Historical Research, 1969), p. 534.

38 *The York Sede Vacante Register 1423–1426: A calendar*, edited by Joan Kirby (York: Borthwick Publications, 2009), p. 55. I am indebted to Jessica Knowles for bringing this reference to my attention. An anchorite's cell was constructed at the west end of All Saints North Street c. 1910, supposedly on the site of Rawghton's enclosure.

39 The Rous Roll has also been digitised in full by the British Library: see www.bl.uk/collection-items/the-rous-roll.

This lord was master to King Harry the Sixth in his tender age, and with the help of the land crowned him twice: at Westminster as for king of England, and at Paris for king of France. He made certain where afore was uncertain at Gybclif [*Guy's Cliffe*] a chantry of two priests, that God would send him heir male. He did it by the stirring of a holy anchoress named Dame Em. Rawghtone, dwelling at All Hallows in the Northstreet of York, and for it to her appeared Our Lady seven times in one year, and said that in time to come it should be a regal college of the Trinity of a king's foundation, and it should be a gracious place to seek to for any diseases or grief, and one of St Guy's heirs should bring his relics again to the same place.[40]

(ii) Here [*sc.* This illustration] shows how King Henry was after crowned king of France at St Denis beside Paris. Of the which coronation in France, and also the said earl to have the rule of his noble person unto he were of the age of sixteen years, it was the will and ordinance of almighty God, as our Blessed Lady showed by revelation unto Dame Emma Rawhton, recluse at All Hallows in Northgate Street of York, and she said that through the realm of England was no person, lord nor other, like to him in ability of grace and true faithfulness to virtuously nourish [*bring up, nurture*] and govern his noble person according to his royal estate. Also, she put great commendation by the ordinance of God of his great benefits in time to come, of devout comers to the place of Guy's Cliff, otherwise called Gibclyff, which in process of time shall grow to a place of great worship, one of the most named [*those with the greatest name*] in England.

27. On sleeping and dreaming, from *Walter's Rule*

For *Walter's Rule* see [**20**]. Another discussion of sleep, dreams and night-time temptations can be found in Richard Rolle's *Form of Living* [**21**], chapter 2.

Translated from the Latin, chapters 19–20, edited by Oliger, '*Regula Reclusorum* Angliae', pp. 71–2.

The right way to sleep

No one should presume that, when he enters into the reclusive life, he should be able to continue in the same kind of life as before, and lie on comfortable furnishings, nor that there should be a special place set

40 For more on Guy of Warwick, the dynasty's legendary forebear, see [**75**].

aside for him to rest; but his practice should be to lie down now in one place, now in another, sometimes on the step, sometimes in his cell, or else he should rest his head on his arm against the wall, and in this attitude wait for the attacks and ambushes of his Enemy. Varying his discomfort in this way will make things easier. For while we are sleeping the Enemy schemes and probes to find out which aspect of our spirit is weaker and more inclined to evil while we sleep, and then you can be sure that he will try and tempt us in it when we are awake: for he is not able to find out what we are thinking when we are awake, unless by some chance we want to let in a sinful impulse that he himself has sent.

No recluse should be so sure of himself that he dares to lie completely flat on the ground to sleep (unless infirmity demands it or some other reasonable need has arisen), lest when he is weighed down by the fug of sleep he should provide an easier way in for the Enemy to come and injure him. The name 'recluse' is great above the names of all other states of religious life; and for that reason his efforts should be equally great, in order that he should not be put to everlasting reproach. He should sit, or sleep, or lie on a rush mat, and refuse any softer covering, except for a small pillow under his arm, or underneath his bottom when he is awake, if it is necessary due to spending so much time sitting. He must always try to ensure that his life is greater than people's tongues. And when people feel the need to praise him (whether he wants them to or not), he should not let his heart be swayed by that; he should stop his ears, and forget about it as quickly as he can.

The Enemy has a way of sending feelings of lethargy outside the proper times for sleeping. As soon as he feels this, the man of God should put himself on the alert and make his prayer to God and (except in those times set aside for sleep) shake off the weariness of his body. No one should think that what I say is impossible, for to those who practise it, it is most enjoyable. When he is at rest the hardness of his bed often keeps him awake and is not conducive to the relaxation that would quickly allow him to get to sleep; but when he wants to pray it allows him to overcome sleep. And sometimes, when he is resting, one of his limbs will start to drop off to sleep, but he need not fear any evil attack as a result of that. The only effective remedy for it is sprinkling water on the affected part.

The attacks of the Enemy

Every night he should keep a lamp burning, at least when he is performing the night office. He should pay no attention to dreams, even if a vision seems to be conveying something very holy, and he should rebuke those who do take notice of them. The devil often prompts people to do good things while they are sleeping, but when they wake up and do them, he brings about their downfall. Everyone knows that the devil is able through his devious nature to foresee certain future events, and that souls can be harmed if they do not carry out the good deeds to which they are inspired in dreams. And therefore in a night-time vision he transforms himself into an angel of light, so that he can murder the soul of an innocent person later, when he wakes up. Sometimes the Enemy appears in a night-vision to sick people and tells them that they should seek blessings or prayers or food from a recluse, and then they will be made well. The cunning wolf does this so that the recluse's soul will be led into the sin of pride, if he lets himself foolishly believe that this could come about thanks to him. There is no one there who can lay bare the tricks of the Enemy for him, so the recluse must excel in discernment, since he has to live without a teacher or a guide, and still he must withstand all his tricks.

28. The visions of a Winchester anchoress

Richard Beauchamp, earl of Warwick, a few years before his association with Emma Rawghton [**26**], consulted with another anchoress. Early in 1421 he sent two men (one of them the chaplain of Guy's Cliffe [**26**], [**75**]) to visit an anchoress in Winchester, and in May of that year he arranged for her to be brought to London so that he could consult with her there in person. She was almost certainly the same 'holy woman recluse' to whom a vision of purgatory was revealed over three nights in summer 1422. The account is centred on the anchoress's recently deceased friend Margaret, a former nun of St Mary's, Winchester (known as Nunnaminster). Although the three visions chart Margaret's passage through purgatory and conclude with her reception into heaven, they are most memorable for the horrific punishments that are envisaged for the suffering souls. The most gruesome of these are reserved for priests (both secular and religious) who have proved unworthy of their office, and the work is best understood in the context of the early fifteenth-century discourse of clerical reform. The text takes the form of a letter to one of the anchoress's spiritual advisers, probably John London, recluse at Westminster Abbey, and it references a number of other prominent figures in the orthodox reform movement associated with the reign of Henry V.[41] This is its opening.

Modernised from the English in Marta Powell Harley, ed., *A Revelation of Purgatory by an Unknown, Fifteenth-century Woman Visionary* (Lewiston, NY: Edwin Mellen Press, 1985), lines 8–56.[42]

My dear father, I give you to understand what great tribulation I had in my sleep upon St Lawrence's Day [10 Aug.] at night, the year of our Lord 1422. I went to my bed at eight o'clock and so I fell asleep. And father, between nine and ten it seemed to me that I was rapt into purgatory,[43] and suddenly I saw all the pains which were shown to me many times before – as you, father, know well by my telling [*my account of them*]. But sir, I was not shown the sight [*vision*] of them by any such spirit [*as in previous revelations*] on this night of St Lawrence. But suddenly, father, it seemed that I saw them, and forsooth, father, I was never so evil afraid when I woke for showing of the pains as I was then, and the cause was that I was led by no spirit that I knew before, that might have comforted me.

And in this vision of purgatory it seemed that I saw three great fires, and it seemed that each fire adjoined the next. But sir, there was no departing [*division*] between them, but each one added to the other. And these three fires were wonderful and horrible, and especially the most of all [*the biggest of them*], for that fire was so horrible and stinking that all the creatures in the world might not tell [*reckon*] the wicked smelling thereof. For there was pitch and tar, lead and brimstone, oil and all manner of things that might burn, and all manner of pains that one could think, and all manner of Christian men and women that lived here in this world, of what degree they were [*of every degree*].

But among all the pains that I saw of all men and women, it seemed that priests that had been lecherous in their lives, and their women with them – whether they were religious men and women or seculars: ordained men and women – it seemed to me in that vision, they had

41 The context for the work is vividly reconstructed by Mary C. Erler, '"A Revelation of Purgatory" (1422): Reform and the politics of female visions', *Viator* 38 (2007): 321–83.

42 There is a new edition and translation, based on a different manuscript, by Liz Herbert McAvoy, *A Revelation of Purgatory* (Cambridge: D.S. Brewer, 2017).

43 The author narrates her perception of her visions repeatedly using the phrase 'methought', which I have translated as 'it seemed to me', or simply 'it seemed'.

the most pain.[44] And in that great fire it seemed I saw the spirit of a woman that I knew before, which was in her life a sister of a house of religious, the which woman while she lived was called Margaret, which it seemed I saw in this horrible fire and had so great pains that for dread I might not describe them at that time.

And in fearful dread I awoke. And by the time it struck the hour of ten before midnight, and for dread and fear to sleep again, I rose up, and a little maid child with me, and we two said the seven [*penitential*] psalms and the litany. And by the time we had said *Agnus Dei* ['Lamb of God, thou takest away the sins of the world'], I was so heavy with sleep I might not make an end, but bade my child go to bed, and so did I. And by the time it struck eleven, and I had told [*counted*] the last stroke, I began to sleep.

44 The syntax of this sentence is confusing, and possibly garbled, in the manuscript used for Harley's edition, and in McAvoy's.

IV: FOR THE WHOLE TERM OF THIS LIFE[1]

Introduction

The fifteenth-century rule for anchorites, *Speculum Inclusorum* or *Mirror for Recluses*, is at pains to stress to its readers, and in particular to anyone contemplating taking on the life of an anchorite, the seriousness of such a decision. 'After an absolute vow has been made, or this kind of life taken on with deliberation,' the author reminds us, 'it must of necessity be observed until the end, on pain of eternal damnation' [**1**]. For the anchorite, 'the end' was always in view. As we saw in Chapter I, the rite for enclosing an anchorite [**5**] dramatised the process of enclosure as a death and burial. Some versions of the rite specify that the reclusory should contain an open grave, in which the postulant lies down while the celebrant sprinkles earth on him, intoning burial antiphons. The reclusory attached to the church of St Anne, Lewes (Sussex), had a squint so positioned that, in order to see the high altar, the anchoress there would have had to kneel in her own grave [**29**]. *Ancrene Wisse* elaborates upon the practical and spiritual rationale for the open grave:

> Admiring their own white hands is bad for many anchoresses who keep them too beautiful, such as those who have too little to do; they should scrape up the earth every day from the grave in which they will rot. Certainly that grave does a great deal of good to many anchoresses; for as Solomon says, *Remember your last things and you will never sin again* [Ecclus. 7:36].[2]

The grave is there not just as a *memento mori*, however. The London anchorite Simon Appulby planned to be buried in the tomb within his cell [**35b**], and a skeleton discovered beneath the Lewes anchorhold [**29**] probably belonged to its thirteenth-century occupant.[3]

1 The phrase is from chapter 3 of the *Speculum Inclusorum*: 'Recluses' second motive or principal intention may be a fervent desire to do penance for their sins for the whole term of this life.' [**1**]

2 *Ancrene Wisse*, trans. Millett, pp. 46–7.

3 For more on the 'rhetoric of death' in medieval English anchoritism, see my 'Ceremonies of Enclosure: Rite, rhetoric and reality' in *Rhetoric of the Anchorhold: Space, place and body within the discourses of enclosure*, edited by Liz Herbert McAvoy (Cardiff: University of Wales Press, 2008), pp. 34–49.

To spend the rest of one's life in an anchorhold is an impressive and (for most modern people) a horrific commitment. But what did it really mean? Making a vow to die and be buried in one's cell has some of the superficial appeal of a grand gesture; but enclosure was a life-sentence not a death-sentence. Anchorites had ample leisure in which to repent of their decision, and could have plenty of time for second thoughts. In this section, we encounter Katherine Ditton, who was enclosed for sixteen years, Agnes Vertesaws for at least twenty, and Simon Appulby for twenty-four. We have already met Alice Bernard, anchoress at Exeter for thirty years or more [**16**], and Wymark, enclosed at Frodsham [**14**] for fifty. To grow old, ill, infirm of body and/or of mind, whilst committed to strict and perpetual solitude, is a desolate and frightening prospect. In this section we see an anchorite trying to make plans for his future infirmity [**34**] and another who is now too ill to manage her own affairs [**33**]. In neither case, however, does being released from enclosure seem to have been an option. No wonder the authorities were so insistent that the vocation should be taken on only after serious and prolonged consideration [**3**].

In fact, the early fifteenth-century *Dives and Pauper* suggests that anchoritic apostasy was a significant problem, and enumerates a range of reasons that an anchoritic vocation might fail:

> We see that, when men set out to be anchorites or recluses, within a few years they succumb to madness or fall into heresies; or they break out on account of love for a woman, or because they are fed up with their way of life, or due to some temptation of the devil.

The sources actually contain very few records of anchorites who left their enclosure, and fewer individuals still who were clearly apostate. *Dives and Pauper* then goes on to draw an interesting distinction:

> But you rarely hear of any of these failings in women anchorites enclosed in this way; on the contrary, they begin in holiness, and in holiness they conclude.[4]

Unfortunately, such apostates as have so far come to modern attention were women. The best known (at least today) is Christine Carpenter, who was enclosed at Shere (Surrey) in 1329, but left her enclosure

4 *Dives and Pauper*, edited by P.H. Barnum, Vol. 1, part 2, EETS o.s., 280 (1980), p. 92. See also p. 93 for a passage on men's hypocritical reasons for becoming anchorites. *Dives and Pauper* is often discussed alongside Lollard texts, and these not infrequently articulate strikingly pro-feminist attitudes; but whether this is an accurate reflection of Lollardy's attitudes to women, or part of a broader rhetorical contrarianism, remains a matter of debate.

within a year or two. In 1332 she decided (or was persuaded? or forced?) to return, and petitioned to be re-enclosed. Her petition was allowed, and that is the last we hear of her.[5] Her story has inspired Arnold Wesker's play *Caritas* (1981) and (in collaboration with Robert Saxton) the opera of the same name (1991), and independently the film *Anchoress* (dir. Chris Newby, British Film Institute, 1993), and a novel, *Anchoress of Shere*, by Paul L. Moorcraft (2000). Modern treatments speculate on the psychopathology behind Carpenter's broken vows, but the medieval documents are silent on the matter. When Isolda de Heton left the reclusory at Whalley (Lancs.) in the early 1440s, it was to defend the interests of the children she had left behind at her enclosure [**32**]. We do not know why Agnes de Littlemore's dreams of becoming an anchoress came to nothing [**31**] but, whatever her reason, she seems to have met with sympathy rather than condemnation from the authorities.

This section concludes with a couple of examples of anchorite's wills. Though symbolically we are encouraged to think of anchorites as 'non-persons' who were already dead, they were allowed to own property, as William Lyndwood noted [**2**], and by extension therefore to dispose of it in a will. Simon Appulby [**35b**] was comparatively well-to-do and a significant figure in the wider life of his parish, while Katherine Ditton's [**35a**] bequests totalled less than 3s and her circle of documented acquaintance was small, though none the less revealing.

29. The anchorite's cell at Lewes

The female anchorite at the church of St Mary Westout in Lewes[6] was left 5s in the will of St Richard Wyche, bishop of Chichester, who died in 1253. Her cell was rediscovered in 1927 during the building of a new vestry south of the chancel. A number of features were uncovered in the chancel wall: an opening 33 by 18 cm, with splayed reveals to the external wall, where the fittings for a hatch or shutter were still in evidence; a niche or cupboard, and a squint focused on the high altar.

5 For Christine Carpenter see Miri Rubin, 'An English Anchorite: The making, unmaking and remaking of Christine Carpenter' in *Pragmatic Utopias. Ideals and communities, 1200–1630* edited by Rosemary Horrox and Sarah Rees Jones (Cambridge: Cambridge University Press, 2001), pp. 204–23, and Liz Herbert McAvoy, 'Gender, Rhetoric and Space in the *Speculum Inclusorum, Letter to a Bury Recluse* and the Strange Case of Christina Carpenter' in McAvoy, *Rhetoric of the Anchorhold*, pp. 111–26, which includes translations of the documents.

6 The church is in Lewes High Street, and is now dedicated to St Anne.

Though the squint itself was narrow, the walls were splayed widely so as to allow the anchorite to kneel in the recess. As investigators cleared the recess of rubble they realised that it continued below ground level. Here they found a woman's body. The grave had evidently lain open

(i) Plan of church

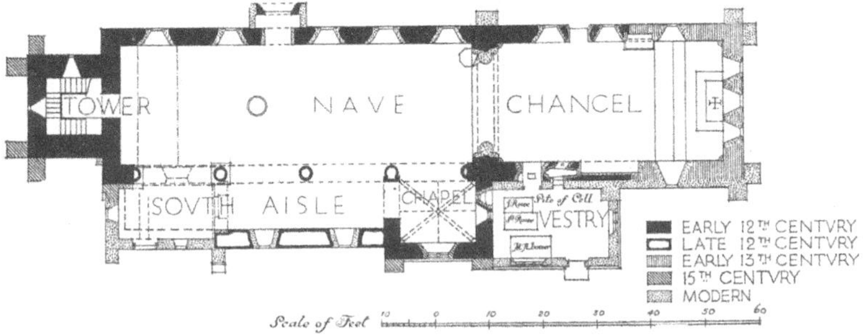

(ii) The anchorite's cell: detail

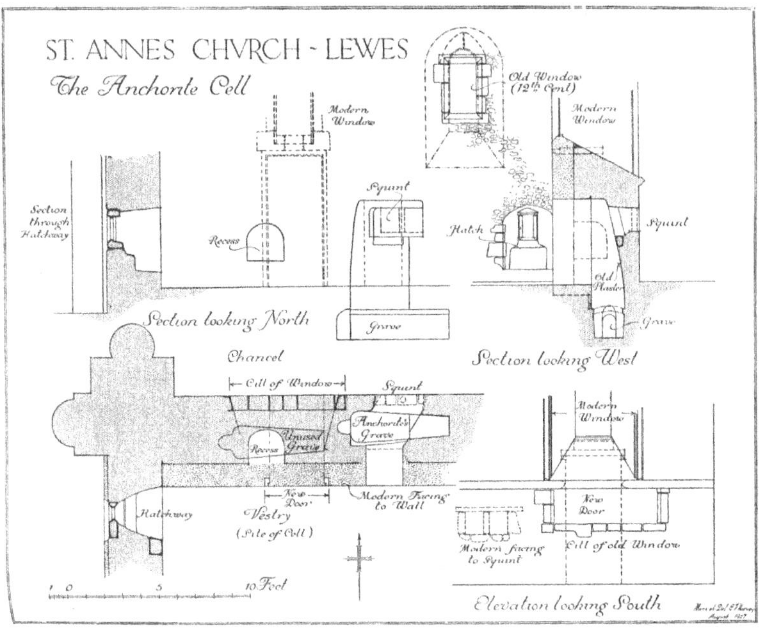

ever since the anchoress was enclosed in her cell; she knelt in it to participate in the sacraments, and when she died she was buried in it. A second, empty grave was also discovered at this time, and was interpreted as belonging to an earlier occupant of the cell.

(i) from Walter H. Godfrey, 'Church of St. Anne, Lewes: An anchorite's cell and other discoveries', *Sussex Archaeological Collections* 69 (1928): 159–69, p. 160. (ii) from Godfrey, 'Church of St. Anne, Lewes', p. 164. Reproduced by permission of the Sussex Archaeological Society.

30. Memorial before the tomb, from *Walter's Rule*

Like *Ancrene Wisse*, the thirteenth-century *Walter's Rule* [**20**], [**27**] sees the grave within the cell as a focus for thoughts of death and penitential meditation. More creepily, it also imagines the grave calling out to the anchorite, summoning him to be reincorporated back into the earth: 'What else do the lips of the tomb call out but, "Hurry to me, hurry. Come, come; hurry, hurry. For this was our agreement when you enclosed yourself in our little house".'[7] These ideas are picked up towards the end of the work in the 'Memorial before the Tomb', which is translated here.

Translated from the Latin, chapter 30, edited by Livarius Oliger, 'Regula Reclusorum Angliae et Quaestiones tres de Vita solitaria saec. XIII–XIV', *Antonianum* 9 (1934): 37–84; 243–68, pp. 81–3, with a few emendations.

O earth, earth, why do you scare me? It seems to me that you are making sounds, because with my eyes I can see and with my hands I can feel you calling. You are always crying out, 'Look, this is your place, this is your dwelling. When you come down into me it will be too late for penitence. You will not come up from here to make your amends until, with the workers in the vineyard, you receive your reward.'[8]

O earth, earth, your throat is always gaping, your lips stretched wide, ready to swallow me. Why did I emerge from my mother's womb, only for your womb to convert me into muck? Alas, my mother, after you spewed me out into this world, you worked hard to rear me as your son. But look, all that work is turned into food for worms, and the thing you thought so precious has become a pile of dung. Already you are start-

7 The passage quoted is on p. 68 of Oliger's edition; quoted and discussed in my 'Ceremonies of Enclosure', pp. 42–3.

8 That is, at the Last Judgement. Cf. the parable of the vineyard, Matt. 20.

ing to shrink away as you see the lips you used to kiss; all their beauty is perishing, for what began as filth will presently turn to filth again. O earth, earth, towards you I turn. And you are always ready to lead me into the darkness. Your jaws make me cry out with fear when, in human likeness, they stretch themselves to my length and breadth, and offer me a place, leaving me no hope of escaping your looming walls. And certainly I shall not escape them. And, o earth, however much you draw me into yourself when I am dead, you will force me to be spewed out again, alive once more, when our true Father comes in judgement.

O earth, earth, still you make me tremble, for you do not cease to scare me. I recall that it is your role, for as long as the final judgement is put off, to humble the eyes of the arrogant man [cf. Isaiah 1:11] and to order the shameless tongue to be silent, to give stench and worms in place of perfume, to turn delicious tastes into the bitterness of gall, to make strong hands weak and useless, and to fix nimble feet in immobility. In you the once sleek flesh decays, teems with worms, and fails, deprived of power and of vigour too. The bones lose their former strength and the body is turned entirely into muck.

What shall I do then, a wretched man, when I see this miserable fate awaiting me, not knowing whether I will be deemed worthy of love or hate?[9] I direct my steps to that place where penitence will meet no reward. Alas, why am I deceived with no reason? Behold, I die daily, as my life ebbs away, and yet I remain in a stupor, without a care, as if I believed that, during the course of my life, that life could be prolonged: 'For my days are vanished like smoke' [Ps. 101:4], because they pass away as smoke does. The smoke has damaged my eyes; my life and my days have offended God and his angels. And smoke, again, fills the darkness, and the many days of my life have dispersed into the darkness of sin. Alas, oh alas, why are there no rivers of tears coming from my eyes, nor from my heart an immense groan? You will be deceived, o man, truly you will be deceived, for whatever you believe to be good does the work of the Deceiver.

31. A failed attempt at the anchoritic life

Agnes de Littlemore was a laysister of the small and poor Benedictine nunnery at Little Marlow (Bucks.), who left to pursue the solitary life

9 Cf. Ecclesiastes 9:1, 'All these things have I considered in my heart, that I might carefully understand them: there are just men and wise men, and their works are in the hand of God: and yet man knoweth not whether he be worthy of love, or hatred.'

(we do not know where), but had to petition to be allowed to return. Eileen Power, who first commented on the case, branded Agnes a 'faint-heart', who attempted the life of an anchorite and then 'repented of her decision'.[10] But we do not know the full facts. If Agnes had taken her final vows, then it would be surprising to find her being readmitted to Marlow so comparatively easily. Perhaps she had embarked upon a year of probation, and found that the life was not for her; or perhaps the material arrangements she had put in place for her support had fallen through at the last moment.

Translated from the Latin entry in the register of memoranda of John Dalderby, bishop of Lincoln 1300–20: Lincolnshire Archives, Episcopal Register 3, fol. 10r.

In favour of Agnes de Littlemore, laysister of the house of Marlow.

John [Dalderby] etc. to his beloved daughters in Christ the prioress and nuns of Marlow, [wishing you] health, etc.

Whereas Agnes de Littlemore, a laysister of your house, who declares that she left your house in order to attempt the life of an anchorite, in which she desired to serve the Lord; because she is unable to fulfil her intention in this regard, desires (as she says) humbly to return to the same; we command that, when this same Agnes returns to you, you should be sure to admit her, unless there is some canonical impediment, and to deal with her according to your rule with sincere charity in the Lord.

Given at [Great] Missenden [Bucks.], 2 July 1300.

32. The anchoress of Whalley breaks her enclosure

The document recording Henry duke of Lancaster's establishment of a reclusory at Whalley, and his arrangements for the support of the anchorites enclosed there, was included in a previous chapter [**13**]. The foundation came to an end in about 1443, when the monks of Whalley Abbey successfully petitioned Henry VI for its dissolution, citing the laxity and immorality of successive occupants, and specifically the scandalous apostasy of the most recent, Isolda de Heton, a widow who had been enclosed in 1437. Thomas Whitaker, the nineteenth-century

10 Eileen Power, *Medieval English Nunneries, c. 1275 to 1535* (Cambridge: Cambridge University Press, 1922), p. 366.

historian of Whalley and its vicar from 1809 to 1821, shared the monks' point of view, speculating that Isolda's vow 'was probably taken in the first fervours of sorrow, which soon wore off, so that the widow grew weary of her confinement, and broke loose from her vows and her cell together'.[11] The truth is probably more complex. More recent discoveries have shown that the monks of Whalley seem to have resented having the anchorites imposed upon them, and they were probably ready to jump at any opportunity to get rid of them. There was also more to Isolda de Heton's situation than Whitaker realised. When she entered her enclosure, she left four children, a ten-year-old heir and his brother and two sisters. When their grandfather struck a deal with a local landowner, Richard Barton, for the heir's wardship and marriage – an arrangement that was likely to leave Isolda's other children penniless – she sought to intervene. Unfortunately the records leave the issue unresolved. Alongside Isolda's petition to the Lord Chancellor, we also have the petition of Richard Barton (not included here), in which he complains that Isolda of Heton and her brother had abducted and were concealing the young heir, who was contracted to marry his daughter.[12] We do not know what the Lord Chancellor decided, but we do know that, soon afterwards, Henry VI complied with the monks' request and dissolved the Whalley reclusory, and used its revenues to found a chantry in Whalley Church for the souls of Henry duke of Lancaster and himself.

(i) is modernised from the English printed by Whitaker, *An History of the Original Parish of Whalley*, vol.1, p. 102; (ii) from the English in 'The Last Ancress of Whalley', pp. 271–2, checked against the manuscript, TNA C 1/142/40, which is illegible in places.

(i) The monks' petition, c. 1443

To the king, our sovereign lord, etc.

Be it remembered that the place and habitation of the said recluse[13] is within a hallowed place, and near to the gate of the said monastery, and that the women that have been attending and acquainted to the said

11 Thomas D. Whitaker, *An History of the Original Parish of Whalley and Honor of Clitheroe. … To which is subjoined an account of the Parish of Cartmell*, 4th edition (2 vols, London: George Routledge & Sons, 1872–76), Vol.1, p. 102.

12 Anon., 'The Last Ancress of Whalley', *Historic Society of Lancashire and Cheshire* 64 (1912): 268–72, p. 270.

13 Whitaker transcribed the petition from one of the Abbey's registers, which is now lost. It sounds as though some preamble detailing the foundation and its history has been omitted.

recluse have recourse daily into the said monastery for the allowance of bread, ale, 'kitchen meat'[14] and other things for the support of the said recluse according to the indenture rehearsed above. The which is not appropriate to be had within such religious places.

And how that diverse of those that have been anchorites and recluses in the said place aforetimes, contrary to their own oath and profession, have broken out of the said place wherein they were enclosed, and departed from there without any restoration.

And in especial how that now Isolda of Heton that was most recently enclosed in the said place, by the nomination and preferment of our sovereign lord and King that now is, has broken out of the said place, and has departed from there contrary to her own oath and profession, not willing or intending to be restored again, and thus living at her own liberty for these two years and more, like as she had never been professed.

And that diverse of the women that have been servants there, and attending to the recluses aforetimes, have been misgoverned, and got with child within that hallowed place, to the great vexation in hurt and scandal of the aforesaid abbey.

May it please your highness of our especial grace to grant your suppliants the Abbot etc. ...[15]

(ii) Isolda's petition, c. 1443

To the most worshipful father in God and most gracious lord the archbishop of Canterbury, Chancellor of England,[16] your poor petitioner Isolda, that was the wife of one Richard Heton, now being an anchoress enclosed at Whalley in the county of Lancashire, pleads that:

> Whereas one William Heton, father of the said Richard, ... [*agreed with?*] ... your said petitioner to have William, son and heir of the said Richard and your petitioner, to marry and provide for according to his discretion, promising your said petitioner 40 marks for her good will;
>
> your petitioner, seeing that her son was to be married against his will and all his friends' will, and also under age, and moreover that

14 Literally, food from the kitchen – used to refer to any food (fish, cheese, etc.) eaten as a relish or accompaniment with bread or another staple.

15 Whitaker omits the rest of the formulaic conclusion.

16 John Stafford was archbishop of Canterbury 1443–52, and lord chancellor 1432–50.

she had great charge daily with other of her children, that is to say a son and [two?] daughters ... unmarried; and also, whereas she was proffered for the marriage of her said son 300 marks [£200], with which she thought to have helped her other children, utterly refused.

The said William, father of the said Richard, seeing soon after that your petitioner was disposed to be an anchoress and enclosed, and would have no power to maintain action at law against him, came with great power and took away the said William her son and married him[17] against the will of your said petitioner and of all her friends, to the great hurt and distress of your petitioner, and also to the utter undoing and ruin of her said children remaining helpless, as described above:

That it please your gracious lordship, considering these things aforesaid, and that your petitioner has no remedy in the law to sue for recovery against him, and also that she does not have power or means to take steps herself nor to get a protector to maintain her in her right, but utterly to her undoing and her children's also, without your gracious help and protection in this case; and that you will of your gracious lordship grant a writ of *subpoena* directed to the said William father of the said Richard to appear before you in the Chancery at a certain day ... and under a certain penalty, and there to be examined and to do as truth and conscience require.

For the love of God and in the way of charity.[18]

33. An ailing anchorite

This is the only record we have of Joan, a thirteenth-century anchorite enclosed somewhere near Blyth (Notts.). How long she had been enclosed before her health gave out is unknown. On a bishop's responsibilities towards the anchorites in his diocese, see [**2**].

Translated from the Latin in *The Register of William Wickwane, Lord Archbishop of York 1279–85*, edited by W. Brown, Surtees Society 114 (1907), p. 74.

1 Jan. [1281], Scrooby.[19] W[illiam Wickwane, archbishop of York] to the vicar of Blyth, [wishing you] health, etc.

17 That is, entered into an agreement for his marriage.

18 A formulaic conclusion.

19 The archbishops of York had a palace at Scrooby (Notts.), which is a few miles north-east of Blyth.

We have heard, and with paternal affection feel sympathy for her predicament, that our beloved daughter in Christ, Lady Joan, who practises the solitary religious life in a solemnly dedicated place near Blyth, with the approval of ourselves and our predecessor Walter,[20] has been, whilst enclosed within her walls as is appropriate, afflicted for a long time now by multiple illnesses, so that it is evident that, while she is languishing wretchedly in her little cell, she barely has enough of the things she needs to sustain her body, and, while she is incapacitated in this way, she has had to cease those lawful occupations that she would sometimes take on in return for supplies of food.

In order that no one whom we have determined in the zeal of our charity to receive into our protection should be lost through thoughtless neglect, with supreme confidence in your careful and extensive effort, we commit and hereby command you to assume the care and custody of the aforementioned religious woman, her household and her goods; on condition that all of it (both people and property, those that remain and those that are taken off in the mean time), having always been kept completely honestly, should be managed carefully in all respects to her benefit; and we desire that you will render a strict account to this effect, whenever we are moved to require it of you.

34. Making a door for the anchorite's cell at Oath

This document is our only witness to an intriguing anchoritic establishment. The chapel, at Oath in the parish of Aller in the Somerset Levels, seems to have been the home of two early fourteenth-century hermits. Perhaps, like many of their fellow hermits, they worked on the bridges and causeways that made the region's low-lying wetlands passable (see further Chapter V, especially [**37**]). After some time, however, one of them decided to 'graduate' to the stricter life of an enclosed anchorite. His fellow hermit evidently did not follow him into reclusion, but remained at the chapel as his link to the outside world. Although this petition of 1328 shows a recently made anchorite starting to make provision for the practicalities of infirmity and death, he may have acted prematurely: the 'brothers of Oath' were left money in a local landowner's will in 1340. But the chapel was in disrepair by

20 Walter Giffard, archbishop 1266–79.

1373, and had fallen out of use by the sixteenth century. No trace of it now remains.[21]

Translated from the Latin in the register of John Droxford, bishop of Bath and Wells 1309–29, Somerset Record Office, D/D/B. Reg. 1, fol. 277a.[22]

Commission issued to the vicar of Muchelney[23] to visit an enclosed hermit and hear his confessions.

J[ohn], by divine permission bishop of Bath and Wells, to our beloved son in Christ the perpetual vicar of the parish church of Muchelney, [wishing you] health, grace and blessing.

A petition that has been shown to us from our beloved son in Christ Brother Thomas, hermit in the hermitage of Oath in the parish of Aller in our diocese, and recently (due to his great devotion and with our authority) enclosed as an anchorite, contained the following:

> that whereas, since the time of his enclosure no one is able to visit or see him, even if he is laid low by sickness of whatever kind or however serious, he humbly besought us that, with our licence and good will, for the increase of his life and the profit of his soul, a door might be made by which you (or someone else deputed by you for this purpose) might have a way in for visiting the said recluse in times of need, and hearing his confessions, granting absolution and enjoining penance, whenever his fellow hermit asks you; and moreover, that when, by divine disposition, the aforesaid recluse shall depart this life, he may be buried in the church of Aller, or the cemetery of the same, or wherever else (in consecrated ground) he chooses to have his burial.

We, wishing to look after the health of both the body and soul of this recluse, and having taken the advice of experts, have graciously given our assent to his aforesaid petition in the form given below:

> that is, that such a door should be made under your supervision, and [secured] with a strong lock whose key should remain in your possession; and that you should come to him in person, for visiting him, and hearing his confessions, and doing the other things in this

21 R.W. Dunning, ed., *A History of the County of Somerset: Vol. 3* (London: Oxford University Press for the Institute of Historical Research, 1974), pp. 61–71.

22 Noted in *Calendar of the Register of John De Drokensford, Bishop of Bath and Wells, A.D. 1309–1329*, edited by E. Hobhouse, Somerset Record Society 1 (1887), p. 284.

23 Muchelney is about 4 miles from Aller.

regard as described above, when you are reasonably summoned by his said fellow hermit, as often as necessary.

We hereby grant our special licence and permission both to the said recluse and to you for faithfully doing and performing these things, to last during our pleasure.

Given at Aller, 5 April 1328.

35. Two anchorites' wills

A pair of wills that are dated a century apart, and whose testators are separated also by gender and social status.

35a. Katherine Ditton, 1437

Two churches in St Albans (Herts.) had anchorites' cells in more or less continuous occupation during the fifteenth century.[24] The church of St Peter was much altered in the nineteenth century, and no trace of an anchorhold remains, but at St Michael's on the south-west fringe of the city some unusual features in the south wall of the chancel (including a 'lowside window', tomb recess, coffin lid and small, locker-like recess) may be connected with the anchorites.[25] Katherine Ditton was enclosed here by 1421, and received regular gifts from local people in their wills. She made her own will in 1437. In itself, the document is unremarkable. Her bequests are focused, as one might expect, almost entirely on the church where she had spent the last sixteen or more years of her life. The amounts involved are small, and there was probably not much left over for her three executors. One of these was a member of her family; the two women named alongside him are worth considering more closely. Several bequests during the 1420s mention Katherine's servants or companions; in 1424 Emma Gowle of St Albans left money to Katherine the anchorite at St Michael's, and Joan Gerard and Agnes Vertesaws dwelling with her.[26] Perhaps they were the two female serv-

24 For a list of anchorites there, see my 'Christina of Markyate and the *Hermits and Anchorites of England*' in *Christina of Markyate: A twelfth-century holy woman* edited by Samuel Fanous and Henrietta Leyser (London: Routledge, 2004), pp. 229–53 at pp. 233, 245–6.

25 For possible remains of the cell at St Michael's see William Page, ed., *A History of the County of Hertford: Vol. 2* (London: Archibald Constable and Company Limited, 1908), p. 403.

26 William Brigg, ed., *The Herts Genealogist and Antiquary*, 3 vols (Harpenden: William Brigg, 1895–99), Vol. 1, p. 67 and cf. p. 106.

ants, one older and one younger, envisaged by Aelred [**12a**]. Agnes must have been inspired by the time she spent with Ditton, because she went on to become the anchorite at St Michael's herself. (Because of gaps in the record, we do not know whether she succeeded her mistress immediately, or returned to St Michael's later in life.) She is named as anchoress in 1452 and again in 1472, almost fifty years after her first appearance at St Michael's.

Translated from the Latin of the registered will in Hertfordshire Archives and Local Studies, 1AR, fol. 31v.

In the name of God etc.

In the year of our Lord 1437, on the 11th day of the month of June, on the feast of St Barnabas, I, Katherine Dytton, anchorite at the church of Saint Michael in the town of St Albans, being of sound mind, draw up my testament in this manner, etc.

Item I leave my lined cloak in place of my mortuary payment.[27] *Item* 12d to the high altar of the same church and 6d to the parish clerk of the same. *Item* 8d to the lights of the aforesaid church. *Item* 8d for the repair of the body of the same.

The residue of my goods I give severally to Joan Gerard and Agnes Verdesaus and John Ditton my nephew, the three of whom I make my executors.

35b. Simon Appulby, anchorite of All Hallows London Wall, 1537

We have already encountered Simon Appulby, who made his profession as an anchorite in June 1513 [**6a**]. He spent the next twenty-four years in his cell at All Hallows, becoming a fixture of parish life, and a benefactor of his parish church. He contributed 40s to building work there in the late 1520s, and also presented a chalice weighing 8 ounces and other money gifts. He was the author of a series of meditations on Christ's life and death entitled *The Fruyte of Redempcion*, printed in 1514. It was a work of no great theological or spiritual ambition, but some popularity: it had run through another four editions by 1532.[28] No date is given for probate of Appulby's will, but the anchorite's house was empty and granted to the swordbearer of London in July 1538.

27 Parishioners were expected to make a gift from their estate to the parish priest.

28 Mary C. Erler, *Reading and Writing During the Dissolution: Monks, Friars, and Nuns 1530–1558* (Cambridge: Cambridge University Press, 2013), chapter 1.

Modernised from the English printed by Erler, *Reading and Writing During the Dissolution*, pp. 148–9.

In the name of God, Amen.

On the 6th day of June in the year of our Lord God 1537, and the 29th year of the reign of our sovereign lord King Henry the 8th, I Simon Appulby, priest, anchorite in the house or anchorage adjoining the parish church of All Hallows in London Wall, being of good and perfect mind (thanks and praise be to Almighty God), make, ordain and dispose this my present testament and last will in the manner and form following, that is to say:

First, I commend my soul to Almighty God my maker, my saviour and redeemer; and my body to be buried in the tomb already appointed and made within the aforementioned anchorage.

Item I will that the priests of Pappey come and be at my burial, and I bequeath to each of them that comes twenty pence; and similarly I bequeath to the clerks of the fraternity that come to my burial, according to their usual custom and manner, twenty pence.[29]

Item I bequeath to 14 children carrying 14 tapers (which I have already arranged for and bought) at my said burial, 2s 4d – that is to say, to each one of those 14 children for their trouble, 2d.

Item I bequeath a further 2s 4d to 14 poor people who live within the said parish of All Hallows, that is to say, 2d to each of them.

Item I will that eight shillings and four pence be spent at the time of my burial on buns, cheese and ale for the company that attends my burial.

Item I will that on the day that falls one month after my decease five shillings should be spent at the discretion of my executor and supervisor named below.

Moreover it is my true intention and will that all the books and vestments that there are now within the chapel of the said anchorage shall remain there perpetually for the use of the anchorite that after my decease shall occupy the same position, so long as that position of anchorite there is filled within a year and a day of my decease; otherwise, if that does not happen, I will that all those books and vestments be given over to whatever use seems good to my executor.

29 The fraternity of St Augustine Pappey in the parish of All Hallows had been founded in 1442 as a home for up to sixty old and infirm priests, and Appulby had been one of its two wardens between 1505 and 1507, before his enclosure.

I will that all the residue of my goods, except for the goods that I recently conveyed to John Drinkmilk by written grant, and once my burial has been completed in the manner described above, be distributed in works of mercy and charity by my executor named below, in whatever way seems best to his discretion.

And I make and ordain as the executor of this my present testament and last will John Davell, citizen and wax-chandler[30] of London. And I bequeath to the same John for his trouble in the foregoing three shillings and four pence. And I make and ordain as the supervisor of my same testament Thomas Hygson, citizen and fletcher[31] of London. And I bequeath to the same Thomas for his trouble in that regard three shillings and four pence.

30 A maker or seller of wax candles.

31 A maker of arrows.

V: SCENES OF EREMITICAL LIFE

Introduction

The life of the hermit was less constrained than that of the anchorite, not only in the obvious sense – hermits were not confined within cell walls, but free to wander – but also in the absence of a rigid regulatory framework or precise set of expectations about what it should involve. (The late Middle Ages did see moves towards the regulation of hermits, and these are treated in the next section.) The lack of a clear definition of the vocation meant that hermits could be accused of simply living as they pleased under the cloak of piety [**36**], but it also allowed for a great variety in the realisation of the vocation, and it is this that the present section seeks to illustrate.

In medieval romance, hermits are found in the forest of adventure; and the popular imagination (medieval and modern) puts hermits in romantic, secluded spots – most evocatively, perhaps, cave dwellings like St Robert of Knaresborough's chapel and hermitage carved out of the rock beside the River Nidd in Knaresborough (N. Yorks.), or the cave hermitage associated with the legend of Guy of Warwick at Guy's Cliffe (Warks.) [**26**], [**75**].[1] Some of the hermits in this section occupied rural ([**38b**], [**43**]) or other lonely situations [**41**], but (in common with late medieval anchorites) many were found in and around urban locations [**38a**]: adjoining, or even in, town walls [**40**], or in bridge or wayside chapels [**39**], [**42**]. As in the case of anchorites, contemporaries sometimes struggled to square the lifestyles and situations of these present-day hermits with their forebears, the Fathers of the Egyptian deserts [**1**], [**36**].

Some hermits were ordained priests, but the majority were not. When a hermit is associated with a chapel (e.g. [**38a**], [**38b**], [**43**]) he may have been its chaplain, but in the absence of any reference to the celebration of divine service he is as likely to have served merely as a

1 On this tendency to impute the presence of a hermit to any likely feature of the landscape, see my 'Hidden Lives: Methodological reflections on a new database of the hermits and anchorites of medieval England', *Medieval Prosopography* 28 (2013): 17–34. For another cave hermitage, see [**76**].

caretaker, like the hermit of St Margaret's, Westminster, who was paid 3d in 1469–70 'for watching and making clean of the church'.[2] This was undoubtedly the case at the chapel of St Mary on Derby Bridge [**42**], where Sir John Dale was priest, whilst the goods and furniture were in the custody of John Shenton, hermit, and his wife. (For married hermits, see [**51**], [**52c**].) But not every hermit dwelt in a chapel,[3] and some were probably itinerant.

As this already begins to suggest, hermits of this period were typically men of no great social standing or spiritual aspiration.[4] Most would have been engaged in what we now think of as public works, soliciting alms towards their projects and performing the labour with their own hands. Most characteristically, we find them building and maintaining roads and causeways [**37**], [**39**], or working on bridges [**37**], [**42**]. We might not find it too difficult to accept such work as charitable, but it is less usual today to think of it as *pious*. The Middle Ages, however, was used to thinking allegorically of life as a journey or pilgrimage to our home in heaven, and of an earthly journey, with its perils and discomforts, as a microcosm of (as Chaucer's Parson calls it) that 'perfect glorious pilgrimage / That hight [*is called*] Jerusalem celestial'.[5] To ease the passage of one's fellow Christians to their earthly destination was to advance one's own heavenly pilgrimage. Many medieval bridges were furnished with chapels: the medieval London Bridge had a row of houses built on it, as well as its chapel dedicated to St Thomas Becket, and there are surviving bridge-chapels at several locations besides the chapel of St Mary, Derby, that is included here [**42**].[6] The connection of hermits, as religious wanderers, with travel and communication seems to have been a strong one. As well as roads and bridges, hermits manned the ferry over the River Darent at Dartford (Kent) from 1235 into the

2 H.F. Westlake, *St. Margaret's Westminster: The church of the House of Commons* (London: Smith, Elder & Co., 1914), p. 20.

3 On the somewhat fluid definition of the term, see Nicholas Orme, 'Church and Chapel in Medieval England', *Transactions of the Royal Historical Society* 6 (1996): 75–102.

4 For a glimpse of hermit spirituality, see [**46**]. In this, as in other aspects of his religious identity, Richard Rolle seems to have been something of a throwback to an earlier age.

5 *Canterbury Tales*, X.50–1, in *The Riverside Chaucer* edited by Larry D. Benson et al., 3rd ed. (Boston: Houghton Mifflin, 1987), p. 287.

6 For bridges as religious buildings, see Eamon Duffy, *The Stripping of the Altars: Traditional religion in England 1400–1580* (2nd edition, New Haven, CT: Yale University Press, 2005), pp. 367–8.

sixteenth century,[7] and there are several other examples of lighthouse hermitages to place alongside the example of Ravenspur included here [**41**].[8] Hermits might frequent the popular pilgrim routes. A hermit named Reynald acts as chaperone to Margery Kempe on a visit to the shrine of Our Lady of Walsingham. They continue on their journey together to Norwich and Ipswich. Later, Kempe encounters Reynald again, when they have both come to Syon Abbey, beside the Thames near Isleworth (Middlesex), for the popular Lammastide indulgence, and (with some persuasion) he accompanies her home again to Lynn.[9]

It was normal, then, for most late medieval hermits to spend much of their time on the road, begging for support for themselves and the projects on which they might be employed. A minority might occupy an endowed hermitage and live off its income: the chapel of the hermits of Cripplegate, London [**40**], was sufficiently well furnished at the end of the thirteenth century to be worth plundering, and the hermit himself was in a position to lend money to a group of substantial London merchants. But most hermit-chapels would have been in the same position as the hermitage on Highgate Hill [**39**], having 'no yearly rents of its own', and entirely dependent, therefore, on the support of the faithful. The hermits could beg from passers-by, of course, and achieve some success. In 1531 a hermit secured a modest gift from Henry VIII, who encountered him 'upon the way' [**44**]. But there was considerable debate around mendicancy in the Middle Ages, and unease in particular about 'sturdy beggars', who looked as if they ought to be able to work for their living. William Langland memorably voices his contempt for those *soi-disant* hermits who 'hang around by the highway', scrounging off the unsuspecting traveller [**36**]. To reassure the faithful that their money was not going to be wasted, a hermit could produce some sort of documentation. From the Church he could seek an indulgence towards his maintenance and the upkeep of his chapel or hermitage [**38**]. Though indulgences receive a bad press, they represented a key strand in the fabric of charitable giving in the Middle Ages. With so many demands on the charity of the faithful, an indulgence was a way of certifying particular individuals or projects as *bona fide* good causes, and worthy recipients of support. Alternatively, a hermit could seek validation for himself and his project

7 John Dunkin, *The History and Antiquities of Dartford* (London: privately printed, 1844), pp. 187–90.

8 For other examples, see Clay, *Hermits and Anchorites*, pp. 49–56.

9 See *The Book of Margery* Kempe, trans. B.A. Windeatt (Harmondsworth: Penguin, 1985), book II, chapters 2 and 10.

from the secular authorities, in the form of letters of protection [37], inviting the king's subjects to look kindly on his requests for assistance. In the aftermath of the Black Death of 1349, when labour shortages contributed to a more repressive social environment, it became harder to secure such endorsement. In particular, the authorities were much less likely to offer the 'blank cheque' of a licence to beg; instead hermits were granted the right to request tolls such as pavage or pontage, which specified precisely the good cause to which the money collected would go, and also encouraged the hermit to remain in one place and collect his tolls in person, rather than 'gadding about or wandering around the country' [56].[10] Additions to the Statute of Labourers made at Cambridge in 1388 threatened fines and punishments for anyone found outside their hundred, borough or city unless they could provide evidence that their absence was licensed. Among those exempt from its penalties were 'people of religion and approved hermits having letters testimonial from their ordinary' (i.e. their religious superior).[11] Fifteenth-century moves to formalise such mechanisms of approval are the subject of Chapter VI.

36. Vagabond hermits, from *Piers Plowman*

William Langland's great poem wrestles incessantly with some of the biggest religious and social questions of the late fourteenth century. From the very opening of the poem, when his narrator Will appears 'In habite as a heremite unholy of werkes', hermits are a recurrent concern, representing both the purest ideal of the religious life and its worst abuses. In his final revision of *Piers*, the C-Text, written probably in the late 1380s, Langland augments the role of hermits considerably. In an 'autobiographical' passage in Passus V he presents himself as just the kind of idle layabout with eremitic pretensions that he elsewhere castigates and that the authorities were beginning to crack down upon.[12] He also rewrites and expands the episode of Piers's Pardon that concludes the *Visio* section of the poem, with a new and insistent focus on the problem of 'sturdy beggars' and the undeserving

10 For changes over the course of the fourteenth century, see my 'Langland and Hermits', *Yearbook of Langland Studies* 11 (1997): 67–86.

11 *Statutes of the Realm* (11 vols, London: Dawsons of Pall Mall, 1810–28), Vol. 2, p. 58.

12 On the context for this episode, see Anne Middleton, 'Acts of Vagrancy: The C Version "Autobiography" and the statute of 1388' in *Written Work: Langland, Labor, and Authorship* edited by Steven Justice and Kathryn Kerby-Fulton (Philadelphia: University of Pennsylvania Press, 1997), pp. 208–317. See also [63].

poor. Once more, hermits feature strongly, and Langland makes explicit the contrast between the 'lewd hermits' of his day and the ideal of the Desert Fathers.[13]

Translated from the Middle English verse, William Langland, *Piers Plowman: The C-Text*, edited by Derek Pearsall (Exeter: University of Exeter Press, 1994), IX.58–60; 187–212.

All the world's labourers that truly and lawfully live
By the work of their hands, our lord Truth grants them
Perpetual pardon, the same as Piers the Plowman.
...
And all holy hermits shall have the same.
But hermits that hang around by the highway
And in towns among tavern-women, and beg in churches?
Holy hermits hated and despised all that –
Riches, deference, alms from the rich, and so on –
These idlers, sneak-thieves, apologies for hermits,[14]
Want just the reverse, for they live like any villager.
They're nothing but beer-swilling layabouts:
No breeding or education, nor holy like [real] hermits
That used to live in the woods with bears and lions.
Some were born with enough, and needed nothing more,
And some lived by their learning and the work of their hands,
And strangers were like friends to some, and sent them food,
And birds brought bread to some, and they lived on that.
Holy hermits who hailed from a fine family
Relinquished their lands and lordship, and all bodily comforts.
But these hermits that 'edify' by the highway[15]
Used to be workmen, weavers and tailors,
And carter's mates and out-of-work clerics:
They kept a hungry house and lacked for most things –
Long labour and not much to show for it – till they noticed
That loafers dressed as friars had fat cheeks.
And so they left their labour, these good-for-nothings,
And slipped into copes, as if they were clergy,

13 For hermits in *Piers Plowman*, see Ralph Hanna, 'Will's Work' in *Written Work*, pp. 23–66, and my 'Langland and Hermits'.

14 Langland calls them *lewed* hermits, where *lewed* means both 'lay, not clerical' and 'ignorant, good-for-nothing'.

15 There is a pun on *edify*, which means both to provide edifying instruction and to be engaged in construction work. Langland's hermits are concerned only with the latter.

Or part of a holy order, or a prophet perhaps,
Against the law of Levi.[16]

37. Support from the state: letters of protection for hermits

Medieval culture was suspicious of strangers. Anyone found outside her or his home manor or vill was liable to arouse official interest, and that interest would grow increasingly hostile as the Middle Ages went on. Royal letters of protection were a kind of 'internal passport' or safe-conduct, guaranteeing that the bearer was a reputable person on *bona fide* business. Typical recipients included foreign merchants, soldiers *en route* to or from the wars and various kinds of pilgrim and religious mendicant. Hermits, of course, fell into the latter category. The patent rolls record the issuing of letters of protection. The letters themselves bearing the royal seal would be carried by the hermit as a certificate of approval. In several cases they are also explicitly a licence to beg: these are the letters (like the first example below) that include the clause *Rogamus* ('We ask') which request that the bearer should be favoured with alms. The details given provide a snapshot of the range of charitable activities in which hermits could be engaged.

The original language of the letters is Latin. (i) is translated from the full text on the patent roll, TNA C66/89, m.14.[17] Succeeding entries are quoted from the summaries printed in (ii) *Cal. Pat. Rolls 1327–1330*, p. 252; (iii–iv) *Cal. Pat. Rolls 1330–1334*, p. 1, p. 464; (v–vi) *Cal. Pat. Rolls 1334–1338*, p. 72, p. 154; (vii) *Cal. Pat. Rolls 1338–1340*, p. 204; (viii) *Cal. Pat. Rolls 1348–1350*, p. 91; (ix) *Cal. Pat. Rolls 1358–1361*, p. 313; (x) *Cal. Pat. Rolls 1374–1377*, p. 280; (xi) *Cal. Pat. Rolls 1405–1408*, p. 336. They have been edited slightly in a few cases, and where possible all place-names have been replaced with their modern forms, and the county added.

(i) 1271

Brother William,[18] hermit of Gamlingay,[19] has letters of protection from the king, lasting for four years, including this clause: 'We ask you

16 In Jewish tradition, priests could be drawn only from among the Levites, descendants of Levi; presumably Langland intends a contrast with the opportunistic 'hermits' that he is describing.

17 Calendared in *Cal. Pat. Rolls 1266–1272*, p. 538.

18 In the calendared version, the hermit is named as William Westminster, but the spurious surname appears to have arisen out of confusion with a neighbouring entry.

19 Gamlingay is in Cambridgeshire, near the border with Bedfordshire. The surrounding land is low-lying and often boggy, and it is probable that Brother William, like most of the other hermits in this selection, was engaged in work to keep the roads passable.

that, when the aforesaid Brother William comes to you, you will wish to let him have some of those goods that God has in turn bestowed upon you, so that you should be worthy to receive a fitting reward from God and our thanks.'

In witness of which, etc.

Given at Westminster, on the second day of June.

(ii) 13 March 1328
Protection and safe-conduct, for as long as he shall be employed therein, for brother Robert de Skytheby [Skeeby (N. Yorks.)], hermit of the chapel of St Augustine, Skeeby, travelling in search of carriage and alms towards the construction of a bridge over the stream of Gillyngbeck at Skeeby, co. York.

(iii) 15 September 1330
Protection and safe conduct until the work is finished for Adam de Quenby, hermit of the chapel of St Helen, Shipton (N. Yorks.), while seeking means of carriage and alms to enable him to make a safe way in the forest of Galtres at a place called 'les Polles' where many accidents have occurred by reason of the depth of the ways.[20]

(iv) 12 August 1333
Protection and safe conduct for Robert de Skitheby,[21] hermit of the chapel of St Augustine, Huntington by York, while seeking carriage and alms for making a safe way at a place called 'Les Polles', in the forest of Galtres, hitherto very dangerous on account of the depth of the ways there.

(v) 26 January 1335
Protection for two years for brother John le Mareschal, a hermit, staying at the chapel of St Michael by Blyth (Notts.), about the making of a causey between Blyth and Mattersey and a bridge for the town of Mattersey, who is dependent upon charity for the sustenance of himself and the men working at the causey and bridge, and is going to divers parts of the realm to collect alms.

20 Renewed 16 October 1332: *Cal. Pat. Rolls 1330–1334*, p. 359. Galtres was an area of royal forest immediately to the north of the city of York.

21 This hermit may be the same man as in (ii), though now found some 50 miles further south.

(vi) 17 July 1335
Protection with clause *rogamus*, for one year, for brother Thomas, hermit of Skip Bridge, who has spent great sums in the repair of the bridges and causeys over the moor of Hessay (N. Yorks.) now in a dangerous state, collecting alms to complete the work.[22]

(vii) 9 February 1339
Protection with clause *rogamus*, for one year, for Alan de Elsefeld, a poor hermit of Wargrave (Berks.), collecting alms in churches to build a chapel there in honour of Corpus Christi.

(viii) 16 May 1348
Protection with clause *rogamus*, for two years, for brother Richard Dryng, hermit of the hermitage of St Mary, Nettleton by Thwangcastre [Caistor, Lincs.], now engaged about the making of a causeway between those towns, who has not means to support himself and his labourers, and is going to divers parts of England to collect alms.

(ix) 3 January 1359
Protection with clause *rogamus* for John Canes of Brantham (Suffolk) and brother John atte Welle, hermit of Cattawade (Suffolk), keepers of the bridge and causeway between Manningtree (Essex) and Cattawade, who have not whereof to keep up the works of the bridge and causeway and build a chapel there in honour of the Virgin Mary for the perpetual celebration of divine offices therein for all benefactors of the bridge and causeway, unless assisted by the charitable, seeking alms for the sustenance of them and the works.

(x) 14 June 1376
Grant to William de Raby, hermit, of pontage[23] for one year in aid of the repair of a bridge called 'Le Petypount' by Oxford, which is broken down.

(xi) 17 June 1407
Grant to Thomas Kendale, hermit, of pontage for two years for the repair of the bridges called 'Smalebrigges' and the causey [causeway] between the town of Cambridge and the town of Barton (Cambs).[24]

22 Renewed 24 November 1336: see *Cal. Pat. Rolls 1334–1338*, p. 337.

23 The right to charge a toll for using the bridge.

24 Hermits are recorded at Small Bridges from 1396. In 1428 the hermit was permitted to cut willow for mending the road. See 'The City of Cambridge: Bridges' in *A*

38. Two episcopal indulgences in favour of hermits

Though sin could be absolved in this present life through the sacrament of penance, there remained a penalty to be paid in purgatory. Descriptions and depictions of the torments to be suffered there provided an unfailing stimulus to the medieval imagination (see [**28**] for an example). Contrary to popular belief, indulgences offered not forgiveness of sins but remission of the penalty still to be paid for those sins in purgatory, once they had been absolved. Bishops were allowed to grant remission of up to forty days. (See [**39**] for a more generous papal indulgence.)

38a. For the hermit of St Cyriac, Chichester

The chapel of St Cyriac was located just inside the city walls of Chichester, at a site now marked by St Cyriac's car park, and probably not much less bustling then than now.[25] The source records the full text of the indulgence. Presumably the hermit displayed it at his chapel, or exhibited it to passers-by, as he solicited them for alms. The preamble alludes to the notion of the 'treasury of the Church': that is, that Christ and his saints had, through their virtuous lives, accrued a superabundance of merit; and ordinary Christians could be allowed to draw on this surplus in order to speed their own passage through purgatory.

Translation of the Latin by Cecil Deedes in *The Episcopal Register of Robert Rede, ordinis predicatorum, Lord Bishop of Chichester, 1397–1415. Part I*, Sussex Record Society 8 (1908), pp. 54–5, reproduced with slight modifications.

A Letter Granted to a Poor Hermit

To all sons of holy Mother Church to whom the present letters shall come, Robert etc. wishes eternal health in the Lord.

We believe that we do a service pleasing to God as often as we stir up more readily the minds of the faithful to works of piety and charity by the attractive grants of indulgences. Therefore, of the mercy of Almighty God, and trusting in the merits and prayers of the glorious Virgin Mary his mother and of the blessed apostles Peter and Paul, and

History of the County of Cambridge and the Isle of Ely: Vol. 3: The City and University of Cambridge edited by J.P.C. Roach (London: Oxford University Press for the Institute of Historical Research, 1959), p. 114.

25 Alison McCann, 'The Chapel of St. Cyriac, Chichester', *Sussex Archaeological Collections* 113 (1975), pp. 197–9.

also of the most blessed confessor St Richard our patron,[26] and of all the saints, we grant by these present [letters] 40 days of indulgence to all Christ's worshippers through our diocese wherever they may be (and to others whose diocesans shall ratify and accept this our indulgence), being truly contrite and confessed of their sins, who have contributed or in any way assigned any of the goods conferred on them by God as charitable supplies towards the support of Richard Petevyne, hermit of the chapel of St Cyriac founded in our city of Chichester, and to the repairs of the same chapel.

In witness hereof our seal is attached to these present [letters]. Given in our manor of Drungewick,[27] April 3 1405, and in the ninth year of our translation.

38b. For repairs to the hermitage of Barmore, following a fire

In contrast to the previous example, the hermitage of Barmore in Co. Durham was a rural hermitage in the large straggling parish of Gainford, just north of Darlington. And whereas the grant to the hermit of St Cyriac seems to offer routine maintenance, the Barmore hermit, Robert Perules, had been the victim of a disastrous fire in which he had lost everything. This is the only record we have of Perules, but the indulgence in his favour evidently had the desired effect: another hermit is recorded here later in the fifteenth century, and the site was still in use in the sixteenth.[28]

Translated from the Latin of the register of Thomas Langley: Durham University, Durham Cathedral Archive, Reg. Lang. fol. 217.[29]

Indulgence

On the first day of the month of February in the same year [viz. 1435], the lord [bishop] in his manor of [Bishop's] Aukland granted letters of indulgence to Robert Perules, hermit of the chapel of the Blessed Mary Magdalen of Barmore in the parish of Gainford in his diocese, whose house adjoining the same chapel together with the chapel itself

26 St Richard Wych (d. 1253), buried in Chichester Cathedral.

27 One of the bishop's residences, about 25 miles north-east of Chichester, near Billingshurst.

28 The site is no. 12 in the list for Durham in Clay, *Hermits and Anchorites*, pp. 214–15, where the references to later occupants will be found.

29 Calendared by R.L. Storey in *The Register of Thomas Langley, Bishop of Durham 1406–1437*, Vol. 4, Surtees Society 170 (1961), p. 150 (no. 1137).

and all his goods present in the same house and chapel have recently been destroyed in a conflagration of fire, so that nothing remains with which he can repair the aforesaid house and chapel or support himself in any way unless Christ's faithful devoutly come to his aid with their alms in this regard. To last for one year only.

39. Papal indulgence for the hermit of Highgate Hill

The hermit-chapel of St Michael in Highgate, north of London, is first recorded in the mid-fourteenth century; probably the last hermit was appointed in 1531. It stood near the top of Highgate Hill, on the Great North Road, the main road from London to York.[30] Some of the dangers, of both natural and human origin, incident upon medieval road travel can be gleaned from the present document. While hermits were frequently the beneficiaries of indulgences from their local bishop [**38**], a papal indulgence is more rare, and suggests that the chapel was already of some importance and was attracting significant numbers of pilgrims. (See also [**58**].) The generous indulgence (5 years 200 days, against the 40 days maximum that a bishop could grant) would only have increased its appeal.

Quoted from J.A. Twemlow, ed., *Calendar of Entries in the Papal Registers Relating to Great Britain and Ireland, Vol. 12: 1458–1471* (London: HMSO, 1933), p. 411.

Rome, 28 September 1464.

To all Christ's faithful. Relaxation in perpetuity of five years and five quarantines of enjoined penance to all, being penitent and having confessed, who on the feast of the Assumption of St Mary [15 Aug.] and the feast of St Michael the Archangel in September [29 Sept.] visit and give alms for the completion, conservation and augmentation of the chapel of the said Archangel, situate within the parish of the parish church of St Mary the Virgin, Harnsay [Hornsey], in the diocese of London, and in a solitary place; which chapel has been wont, with the consent of the rector and parishioners of the said church, to be governed by persons who lead a solitary life, devote themselves to the repair of decayed bridges and ways and the burial of the bodies of persons slain by robbers, and exercise many other works of piety,

30 For other references to the hermitage, see 'Hornsey, including Highgate: Churches' in *A History of the County of Middlesex: Vol. 6: Friern Barnet, Finchley, Hornsey with Highgate* edited by T.F.T. Baker (London: Oxford University Press for the Institute of Historical Research, 1980), pp. 103, 178.

and is governed at present by John Cledro, who leads the said life, in which masses and other divine offices are celebrated daily, in which by the intercession, as is believed, of the said Archangel, the Most High manifests divers miracles, so that there is great devotion and resort thereto, and whose buildings are not yet complete, nor do the resources of the said chapel, which has no yearly rents of its own, suffice for such completion, as well as for the said works of piety.

40. The hermitage of St James, Cripplegate

Cripplegate was one of the medieval gates into London, situated in the north-western corner of the city wall, in the area where the Barbican Centre and Museum of London now stand. It also gave its name to the immediately surrounding area of the city, both within and without the wall. There was a hermitage here at the beginning of the thirteenth century: a hermit named Warin died in 1205. Perhaps already in 1205, and certainly by the second half of the thirteenth century, the hermitage was in the patronage of the Crown. It was known as the hermitage of St James in the Wall, and the hermit may have lived in one of the bastions or defensive towers that formed part of the structure of the wall itself. (There was also a hermitage 'in the wall' near Aldgate in the thirteenth century, and another 'within Bishopsgate' in the fourteenth.) The sequence of records printed here shows a succession of hermits, with some incidental details of their lives and means of support. Particularly intriguing is the appointment in 1291 of William Winterburn not only as the new incumbent of the hermitage but also to be his predecessor's carer. The records do not consistently identify the occupants of the hermitage with the title 'hermit'. John de Bello (1296) may not have intended to live here as a hermit; William de Rogate (1300) almost certainly did not. By 1341 the chapel was no longer being used as a hermitage, and Edward III granted it to the Cistercian abbey of Garendon (in Leicestershire), on condition that they 'find a chaplain to celebrate divine service daily therein for the good estate of the king in life, for his soul after death and for the souls of his heirs and progenitors'.[31]

31 For the history of the hermitage, see further 'Alien Houses: Hermits and anchorites of London' in *The Victoria History of the County of London. Vol. One: Including London within the Bars, Westminster and Southwark* edited by William Page (London: The University of London, 1909), p. 586. Cripplegate is shown on the 'Agas' map of London (1560s), in square B5 in the reproduction available at http://mapoflondon.uvic.ca/.

Summaries quoted from (i) *Cal. Pat. Rolls 1272–81*, p. 99, corrected against the manuscript (TNA C66/94, m. 16); (ii) Reginald R. Sharpe, *Calendar of Letter-Books of the City of London: A, 1275–1298* (London: HMSO, 1899), p. 118; (iii) *Cal. Pat. Rolls 1281–1292*, p. 445; (iv) *Cal. Pat. Rolls 1281–1292*, p. 464; (v) *Cal. Pat. Rolls 1281–1292*, p. 479; (vi) *Cal. Pat. Rolls 1292–1301*, p. 185; (vii) *Cal. Pat. Rolls 1292–1301*, p. 532.

(i) 12 July 1275
Whereas the chalices, books, vestments, images, bells and other ornaments and goods of the hermitage near Cripelgate, which is of the king's advowson, and which Henry III gave to Robert de Sancto Laurencio to dwell in for life, are wont, in time of voidance after the decease of hermits thereof, to be carried away by clerical and lay persons, because of the hermitage not being under any definite custody and protection, the king deputes, during pleasure, the mayor of London for the time being as keeper to protect, in the king's name, the persons dwelling therein, the rents and all other things belonging thereto, and if any injury should be done to them he is to cause amends to be made without delay.[32]

(ii) 22 November 1289
The following Friday came Henry de Durham, William Servad and Paul Godchep,[33] and acknowledged themselves bound to Friar[34] Robert, the hermit of Crepelgate, in the sum of 10 marks; to be paid on Easter Eve.

(iii) 18 September 1291
Admission of William de Wyntreburn, chaplain, upon testimony of his good conversation [*behaviour*], to the custody of the hermitage by Cripelegate, London, provided that he behave himself well and honourably, that he devote himself to his sacred office, minister to brother Robert, the hermit of the place, who is feeble, and maintain him in a fitting manner for as long as he lives.

32 In 1281 the constable of the Tower of London was appointed keeper. See *Cal. Pat. Rolls 1272–81*, p. 450.

33 All three were prominent citizens. Servad and Durham would go on to serve as aldermen in the early fourteenth century.

34 That is, 'brother'. There is no reason to suppose that Robert was a member of one of the orders of friars.

(iv) 11 December 1292
Grant to William de Wyntreburne of the hermitage by Cripelgate, London, void by the death of brother Robert de Sancto Laurencio.

(v) 6 February 1293
Licence for the alienation in mortmain[35] by the executors of the will of Robert, sometime hermit of the hermitage of Crupelgate, London, to William de Wynterburn, present hermit, of three messuages with a void plot adjoining and 4d rent from a messuage late of Christiana, relict of Simon de Bereford, in Abbeychurche Lane in the parish of St Nicholas Akun, and 2d rent, from a messuage late of John le Chaloner in the parish of Fanchirche.

(vi) 25 March 1296
Grant to Master John de Bello of the hermitage by Cripelgate, London, void by the resignation of Brother William de Wynterburn, late hermit of that place.

(vii) 25 September 1300
Grant to William de Rogate, clerk of Edward the king's son, of the custody, for life, of the hermitage in London within Crupelgate, on condition that he find a chaplain to celebrate divine service in the chapel every day for the soul of the king, his ancestors and heirs and all the faithful departed, and that he increase the hermitage with 2 marks a year in rent for ever.

41. The hermitage and lighthouse at Ravenspur

For the modern imagination, nothing evokes solitude so much as a lighthouse; and there is perhaps no lighthouse more evocatively situated than the one at Spurn Head, a three-mile spit of sand and shingle that extends southwards from Holderness (E. Yorks.) where the River Humber meets the North Sea. The spit is today no more than 50 m wide in places, but in the Middle Ages it was wider, and supported several settlements, including Ravenspur, though these have since been lost to erosion. It was, as mentioned in (i), on the 'naked shore' at Ravenspur,

35 A statute of 1279 that sought to limit the alienation of property into the 'dead hand' of religious corporations, such as monasteries. A licence had to be secured before such a gift could be made.

in 1399, that Henry Bolingbroke landed on his return to England to spearhead the rebellion against Richard II that ended with his being crowned as Henry IV.[36] There has been a succession of lighthouses on Spurn Head, though there is none in use now; no trace of Reedbarowe's lighthouse remains.[37]

(i) is translated from the Latin in Thomas Rymer, ed., *Foedera* (10 vols, The Hague: Joannes Neulme, 1739–45), Vol. 3 pt 4, p. 163. In (ii), the petition is modernised from the English, and the response translated from the French, in *Rotuli Parliamentorum: ut et petitiones et placita in parliamento Tempore Henrici R. V.* (London: HMSO, 1777), Vol. 4, pp. 364–5. The original is TNA SC 8/25/1232.

(i) The building of the hermitage, 1399
The king [Henry IV] to all those [to whom the present letters shall come]: greetings.

Be it known that whereas Matthew Danthorp, hermit, without having obtained our licence for it, has begun newly to build a certain chapel in a place called Ravenspur where we landed at our most recent coming to England, which (as we have heard) he intends to complete at his great cost and expense;

out of reverence for God and the blessed virgin Mary, in whose honour the aforesaid chapel (thus incomplete) is going to be built, and also that the same Matthew might be encouraged more freely and fervently towards the completion of the same chapel, of our special grace we have pardoned and released the same Matthew of all trespasses and misdemeanours made by him in this regard, and whatever he has forfeited to us or incurred as a result of the foregoing.

And moreover, of the fullness of our grace, we have given and granted to the same Matthew the aforementioned site, to be held by his successors, the hermits of the aforesaid place, together with the aforementioned chapel, when it is built and completed, together with wreck of the sea, waifs,[38] and all other profits and produce that shall arise on the shore for two leagues around the same place, in perpetuity (saving always and reserving to the capital lord of the fee such royal fish[39] as

36 Quotation from Shakespeare's *1 Henry IV*, IV.iii.79.

37 For the lighthouses, see George De Boer, *A History of the Spurn Lighthouses* (York: East Yorkshire Local History Society, 1968). Spurn Head is now owned by the Yorkshire Wildlife Trust: see www.ywt.org.uk/spurn_point.php.

38 Legal rights to any goods that may be washed ashore.

39 Any whale or sturgeon found in English waters were (and still are) the property of the Crown.

might issue there), notwithstanding the statute made against placing lands and tenements into mortmain,[40] or any other cause.

In witness whereof, etc. [*witness clause omitted*]

Attested by the king at Westminster, the first day of October [1399].

By the king himself.

(ii) The building of the lighthouse, 1427
Petition

To the wise commons of this present parliament, your poor beadsman [*petitioner*] Richard Reedbarowe, hermit of the chapel of Our Lady and Saint Anne at Ravenspurn, makes petition that,

Inasmuch as there are many diverse straits and dangers in the entering into the River Humber out of the sea, where oft-times by misadventure many diverse vessels, and men, goods and merchandise, are lost and perished, as well by day as by night, for default of a beacon that should teach the people to hold in the right channel; so that the said Richard, having compassion and pity of the Christian people that oft-times are there perished, and also of the goods and merchandise there lost, has begun, by way of charity, in salvation of Christian people, goods and merchandise coming into the Humber, to make a tower to be in daylight a ready beacon, wherein shall be light given out by night, to all the vessels that come into the said River Humber; the which tower may not be made nor brought to an end without great cost, help and relieving from the shipmen, mariners and vessels coming that way; and at the diligent pursuit [*plea, suit*] of the said Richard, it was prayed by the commons of the parliament held last at Leicester for the making of the said tower to have letters patent of our sovereign lord the king for to take and receive of every vessel laden of 120 tons and over, 12d, and of every vessel of 100 tons 8d, and of every vessel of less tonnage 4d, as oft-times as they come in, to endure 10 years; which is yet the desire and full will of all merchants, shipmen and mariners belonging to Hull, as by their letters patent to this effect openly appears,

That it like to your high and wise discretions to pray to our sovereign lord the king, by assent of his lords spiritual and temporal being in this present parliament, to grant by authority of the said parliament, to the said Richard, by his letters patent to endure 10 years to have

40 The statute of 1279 that sought to limit the alienation of property into the 'dead hand' of religious corporations, such as monasteries.

and to receive of every vessel laden of 120 tons and over 12d, and of every other vessel of 100 tons 8d, and of every other vessel of less tonnage, 4d, as oft-times as they come into the Humber, by the hands of John Tutbury, Thomas Marchall, -------- Fitlyng,[41] Robert Holme and William Robynsson, merchants and mariners of Hull; and that the same money received in form aforesaid be spent and disposed by the governance, disposition and oversight of the said John, Thomas, Robert and William, in and for the making and accomplishment of the tower aforesaid, in comfort, relieving and salvation of all merchants, mariners, vessels, goods and merchandise, and of the king's customs and subsidies for the same goods and merchandise coming there, and for holy charity.

Response
Let letters patent be made under the Great Seal to the mayor of the town of Hull for the time being, that, for the next 10 years, to help towards the completion and construction of the tower begun at Ravenspur, which is mentioned in the petition, he should by himself and his deputies such as he wishes to assign, take and have of each vessel of the capacity of 120 tons and more, coming from the sea into the River Humber, 12d, and of each other vessel of the capacity of 100 tons similarly coming from the sea into the same river, 8d, and of each vessel of less capacity coming in the same way into the same river 4d, as many times as the aforesaid ships and vessels come into the said river from the sea, as is said above. Saving to the lords and all the other subjects of the king, their liberties and franchises granted to them before. Providing always that the pence so taken from the ships and vessels aforesaid be faithfully applied and expended upon the making and construction of the said tower, according to the oversight, disposition and supervision of John Tuttebury, Thomas Marchall, -------- Fitlyng, Robert Holme and William Robinson, merchants and mariners of the said town, or of others assigned for this purpose by the chancellor of England for the time being; and that the same mayor annually during the aforementioned term should make faithful account of the pence thus taken by himself and his deputies, before the said persons so assigned or to be assigned, when he shall be duly required to do so by these people.[42]

41 'Fitlyng' was inserted into the document after its initial writing. The individual's given name is missing both here and in the response, though a John Fitlyng appears in other Hull records of the time.

42 For the letters patent so issued see *Cal. Pat. Rolls 1422–1429*, p. 457.

42. Inventory of the chapel of St Mary on Derby Bridge, 1488

The fourteenth-century bridge-chapel of St Mary, Derby, survives, though the bridge on which it stood has not.[43] It evidently housed an image of the Virgin and Child that was especially popular with the women of the area, perhaps in connection with a townswomen's guild based at the chapel. The gifts of clothes and jewels would have been intended to adorn the statue. This inventory of the chapel's ornaments and the offerings made there offers a fascinating insight into the place of images in the devotion of people from a wide range of society, and the institutional memory, keyed to specific material objects, that kept the names of benefactors in remembrance. As noted in the Introduction to this section, the hermit was probably the chapel's caretaker; he may also have collected alms or tolls for the maintenance of the bridge.

Modernised from the English text in J. Charles Cox, *Notes on the Churches of Derbyshire* (4 vols, Chesterfield: W. Edmunds, 1875–79), Vol. 4, pp. 104–5.[44] There are a few uncertainties in the text that I have been unable to resolve.

Churchwardens' accounts, All Saints Derby, 1488

And the said John and Thomas Oxle[e] at the same time gave their account to the said auditors of all the jewels and ornaments being at the Mary of Bridge [*sic*], that are in the custody of John Shenton, hermit, and his wife, Sir John Dale then their priest.

First, a coat of crimson velvet decorated with gold that my lady Gray gave, and upon it is 66 pennies, 2 gilt pennies, one gilt farthing, 2 coins of 2d, one groat, a bee (?) of silver, 2 shells of silver, a heart of silver, a mound of silver, a brooch of copper and gilt, 2 [arrow-] shafts of silver, one crystal stone enclosed in silver.

Also a coat of blue velvet that my lady Chamberlain gave. Upon it is a crown of silver and gilt that John Boroes gave. *Item* a great brooch of silver and gilt with a stone in it. Also one case of red satin with buttons of silver and gilt. *Item* 60 pennies, 3 gilt pennies, one coin of 2d, one cross of silver. *Item* a case of velvet, one brooch and one penny off it (?), and a crystal stone.

43 The bridge chapel is no. 18990 in the Derbyshire Historic Environment Record (via www.heritagegateway.org.uk).

44 Also printed with discussion in Charles Kerry, 'Hermits, Fords, and Bridge Chapels', *Journal of the Derbyshire Archaeological and Natural History Society* 14 (1892): 54–71, at pp. 59–61.

Item one garment that my lady Longforth gave of blue velvet and red. And on it is a crucifix of silver and gilt, with a ring of gold that Mrs Bonynton gave. Also a ring of silver and gilt, another of copper, 6 -------- [*word uncertain*] a 4d and 6 halfpennies, 3 groats, 3 coins of 2d, 6 flowers of silver and gilt. *Item* 10 coral beads with 2 silver gauds.[45]

Item one coat for our Lord of crimson velvet furred with minever that my lady Longforth gave. Upon it is a shield of silver with 5 bent pennies. *Item* 11 pennies, and 5 gilt pennies, a coin of 2d. *Item* one rosary of silver gauded with coral that Oxlee's wife gave. *Item* one stone enclosed in silver, with one cross of silver, one brooch of silver, 2 other brooches of silver and gilt, with one collar of black pearls with 17 bells of silver and gilt.

Item one rosary of coral, gauded, having gauds of silver and gilt, with 4 rings, and 2 not fixed of silver and gilt, with a crystal stone set in silver, and a stone of coral that Richard Baker's wife gave.

Item another rosary of coral, with gauds of silver and gilt, with one gold ring, and 2 rings of silver and gilt, with 2 crucifixes of silver and gilt, that Richard Sale's wife gave.

Item one rosary of coral, gauded with silver, that Richard Colyar's wife gave. *Item* one rosary of black jet. *Item* one rosary of coral, with a cross stone, with 25 gauds of silver, with a tassel set with pearls that Roger Justice's wife gave.

Item one gilt girdle that Mrs Entwistle gave. *Item* one purple girdle that Edmund Dey's wife gave. *Item* one blue girdle with 7 studs mounted on it, that John Hill's wife gave.

Item one white vestment of damask, with all things that belong to it, and 2 corporasses[46] of red velvet. *Item* 5 altar cloths, 2 of them twill. *Item* 5 towels, one of them twill, and 2 paxbreds.[47] *Item* 4 frontals, one of blue say[48] with stars on it, that Sir James Blounte, knight, gave.

45 A large, ornamental bead that marked each decade of 'aves' in a rosary. From Latin *gaudium* ('joy'), referring to the 'joys of Mary'.

46 A corporas is a cloth, usually of linen, upon which the consecrated elements are placed during the celebration of the mass, and with which the elements, or the remnants of them, are covered after the celebration (*OED*).

47 A tablet of gold, silver, ivory etc., with a projecting handle, depicting the crucifixion or other sacred subject, which is kissed by the celebrating priest and then by the other participants at a mass (*OED*).

48 A fine cloth.

Item in the chapel is 2 mass-books, 1 psalter, 1 chalice of silver and gilt, 2 cruets (one copper); 2 cushions of tapestry work that Alesome Sonkye gave, one pillow of coral, 2 caps for our Lord, one blue velvet, with one rosary gauded with pearls, with 3 stones of coral, and one penny off it. *Item* another of black with crowned ... off it and one flower of silver and gilt. *Item* 2 candlesticks of latten and 19 tapers of wax.

43. Henry Lofte, a sixteenth-century pilgrim hermit

The 'grand voyage' to the Holy Land was the acme of medieval pilgrimage, and the main attraction for pilgrims to Jerusalem was the church of the Holy Sepulchre, built on the site of Calvary itself. The careful measurement of such holy sites was a common devotional practice, and the figures so derived carried an almost mystical power.[49] Towton (N. Yorks.) was a place in need of such sanctification. It had been the site in 1461 of a key battle in the Wars of the Roses, reputed to have been the bloodiest ever fought on English soil. Some years later, Richard III built a chapel here in memory of the many dead.[50]

Translated from the Latin in Rymer, *Foedera*, Vol. 6, part 1, pp. 22–3.[51]

The king [Henry VIII] to all those to whom [the present writing should come]. Greetings.

Be it known that, at the humble request of our petitioner Henry Lofte, of the order of St Paul the Hermit,[52] who was professed by the Archbishop of Rhodes, and has been in pilgrimage to Christ's sepulchre, bringing the length of the same sepulchre back with him to this our realm of England, and continued on to Rome from where (as he says) he has acquired certain indulgences,

we have given and granted of our special grace to the same hermit a certain chapel of St James of Towton in the parish of Saxton in our

49 For pilgrimage to the Holy Sepulchre in general, see Colin Morris, *The Sepulchre of Christ and the Medieval West: From the beginning to 1600* (Oxford: Oxford University Press, 2008), and more precisely Zur Shalev, 'Christian Pilgrimage and Ritual Measurement in Jerusalem', *Micrologus* 19: *La misura/Measuring* (2011), 131–50.

50 On the possible site of the chapel, see http://towtonbattle.free.fr/index.php/chapel-hill/.

51 Summarised in *Letters and Papers, Henry VIII*, Vol. 1, p. 464.

52 For the 'order of St Paul', see Chapter VI.

county of [York];[53] the said Henry to have and hold the same chapel during his life, with the intention that the same Henry should place and leave the aforementioned indulgences in the aforesaid chapel, and that he should especially pray for prosperity for ourself and our most beloved consort the queen, for the souls of our parents the former king and queen of most glorious memory, and also for the souls of each and every one of our progenitors.

[*Witness list omitted*]

By witness of the king at Canterbury, on the fourteenth day of September [1511].

44. Royal alms to an unnamed hermit, 1531

This daily record of Henry VIII's personal expenditure between 1529 and 1532 affords a unique insight into the king's household, his life-style and his current projects and enthusiasms. The latter evidently included the 'lady Anne' (Boleyn), as may be seen from several entries in this account for May 1531. Evidence for the king's piety is less prominent here, though among several pious and charitable gifts was a small alms given to a hermit. On 29 July of the same year the king made a much more substantial donation of £3 6s 8d to the hermit of Deptford towards the repair of his chapel.

Modernised from *The Privy Purse Expences of King Henry the Eighth, from November MDXXIX, to December MDXXXII*, edited by Nicholas Harris Nicolas (London, W. Pickering, 1827), pp. 42–7.[54]

The first day of May paid to a servant of Sr Giles Capell in reward for bringing a doe to the king	10s
Item the same day paid in reward to a servant of my lord of Richmond at his going into Ireland	5s
Item the 5th day of May paid by the king's commandment to Hector Assheley of Hunsdon for to be employed about the king's building at Hunsdon	£200
Item the 6th day paid in alms to a hermit upon the way	4s 8d

53 Rymer has 'Lincoln'.

54 Calendared with a few errors and omissions in *Letters and Papers, Henry VIII*, Vol. 5, p. 749. For the gift to the hermit of Deptford, see *Privy Purse Expences*, p. 150.

Item the 7th day paid to a servant of my lady Parr's in reward for bringing a coat [of] cloth of Kendal[55] for the king's grace 4s 8d

Item the 9th day paid to Doctor Baugh by the king's commandment for to be employed about his grace's charitable alms for 2 months beginning the 14th day of this month £20

Item the same day to Nicholas Clampe for his board, wages and hawk's meat [*food*] as appears by his bill 58s

Item the 10th day paid to the hen-taker for one month's wages 15s

...

Item [the 11th day] to the same Master Hennage for so much money by him paid at the king's commandment to a miner 40s

Item to the same Master Hennage for so much money by him paid to a servant of the Abbot of Gloucester for bringing a sturgeon to the king 10s

Item to the same Master Hennage for so much money by him paid to one of the queen's servants for bringing Cut the king's spaniel again 10s

Item the 12th day paid to Humfrey of the king's privy buck-hounds for his wages for the month now ended 9s 4d

Item the 13th day paid to a servant of my lord Barkeley's in reward for bringing a fresh sturgeon to the king's grace at York Place 40s

Item the 14th day paid to one in reward for bringing home Ball the king's dog that was lost in the forest of Waltham 5s

...

Item the 16th day paid to Culbert the king's apothecary upon the full contents of his bill as it shall appear by the same £30 12s 6d

...

Item the 19th day paid to the gardener of Beaulie in reward for bringing herbs to the king 6s 8d

Item the 20th day paid to Vincent the painter for trimming the king's new barge £15 4s 9d

Item the 21st day paid to Walter Walsh for to pay as well the tailor and skinner for certain stuff and workmanship for my lady Anne; as also to a printer for divers books for the king's grace £59 18s

...

55 A green woollen cloth manufactured in the Cumbrian town. Lady [Maud] Parre, lady in waiting to the queen, was mother of Catherine, Henry's sixth and last wife.

Item the [25th] day paid to Jasper of Beaulie the gardener in reward for bringing strawberries to the king 6s 8d

...

Item the [26th] day paid to 5 poor people the which the king's grace healed of their sickness[56] 37s 6d

Item the same day paid to a servant of my lord of Durham in reward for bringing of a seal[57] 15s

...

Item the 28th day paid to Wodall's servant in reward for bringing crabs to the king's grace 10s

...

Item the [29th] day paid to Scawesby for bows, arrows, shafts, broad heads, a bracer [*wrist guard*] and shooting glove for my lady Anne 23s 4d

Item the last day paid to the king's watermen for 3 day's waiting 32s

45. The hermit of Rye in the 1530s

As a major port in cross-channel trade, Rye (East Sussex) was much involved in the exchange of goods, people and ideas with northern mainland Europe, and it is not surprising that there was early interest in Protestantism here. During the years immediately following Henry VIII's 'Act of Supremacy' (1534), amidst vehement doctrinal debate, the town descended into factionalism and near civil war.[58] Through all this turbulence, the community maintained a steady relationship with a hermit.[59] He received a regular stipend of 16s per annum from the chamberlains for most of the 1530s, and a quarterly payment of 12d from the churchwardens between 1533 and 1540, being employed in caretaking and cleaning duties or taking on occasional odd jobs and

56 A reference to the ritual of the 'royal touch', thought to be a remedy for a number of conditions, including scrofula or the 'King's evil'. The Tudor monarchs were particularly keen to demonstrate their divinely sanctioned power in this way.

57 Seals were eaten, though perhaps what is meant is a porpoise, which was a particular delicacy.

58 See G.R. Elton, *Policy and Police: The enforcement of the Reformation in the age of Thomas Cromwell* (Cambridge: Cambridge University Press, 1972), pp. 85–90. For more on Rye in this period, see Graham Mayhew, *Tudor Rye* (Falmer: Centre for Continuing Education, University of Sussex, 1987).

59 For the anchorite at Rye earlier in the century, see [**10**].

errands. None of them was conspicuously spiritual, and some of them were decidedly material.

Modernised from the English churchwardens' and chamberlains' accounts in the East Sussex Record Office, Lewes: (i) RYE/60/5, fol. 235r; (ii) RYE/147/1, fol. 66v; (iii–v) RYE/60/5, fols 275r, 318r, 332r; (vi) RYE/147/1, fol. 89r.

(i) St Bartholomew's term[60] 1532–3
To the ... hermit for casting over the dung at Baddyng[61] 7s 6d

(ii) Easter term 1533
Paid to the hermit for keeping clean of the churchyard 12d
Paid to the hermit for paring of all the church walls the green grass away 12d

(iii) Christmas term 1534
Paid to the hermit for keeping clean the Strand Gate for his wages 4s

(iv) St Bartholomew's term 1536–7
To the hermit for mending of the churchyard and the alleys at Mr Mayor's commandment 3s

(v) Early 1538
To Father Hermit for making clean the shitting house and for his fee 10s

(vi) 8 Jan. 1540
To the hermit for a piece of timber for the beam in the high chancel 8d

46. A hermit's meditations, from the *Rule of Celestine*

Most of this section has reinforced an impression of hermits as humble labourers of no real spiritual ambition, and we have learnt little of their inner lives. We conclude, however, with a glimpse of a late medieval hermit's devotional practice. The source is the so-called *Rule of*

60 The accounting period beginning on the feast of St Bartholomew (24 August).

61 Baddyng was the part of Rye on the cliff-edge overlooking the sea. This was the accepted method of disposing of sewage from coastal towns in the Middle Ages.

Celestine, a fifteenth-century rule for hermits. The link with St Celestine is entirely spurious. The Sicilian hermit Pietro da Morrone was surprisingly elected as pope in 1294, and took the name Celestine V. But he abdicated (one of the handful of popes to do so) before the year was up, and was subsequently imprisoned, and perhaps murdered, by his successor Boniface VIII. The rule that invokes his name was composed in Latin, and also survives in English translation.[62] The series of affective meditations on Christ's life and passion is standard fare. The way in which they follow the canonical hours recalls Aelred's much earlier set of meditations, written for his anchorite sister.

Translated from the Latin of chapter 20, edited by Livarius Oliger, 'Regulae tres reclusorum et eremitarum angliae saec. XIII–XIV', *Antonianum* 3 (1928): 151–90 and 299–320, at pp. 319–20.

The manner and time of his contemplation or meditation

In the middle of the night, either before Matins or after, you should plumb the depths of humility, considering first the Day of Judgement, and afterwards the birth of Christ and his passion. At Prime, judge yourself to be wretched, and think how Christ was condemned by the Jews for your sake, and of the resurrection. At Terce, prepare your heart for true penitence and the taking of [the?] discipline, and think of Christ's scourging and the sending of the Holy Spirit. At Sext, think how man was made from dust and ashes etc., and [yet] as regards your soul you were made in the image and likeness of God, and of the incarnation of Christ and his crucifixion. At None, of your last hour and the death of Jesus Christ and his ascension. At Vespers, how our prayers (if they are legitimate) can release souls from purgatory, and how before Vespers Christ was pierced with the lance and afterwards taken down from the cross, and of the lamentations of the Blessed Virgin beside the cross. At Compline, of Christ's burial and his sweating blood when he prayed to his Father. After that think similarly of the division of the good and bad at the Day of Judgement, and of the pains of hell and the joys of heaven. And after that, secure in mind, go to your rest in the fear and love of the Lord.

Now at the sixth and ninth hours your contemplation can be briefer than at the other hours, because at these hours the flesh strains with

62 The English versions have been edited by Domenico Pezzini, 'An Edition of Three Late Middle English Versions of a Fourteenth-Century *Regula Heremitarum*', *Leeds Studies in English* 40 (2009): 65–104. For another excerpt from the *Rule*, see [**56**]. The emergence of rules for English hermits is examined more closely in Chapter VI.

desire against the spirit more than at others. For three things above all are necessary for all human flesh, that is food and drink to nourish it, rest and sleep to regulate it, and clothes to cover the body and keep out the cold.

VI: RULES AND REGULATION

Introduction

Some time in the 1320s the young Yorkshireman Richard Rolle dropped out of Oxford and returned home. Soon afterwards, he took two of his sister's dresses and his father's rainhood to a nearby wood and, with a bit of amateur tailoring, fashioned a kind of habit for himself. Putting it on, he arrived at 'a confused likeness to a hermit' [**47**]. The anecdote makes it clear that Rolle knows what a hermit ought to look like, even if his improvised attempts fall comically short. But equally, there is no sense that he might or should have proceeded differently. With no accepted procedure to follow, the early fourteenth-century hermit marked his transition to a new state of life as best he could.

Chapter I of this volume offered evidence for the enquiries and deliberations, the official processes and procedures, and finally the liturgical ceremonial that were involved whenever an individual expressed the intention of becoming an anchorite. By the end of the Middle Ages, a comparable framework was in place for the vocation of hermit, though only as a much more recent development. A system of episcopal scrutiny and supervision of potential anchorites seems to have existed by the end of the twelfth century, and provides a context for the well-known anchoritic rules (Aelred's, and the *Ancrene Wisse*) that also belong to approximately this period. But there is little evidence for any concerted attempt to put hermits on a similarly well-ordered and orderly footing before about 1400. Thereafter, however, things moved quickly and, had Rolle been born a century later, his reception into the eremitic life could have looked strikingly different.

Long associated with the uncompromising repression of heresy, the early fifteenth century is now recognised for its movement of orthodox reform, which saw (amongst other developments) a monastic revival and a renewal of the liturgy.[1] We have already seen evidence

1 See the essays collected in *After Arundel: Religious Writing in Fifteenth-century England*, edited by Vincent Gillespie and Kantik Ghosh (Turnhout: Brepols, 2011), especially Vincent Gillespie, 'Chichele's Church: Vernacular theology in England after Thomas Arundel', pp. 3–42.

of increased scrutiny of potential anchorites in this period (see Chapter I, especially [**2**]), and the attention paid to the solitary vocations in the early fifteenth century may belong alongside these other reformist initiatives. That the curious case of Adam Cressevill, a hermit who had contracted a marriage, was entered into Archbishop Thomas Arundel's register in 1405 [**51**] might suggest an interest within his administration in questions around hermits' legal status. The next decades saw a more formal role for bishops in assessing and approving candidates for the vocation, the development of a new liturgical rite for hermits' profession, and the composition of a number of rules, ranging in character from the entirely rudimentary to the more spiritually advanced.

Like the rite for the enclosing of anchorites, a hermit's profession had to be conducted by a bishop or his designated representative [**48**], [**49**]. It was a relatively simple affair, incorporated within the celebration of the mass of the day, as monastic professions were, and with none of the rhetorical and symbolic elaboration of the corresponding rite for anchorites [**5**]. The two essential elements are the hermit's vow, which is both made orally and recorded in writing, and his vesting in the habit of a hermit.

The prospective hermit, before he reached this stage, would need to have satisfied the authorities of his suitability for the vocation. In most cases this must have been done informally, but when, in 1423, Richard Ludlow expressed his desire to become a hermit at Maidenhead the bishop of Salisbury initiated a careful and lengthy process of inquiry [**50**]. This is the first record of the approval and investiture of a hermit in the Salisbury registers, and the fact that the procedure was described in such detail, and those details recorded so fully in the bishop's register, could suggest that this was the first time it had been employed in the diocese. In any case, it is one of the earliest records we have of a hermit who had been formally recognised by his bishop. Thereafter, bishops' registers often contain records of hermits' professions, though none is as long or as detailed as the example from Maidenhead. The entries typically record the name and status of the candidate, the date and place of his profession, and the precise words of his vow, quoted in the English that he would have used to make it. The majority of hermits were illiterate, and signed their profession only with a cross [**52**].

Medieval monks and nuns made a threefold vow: of stability (that is, to reside in a fixed place, such as a monastery), of personal poverty and perpetual chastity. Hermits committed themselves only to chastity. Vows of chastity occur quite frequently in late medieval bishops' registers, the great majority however made by women, usually widows (who would then become known as vowesses), though some married women also appear. A vow of chastity could not be made unilaterally while both partners were still living. (Margery Kempe's negotiations with her husband John to get him to agree to her commitment to chastity are a well-known case in point.) So on the same day that Henry Andrew became a hermit, his wife Alice became a vowess [**52c**]. Whether they continued to live together (as Margery and John Kempe did, at least at first) is not known.[2]

A number of late medieval hermits professed to follow the rule of St Paul (i.e. Paul the First Hermit, whose life was recorded by St Jerome): see [**43**], [**52a**], [**52b**].[3] This was not a rule in the same sense as the *Rule of St Benedict*, for example – that is, a stable set of precepts enforceable across (and constitutive of) a religious order. When further details are given, they comprise a loose set of guidelines for balancing the daily demands of physical and spiritual occupation, together with some general moral exhortation. The vow that Richard Ludlow made at Maidenhead [**50**] follows a very similar pattern, and the so-called *Rule of St Linus* [**53**] is a somewhat expanded version on the same principles. Though such rules could not be more rudimentary, we should nevertheless recognise the attempt to provide for the freewheeling life of the hermit the same kind of regularity and structure that the monastic *horarium* offered the traditional religious orders, albeit with the basic prayers of the Church replacing the round of Latin prayers and psalms that the literate clergy would have recited. (Something similar was done for anchorites a couple of centuries earlier; compare [**19**].) The stand-alone texts known as the *Cambridge Rule* and *Rule of Celestine* are more elaborate [**54**], [**56**] and, though their spiritual trajectory remains comparatively low, their links to Aelred's *Rule of Life for a Recluse* connect them directly with the literature of anchoritic guidance and regulation that featured in the first half of this volume.

These late medieval developments – of official examination, approval and licensing, supervision and regulation – together bring an inevita-

2 For women's vows of chastity in the late Middle Ages, see Mary C. Erler, 'Margery Kempe's White Clothes', *Medium Aevum* 62 (1993): 78–83. For another married hermit see [**42**].

3 For the 'Rule of St Paul', see Virginia Davis, 'The Rule of St Paul the First Hermit in England in the Later Middle Ages' in *Monks, Hermits and the Ascetic Tradition* edited by W.J. Sheils, Studies in Church History 22 (London: Wiley-Blackwell, 1985), pp. 203–14.

ble paradox: as hermits gained new levels of regularity and structure for their way of life, with the respectability and security that they brought, so they simultaneously lost some of the freedom, anarchic variety and 'edginess' that had always been at the heart of their claim to spiritual and symbolic power.

47. Richard Rolle fashions himself into a hermit

At his death in 1349 Richard Rolle seems to have been something of a local celebrity, and a popular cult quickly sprang up around Hampole, the Cistercian nunnery where he died, and with which he seems to have had some spiritual connection. The nuns hoped to see him recognised as a saint, and put together a collection of readings – anecdotes and excerpts from his writings – that would form the basis of his office. In the event, Rolle was never canonised, but the *Officium* remains as our chief biographical witness to his life.[4] Its first reading describes Rolle's return from Oxford and his inception as a hermit. The hagiographical *topos* of the world's incomprehension of the saint's higher purpose, personified here by Rolle's sister, is a theme that recurs many times in Rolle's life and writings.

Quoted with slight simplifications from the translation by H.E. Allen, in *Writings Ascribed to Richard Rolle Hermit of Hampole and Materials for His Biography* (New York, 1927), pp. 55–6. By permission of the Modern Language Association of America.

First Lesson
The saint of God, the hermit Richard, took his origin in the village of Thornton near Pickering in the diocese of York. In due time he was set to learn his letters by the efforts (or the intention) of his parents. When he was older, Master Thomas de Neville, at one time archdeacon of Durham, honourably maintained him in the University of Oxford, where he was very proficient in study. He desired rather to be imbued more fully and deeply with the theological doctrines of Holy Scripture than with the study of physical and secular science. In his nineteenth year, considering the uncertain term of human life, and the fearful end especially before the fleshly and the worldly, he took thought, by the inspiration of God, providently concerning himself (remembering his

4 For discussion, see Nicholas Watson, *Richard Rolle and the Invention of Authority* (Cambridge: Cambridge University Press, 1991), pp. 31–53.

end), lest he should be taken in the snares of sin. Therefore, when he had returned from Oxford to his father's house, he one day asked his sister (whom he dearly loved) for two of her tunics (a grey and a white) and for his father's rain-hood. At his request (but ignorant of his purposes) she next day brought them to a neighbouring wood. He took them and cut off the sleeves from the grey one and the buttons from the white, and, as he could, fitted the sleeves to the white tunic, that it might suit his purpose. He took off his own clothing, and put his sister's white tunic next his flesh. The grey tunic (with the sleeves cut off) he put over it, and through the openings where the cutting had taken place exposed his arms. He hooded himself in the aforesaid rain-hood, and thus, as far as was then possible to him, he contrived a confused likeness to a hermit. When his sister had understood these things, she cried in astonishment, 'My brother is mad!' When he heard her, he drove her away from him menacingly, and he himself fled at once without delay, lest he should be taken by his friends and acquaintances.

48. Profession of a hermit, from the Clifford Pontifical

The rite for the profession of a hermit was one of a handful of offices added to the Clifford Pontifical [4] after the main body of the book was complete, between 1421 and 1435, when it belonged to Philip Morgan, bishop of Worcester and subsequently of Ely.[5] (The pontifical was a collection of those rites that only a bishop was authorised to perform.) As with the enclosure rite, the text is provided with an illustration at its beginning as a means of ready identification. In this case, bishop and hermit inhabit the initial *D* of *Deus* (God), the first word of the rite's opening prayer. The hermit is grey-haired, bearded and does not have the tonsure that would mark him out as a cleric. He wears a white scapular over a brown robe. The staff that the bishop is holding will be given to the hermit during the ceremony as a symbol of his new status.

From the Clifford Pontifical. Reproduced from Corpus Christi College Cambridge MS 79, fol. 18v, by permission of the Master and Fellows of Corpus Christi College, Cambridge.

5 For the date of these additions to the manuscript, see Kathleen L. Scott, *A Survey of Manuscripts Illuminated in the British Isles: Vol. 6: Later Gothic Manuscripts 1390–1490* (2 vols, London: Harvey Miller, 1996), no. 18, Vol. 2, pp. 80–1.

49. The rite for making a hermit

This version of the rite is of similar date to the one in [48], and its text is also very similar.[6] It is included in a pontifical that was probably

6 For a later and somewhat more complex rite, see Clay, *Hermits and Anchorites*, appendix B; also translated by Frank Bottomley at www.hermitary.com/articles/benediction.html.

made in the second quarter of the fifteenth century, and belonged to Robert Gilbert, bishop of London 1436–48.[7]

Translated from the Latin in Cambridge University Library, MS Mm.3.21, fols 193r–v. Rubrics (written in red in the manuscript) are here printed as italics.

The order according to which a hermit makes his profession

First the psalm Have mercy on me O God [Ps. 50 (51)] *should be said by the bishop, with* Glory be to the Father. *Once this has been said the hermit shall approach with his garments. He shall kneel and place them before the bishop. The latter shall speak to him concerning his vow of chastity. Then he shall read his profession in this manner:*

> I, N., a single man, promise and vow to God and to the Blessed Mary and to all the saints, in the presence of the reverend father lord N. & N. bishop of N., my purpose of perpetual chastity according to the rule of St Paul. In the name of the Father, and of the Son, and of the Holy Spirit. Amen.

Then he shall make the sign of the cross at the end of his profession and pass it to the bishop. Then he shall lie prostrate while the bishop says this prayer over him.

> Almighty God, we beseech you, let the doors of your grace be opened to this your servant who has renounced the pomps of the world, who has left the despicable devil to be under the banner of Christ. When he comes to you, order that he be received with a pleasant countenance, that the Enemy might not be able to triumph over him. Grant him the untiring aid of your arm, protect his mind with the breastplate of faith so that, fortified by such blessed defences, he may rejoice to have forsaken the world. Through Christ our Lord.

Then there shall follow the blessing of his garments, beginning with Let us pray.

> God, whose promise of eternal goods is most faithful and whose fulfilment of his promises is most sure, who have promised to your faithful the vestments of salvation and the apparel of joy, we humbly pray for your mercy, that you will graciously deign to bless these garments, that signify humility of heart and contempt of the world, and by which your servant's holy purpose is given visible form; and

7 See Paul Binski and Patrick Zutshi, *Western Illuminated Manuscripts: A catalogue of the collection in Cambridge University Library* (Cambridge: Cambridge University Press, 2011), no. 236.

that with your protection he may maintain the habit of chastity that (with your aid) he is about to receive, so that he whom you have dressed in the vestments of a venerable profession, you will cause to be forever clothed in blessed immortality. Through our Lord.

Then holy water shall be sprinkled on the vestments. Afterwards he [the bishop] shall give the habit to him [the candidate], and while he is being clothed the bishop shall say

May God strip you of the old man with his deeds and clothe you with the new, who is created in God's likeness in justice and the holiness of truth.

The response

Thanks be to God.

Then he shall lie prostrate before the bishop for the following blessing, beginning with Let us pray.

O Lord, keep your servant in your merciful protection, so that with your protection he may maintain unbroken the holy vow of chastity that, inspired by you, he has undertaken. Through our Lord.

Then there shall follow the bishop's blessing upon him, in which the bishop shall say

May the blessing of Almighty God the Father[8] + the Son + and the Holy Spirit + descend upon you and remain forever. Amen.

And with that he shall withdraw in God's name.

50. The making of a hermit at Maidenhead Bridge

We have seen already that bridge maintenance was a typical occupation for a late medieval hermit (see [**37**] and [**42**]). The bridge over the Thames at Maidenhead, where this hermit intended to reside, was an important crossing on the main road from London to Bath and the West of England. The bishop entrusted the business of approving and professing the hermit to a senior cleric in the vicinity, and this has resulted in the very full account of the process reproduced here. (Shottesbrooke is about 5 miles from Maidenhead.) It was a matter of some delicacy to balance the zealous desire of the would-be hermit against a range of local land-holding and ecclesiastical interests. The

8 Crosses in the text indicate that the bishop here makes the sign of the cross.

river at Maidenhead marked the boundary among several manors, adding to the complexity of the negotiations.

The main text is translated from the Latin, and the hermit's profession modernised from the English, in Wiltshire & Swindon History Centre, Episcopal Registers, 'Register of John Chaundler', fols 40r–41r.

[*Word uncertain*] of the hermitage at the end of the bridge in the town of Maidenhead

The following notification was received on 23 December 1423.

To his reverend father in Christ and lord, Lord John [Chaundler], by grace of God bishop of Salisbury, his humble and devoted son John, warden of the collegiate church of St John the Baptist, Shottesbrooke, in your diocese, [wishing you] grace and the respect due with honour to such a father.

Having recently received your letters of commission, whose contents are given below –

> John, by divine permission bishop of Salisbury, to his beloved son in Christ the Warden of the collegiate church of Shottesbrooke in our diocese: [wishing you] health, grace, and blessing.
>
> Our beloved son in Christ Richard Ludlow has besought us by his humble petition that,
>
> > whereas he, not feigning but truly by the Lord's leading (as he asserts), longing to assume and receive a habit and vestment, and desiring to transfer to the fruit of a better life, wishes piously to observe continence and chastity, and laudably proposes and intends (with the support of Christian people) to build and newly construct a hermitage or hermit's house at the western end of the bridge in the town of Maidenhead in our diocese, in order that he might be more able to serve the most high King of kings there,
>
> we might see fit to grant him consent and assent.
>
> We, conscious of how easily human weakness can fall, and that the enemy who lies in wait throughout our lives can cause something to become disagreeable by repetition, which when done once was pleasing to us; knowing absolutely nothing of the circumstances of the said petitioner, or of the said place intended for a hermitage or hermit's house of this kind, and wishing to ensure indemnity for the rector and parishioners there and for anyone else who might have an interest in this case,

Commission and order you that, going in person to the said bridge where he proposes to establish such a hermitage or house, having first given notice to the aforementioned Richard, and the rector and parishioners in particular, as well as anyone else with an interest, you are diligently to exert yourself to discover the truth, by means of trustworthy men (both clerics and laymen) under legal oath, who have fuller knowledge of the said matters, as to whether this same Richard is of good behaviour [*conversation*] and honest life, such that he is capable of fulfilling his intention of leading this holier form of living; whether he is single or else betrothed or joined to someone in marriage, and whether there will be any prejudice to the rector or the parishioners there, or to either one of them.

And if by this inquiry you find no legitimate reason why the said Richard should not build and construct a hermitage or hermit's house of this kind as aforesaid as he desires, you should diligently, duly and effectively proceed with our authority to clothe and vest him in the appropriate and customary vestments, clothes or habit of a hermit; and do everything else necessary or appropriate in these kinds of cases. And you should duly notify us what you have done to expedite this matter by letters patent to this effect under authority of your seal.

Given in our manor of Potterne,[9] 16 July 1423, and the sixth year since our consecration.

– by the authority of these letters, on Tuesday 29 October in the year given above, I went in person to the bridge in the town of Maidenhead in your said diocese where the aforesaid Richard Ludlow proposes to build and newly construct a hermitage or hermit's house, and in the chapel of Maidenhead located next to the aforementioned bridge I duly made diligent enquiry of trustworthy men (both clerics and laymen) under legal oath, a list of whose names is contained in a document annexed to the present letters, having weighed especially their ability to speak the truth in this case, and having first given notice to those who should be notified, and summoned to that time and place in this case.

By which [*word unclear*] that the aforesaid man is of virtuous behaviour and laudable life, free and single, not betrothed nor joined to anyone in matrimony, or bound by any covenant, as has been known

9 Potterne had belonged to the bishops of Salisbury at least since Domesday. It is some 70 miles from Maidenhead.

and evident in the region for a long time; and there is no prejudice to the rector or the parishioners there, or to any other person, if the same Richard should build and newly construct a hermitage or hermit's house. And furthermore the same Richard has with fervent desire and all zeal begged with almost daily requests that he might be admitted to the state of a hermit so that he might more quickly bring his long-held intention to the desired conclusion, and to hasten this conclusion he has freely, humbly and devoutly, in the presence of the witnesses listed in a document annexed to the present letters, and of others from the towns of Maidenhead, Bray and Cookham then being present, presented the profession he is to make, written in his mother tongue, in a document annexed to the present letters.

Having considered all these things, and taken cognizance of the deliberations had before, and having received no objections, I first of all assigned to him, with the consent of the steward of the duke of Gloucester's manors of Bray and Cookham, who attended in person, and of other worthy men of the aforementioned towns and manors, the aforesaid site for him to build and newly construct his house. Then I enjoined him for his part to make and keep his profession according to the manner and circumstances recited and written therein for as long as he should live; and then I clothed and vested him then and there in a hermit's habit suitable for his status, having previously consecrated it according to the form that is usual in these cases and asperged it with holy water. And thus I have humbly carried out your letters of commission.

Each and every one of these things I make known to you, my father, by these present letters. And in witness to this the common seal of the collegiate church of Shottesbrooke is appended to these present letters.

These are the names of the witnesses mentioned in this matter: Andrew Sperlyng, steward of the manors of Bray and Cookham; John Mustard, beadle there; Sir John Coter ⌈and⌉ Sir Robert, chaplains; Thomas, John Palmer, proctors; James Lynde, John Pynkeney, Thomas Lecceford, John Louches, William Skynnere, Simon Nortone, John Laurence, Richard Bullok, and many others.

The Form of the hermit's profession

In the name of God, Amen.

I, Richard Ludlow, before God and you, commissary of my reverend lord and father John, by grace of God bishop of Salisbury, and also in the presence of all these worshipful men being here, offer up my profession as hermit in this form:

That I, the aforesaid Richard, make protestation and promise from this day forward to be obedient to God and to Holy Church, having the ministers thereof in worship and reverence. Also, to lead my life to my life's end in true continence and chastity, and to eschew all open spectacles, common scot-ales[10] *and taverns, which are unlawful and forbidden by Holy Church, and all other suspect places of sin. Furthermore I grant* [agree] *on my profession every day to hear mass and to say once every day continually Our Lady's Psalter*[11] *and on Sundays and other holy days Our Lady's Psalter twice and also 15 Pater Nosters and Aves in worship and mind of the wounds that our Lord suffered for me and all mankind. Also to fast every Friday in the year, and the 2 vigils of Pentecost and All Hallows, and the five vigils of Our Lady,*[12] *to bread and water. And this foresaid observance (as of hearing mass, praying and fasting) I shall keep truly, unless it be so that any great sickness, or labour, or any other reasonable let or impediment which may not be eschewed, should be a cause to hinder me. And over that, the goods that I may get, either by free gift of Christian people or by quest on testament,*[13] *or by any other reasonable and true way (reserving only things necessary to my subsistence as in meat* [food]*, drink, clothes and fuel) I shall truly without deceit [expend] upon the reparation and amending of the bridge and of [the] common ways belonging to the same town of Maidenhead.*

[signed with a cross] +

Also annexed is an outline order for making a hermit similar to [**49**].

51. Can a hermit marry? A judgement of Archbishop Arundel

Strictly speaking, marriages in the Middle Ages were supposed to be solemnised by the ecclesiastical authorities in church. But the essential components for a legal marriage required the presence only of the

10 A scot-ale was a money-raising event based around drinking.

11 Repetition of the Ave Maria (Hail Mary) 150 times (to correspond with the number of the psalms).

12 All Hallows is 1 Nov., and its vigil or eve (Hallowe'en) is 31 Oct. The five feasts of Our Lady are the Purification (2 Feb.), Annunciation (25 Mar.), Visitation (2 July), Assumption (15 Aug.), and Nativity (8 Sept.). Pentecost (Whit Sunday) is the seventh Sunday after Easter.

13 I.e. by licensed begging.

couple themselves: a verbal contract in which both parties gave their consent, consummated in the act of sexual intercourse. Perhaps inevitably, marriages so contracted could sometimes come into doubt, either from one or both of the partners, or from members of their family or community, and such questions would come before the church courts.[14] A marriage might be declared invalid in cases where the partners were found to be within the proscribed degrees of consanguinity or affinity, or when one of them could be shown to have entered into a prior marriage contract with someone else, or if their contract was trumped by a higher vow, specified in canon law as the reception of Holy Orders or religious profession in one of the apostolically approved orders. This last question was at issue in the present case, though whether the hermit involved was trying to extricate himself from an ill-judged liaison or, on the contrary, seeking legitimation for his unusual domestic arrangements, is unclear.[15]

Translated from the Latin entry in Archbishop Arundel's register, Lambeth Palace Library, LPL 1, fol. 438v.

Licence to a hermit to cause a marriage previously contracted to be solemnised

Thomas [Arundel, archbishop of Canterbury, 1399–1414] etc., to all the sons of holy Mother Church etc., greetings, etc.

Whereas a certain Adam Cressevill of our diocese has, at his urgent request, for the increase of his devotion, received the habit of a hermit, and for some time, according to his pleasure, has continued in the life of a hermit; and subsequently the same Adam has contracted a marriage 'by words of present assent'[16] with a certain Margaret [*space left for surname*] also of our diocese, and this same marriage he has, as he asserts, consummated by carnal union, he has humbly besought us that we might see fit to pronounce on the validity of the said marriage;

We, therefore, considering that the reception of a hermit's habit in this way does not comprise in law either a tacit or an express profession of any religious state approved by the Holy See, in general or in

14 For a review of such questions in the diocese of Ely under Thomas Arundel, see Michael M. Sheehan, 'The Formation and Stability of Marriage in Fourteenth-century England: evidence of an Ely register', *Mediaeval Studies* 33 (1971): 228–63.

15 Married men could become hermits: see the introduction to this section, and examples of married hermits at [**42**], [**52c**].

16 This is the legal formula used to describe a verbal agreement of marriage.

particular, nor does it include in itself holy orders such that marriage, which was instituted in paradise, might be dissolved once it has been contracted,[17] by the authority that we discharge in this respect, declare the said Adam to be effectually obliged and held to the observance of this same marriage contracted as aforesaid, if another canon does not contradict it, the reception of the said habit of a hermit as aforesaid notwithstanding;

which we bring to your notice by the present letters.

In witness of which etc. Given in our manor of Maidstone [Kent], the 28th day of the month of December, AD 1405, and the tenth year of our translation.

52. Records of hermits' professions

This selection covers almost a century of practice from a number of different dioceses. None the less, it will be seen that the essential elements show a high degree of consistency.

52a. The profession of John of Wells, hermit

This mid-fifteenth-century record of a hermit's profession is typical of a number of such entries in late medieval bishops' registers.

Entry predominantly in Latin: translation quoted from H.C. Maxwell-Lyte and M.C.B. Dawes, eds, *The Register of Thomas Bekynton, Bishop of Bath and Wells, 1443–1465*, Somerset Record Society 49–50 (1934–5), Vol.1, p. 190. By permission of Somerset Record Society. I have modernised the English of Wells's vow.

On 9 October [1452] the bishop, immediately before celebrating mass in his chapel in the manor of Woky,[18] ratified and approved the following profession made by a certain John of Wellis, an unmarried man, who desired to lead a hermit's life, serving his Creator in perpetual chastity, to wit:–

17 The considerations cited here are based closely on the relevant passage of canon law. See Sext 2.15.1, in *Corpus iuris canonici*, edited by E. Friedberg, 2 vols (Leipzig: Tauchnitz, 1879–81), Vol. 2, p. 1053.

18 The bishops of Bath and Wells had had a palace at Wookey, a few miles west of Wells, since the thirteenth century.

I, John of Wellis, not wedded, promise and avow to God and Our Lady St Mary and to all the saints of heaven the full purpose of perpetual chastity after the rule of St Paul the Hermit, in presence of you, right reverend father in God Thomas, by the grace of God bishop of Bath and of Wells. In the name of the Father, and of the Son, and of the Holy Spirit, Amen.

He delivered to the bishop the schedule whereon the above protestation was written, marked with the sign of the cross, because he could not write, and thereupon the bishop, after completion of the solemnities requisite in such cases, with his own hands invested him with a habit suitable to the estate of hermit.

52b. A certificate of profession from Lincoln diocese

This is the kind of document that a hermit might produce if challenged by the authorities. That such certificates were issued in significant numbers is suggested by the fact that the text here is taken from a formulary – a collection of model documents in standard form that the clerks of the bishop's chancery could reproduce as required.[19] The use of non-specific *N.* and *B.* to stand for various details of the document reflects this function.

Translated from the Latin, Lincolnshire Archives Office, Formulary 2, fol. 5r.

Letters testimonial on the profession of a hermit according to the Rule of St Paul

To all the sons of holy Mother Church to whom these present letters shall come, William [Alnwick, 1436–50], by divine permission bishop of Lincoln, greetings in the Saviour of all.

By these letters, we give notice to you all that the reverend father Sir Thomas, bishop of Annaghdown, suffragan of our diocese, in our stead and by our authority, on Sunday 26th of *N.* in the year 1452, in a chapel within the prebendal church of *N.* in our diocese, during the celebration of mass in which he was vested as a bishop, solemnly and canonically ordained our beloved son in Christ Richard *B.*, a Catholic man, unmarried, of approved life and behaviour, as a hermit in and according to the Rule of St Paul; and at the same time received a vow of profession to the eremitical life according to the aforesaid rule uttered by the same Richard; and gave the habit and staff befitting and appro-

19 For an example of a hermit who was issued with similar letters testimonial, one week after his profession in the diocese of Exeter, see Davis, 'Rule of St Paul', pp. 206–7.

priate to an eremitical profession of this kind to the same Richard; and at the same time diligently instructed the same Richard (or caused him to be instructed) in the rule of living according to the aforesaid Rule of St Paul.

Therefore we require and ask your worships that, for as long as the aforementioned Richard *B.*, hermit, should remain properly committed to an eremitical life of this kind, you will treat him favourably and charitably as is appropriate.

In witness of which, etc. Given the day, place and year aforesaid.

52c. *A hermit and his wife both take vows*

For married hermits and vows of chastity, see the introduction to this section.

Modernised from the English vows printed in James Raine, ed., *Testamenta Eboracensia. A selection of wills from the Registry of York: Vol. 3*, Surtees Society 45 (1865), pp. 343–4.

2 May 1479
The profession of Henry Andrew, hermit, and Alice his wife

In the name of God, Amen.

I, Henry Andrew, vow to God and to Our Lady, and to all saints, to be chaste from this time forward; and to live in fasting, prayer, and works of piety [*pety*]; and shall never leave this habit while I live, in the presence of you, Laurence [Booth], by the grace of God Archbishop of York, primate of England, and legate of the court of Rome, and promise to live stably in this vow according to the order of hermits during my life.

In witness whereof I with my own hand make here this +

[*There follows in Latin a list of the witnesses.*]

In the name of God, Amen.

I, Alice Andrew, wife of Henry Andrew, vow to God and to Our Lady, and to all saints, in the presence of you, Laurence [Booth], by the grace of God Archbishop of York, primate of England, and legate of the court of Rome, to be chaste from this time forward; and promise to live stably in this vow during my life.

And in witness thereof I with my own hand make here this +

In the name of the Father, and of the Son, and of the Holy Spirit. Amen.

52d. A sixteenth-century hermit's profession

Although (typically) this document does not tell us where the new hermit intended to live, or how he meant to realise his vocation, speculation is tempting: his home village of Abberley is in the Abberley Hills, north of the Malverns, and the sort of place where Langland's Will might have roamed; it is also only a few miles from the cave hermitage at Redstone, still occupied by hermits in the late 1530s [**76**].

Translated from the Latin, and the English vow modernised, from the text in *The Register of Charles Bothe, Bishop of Hereford (1516–1535)* edited by Arthur Thomas Bannister, Cantilupe Society (Hereford: Wilson and Phillips, 1921), p. 238.

The profession of a hermit

On the 12th day of the month of March, in the year of our Lord by the reckoning of the English church 1530, John Evett of Aborley, truly and purely desiring to serve the Most High by choosing a solitary life, devoutly and freely made a vow of perpetual chastity according to the rule and ordinance of St Paul the Hermit, in the presence of the aforesaid reverend father in Christ [Bishop Bothe] in the chapel within his manor of Whitbo[u]rne, and was professed, as follows:

I, John Evett, not wedded, promise and vow to God, to our Blessed Lady, and to all the saints of heaven, in the presence of you, reverend father and lord, Charles, bishop of Hereford, true purpose of perpetual chastity after the rule and ordinance of St Paul the Hermit. In the name of the Father, and of the Son, and of the Holy Spirit. Amen. *In confirmation of the which purpose and vow with my own hand I have put to* [added] *the sign of the cross.*

53. The Rule of St Linus

Linus succeeded St Peter to be the second pope. We can be certain, however, that he had nothing to do with the Middle English 'rule' for hermits that bears his name. (Compare the attribution of the *Rule of Celestine* [**46**].) In fact, this short text is typical of the summaries of a lay hermit's spiritual obligations that are regularly recorded in episcopal documents, often appended to profession rites like [**49**], [**50**]. The owner of the manuscript in which it is recorded is himself of some interest. Thomas Scrope or Bradley was a Carmelite friar and suffragan of the bishop of Norwich during the 1450s, and it was doubtless in such a context that he used the *Rule*. But as a younger man he had spent a decade or so as an anchorite enclosed at the Carmelite house in Norwich.[20]

Complete text modernised from the Middle English, edited by Livarius Oliger, 'Regula Reclusorum Angliae et Quaestiones tres de Vita solitaria saec. XIII–XIV', *Antonianum* 9 (1934): 37–84; 243–68, at pp. 263–5.

Our holy father Linus, pope of Rome, ordained this rule for all solitary men that take the degree [*status*] of a hermit.

He thereby binds himself to spend the night and day in praising of God. The beginning of the day is at midnight, and a hermit shall rise at midnight from Holy Rood Day[21] until Easter Day, and from Easter Day until Holy Rood Day at the dawning of the day. And he shall say in place of Matins of the day 40 Our Fathers, 15 Hail Marys, and 4 Creeds; and for Lauds, 15 Our Fathers, 15 Hail Marys and 1 Creed; and for Prime he shall say 12 Our Fathers, 12 Hail Marys and 1 Creed. And when he has said Prime he shall hear mass. And after mass he shall say, for each [canonical] hour, 10 Our Fathers, 10 Hail Marys and 1 Creed. After that, he shall go to his oratory and have a meditation of the passion of Christ, or of some other holy thing. For mid-day [*i.e. the hour of Nones*] he shall say 10 Our Fathers, 10 Hail Marys and 1 Creed, and then go to his meat [*food*]. After meat he shall say for all his benefactors 30 Our Fathers, 30 Hail Marys and 3 Creeds, and Our Lady's Psalter.[22] For Evensong he shall say 40 Our Fathers, 40 Hail Marys and 1 Creed. For Compline he shall say 10 Our Fathers, 10 Hail Marys, and 1 Creed. And after Compline has been said he shall keep silence.

He shall fast every day in Lent, Advent and the 'Apostles' Fast' – that is to say, from Holy Thursday until Whit Sunday.[23] He shall be shriven and houselled[24] three times in a year, at Christmas, Easter and Whit Sunday. He shall fast on Fridays and Saturdays all through the year, on a Friday to bread, ale and pottage. He shall eat no flesh, except on Christmas Day, Epiphany, [the feasts of] St Paul the First Hermit, St Anthony,[25]

20 See his life by Richard Copsey in *ODNB*.

21 The feast of the Exaltation of the Holy Cross (14 Sept.).

22 150 Hail Marys (just as the psalter contains 150 psalms).

23 Although a period of fasting before Pentecost is frequently specified, the Apostle's Fast (which is still a feature in Orthodox Christianity) normally runs from Pentecost/Whit Sunday until the Feast of Sts Peter and Paul (29 June).

24 That is, be confessed and receive communion.

25 The inclusion of the two desert saints, Paul the First Hermit (10 Jan.) and Anthony (17 Jan.), is noteworthy.

all the feasts of Our Lady, the Ascension, Whit Sunday, the Feast of the Trinity, Corpus Christi, the Nativity of St John the Baptist [24 June], and of Peter and Paul [29 June], the feast of the Angels,[26] the feast of All Hallows [1 Nov.], the feast of the patron saint of his cell, and the dedication of his cell.

Also he shall lie in his kirtle, girded with a girdle or with a cord. He shall wear a hairshirt unless he is weak and may not tolerate it. He shall wear shoes but not hose. And he shall be buried when he is dead in the habit he goes in.

The sum of the Our Fathers over the day is 187 and as many Hail Marys, and 14 Creeds, besides [*over and above*] Our Lady's Psalter.

These are the duties of a hermit's life.

54. A hermit's obedience, from the *Cambridge Rule*

The *Cambridge Rule* is so called, not because of any particular association with hermits of that city, but because its only surviving manuscript is now in Cambridge University Library. It is the most developed and spiritually advanced of the extant English rules for hermits. This chapter, in which the hermit is told that he owes obedience only to God, and not to any earthly superior, reminded earlier commentators of Richard Rolle [**47**], who is said to have composed a *Regula heremitarum.* But that striking opening is quickly qualified, and there is not really anything here that would justify an attribution to him.[27] Although the *Rule* is difficult to date with any precision, it most likely belongs later than Rolle's lifetime; probably, like all the other English rules, it comes from the fifteenth century. About half this section is taken more or less verbatim from Aelred's *Rule of Life for a Recluse*, and that earlier treatise for a female anchorite provides about one-third of the *Rule* as a whole.

Translated from the Latin, edited by Livarius Oliger, 'Regulae tres reclusorum et eremitarum Angliae saec. XIII–XIV', *Antonianum* 3 (1928): 151–90; 299–320, at pp. 304–5.

A hermit is obliged to render obedience only to God, for he is the abbot, prior and provost of the cloister of his heart. But he must inform

26 Probably Michaelmas, the feast of St Michael and all angels, 29 Sept.

27 Arguments against the ascription to Rolle are presented in Watson, *Richard Rolle and the Invention of Authority*, p. 305 n. 21.

the bishop in whose diocese he dwells, or the patron of the place, if he is a prelate or a priest of good discretion. And if they see anything in him that needs amending, he should obey their advice for the sake of Christ, who said to the doctors in Luke 10, 'He that heareth you heareth me' [Luke 10:16]. Alternatively, with the consent of the bishop, a priest may be chosen from a local monastery or church, someone senior, wise, mature in his way of life and of good opinions, from whom he will be able to seek advice when he is in doubt and comfort when he is depressed, and he should duly obey not only his counsels but also his commands (in so far as they do not go against God or the present rule). Of this it is said, 'He became obedient unto death' [Philipp. 2:8]. And the priest in co-operation with the hermit can legitimately give dispensation against the restrictions of the rule concerning food, where there is good reason, as for instance because of great labour or necessity, or indeed because of bodily infirmity. He shall not, however, lightly make any change to the fasts appointed by the Church.

55. The hermit's cell, from Richard Methley's *To Hugh the Hermit*

Richard Methley (1450/1–1527/8) lived a solitary life of his own, as a Carthusian monk at Mount Grace (N. Yorks.). He translated the mystical treatise *The Cloud of Unknowing* and a version of Marguerite Porete's *Mirror of Simple Souls* from Middle English into Latin, and also, in several autobiographical writings, describes mystical gifts and visions that he has received himself.[28] His short *Epistle of Solitary Life Nowadayes, to Hugh the Hermit* was written to a hermit who (as the text reveals) lived in the Lady Chapel that stands high on the hillside overlooking the charterhouse.[29] At the dissolution of Mount Grace it was occupied by the hermit Thomas Parkinson [**74**].

Chapters 2–3, the opening of chapter 8, chapter 9; modernised from the Middle English, edited by Barry Windeatt, *English Mystics of the Middle Ages* (Cambridge: Cambridge University Press, 1994), pp. 265–71, at pp. 266–7, 268, 269–70.

28 See his life by Michael Sargent in *ODNB*.

29 The chapel is still in use as a Marian shrine: see www.ladychapel.org.uk. For its history, see Anthony Storey, *Mount Grace Lady Chapel: An historical enquiry* (Beverley: Highgate Publications, 2001).

Eripe me de inimicis meis Domine; ad te confugi; doce me facere voluntatem tuam, quia Deus meus es tu [Ps. 142:9–10]. That is to say in English thus: 'Lord, deliver me from my enemies; to thee have I fled; teach me for to do thy will, for thou art my God'. These words are pertaining to all Christian people that ask to be delivered from their enemies, bodily and ghostly [*spiritual*], the which flee from the love of the world. But especially they pertain to you, that have fled to God in the wilderness [away] from human fellowship, that you may the better learn to do his will; for he is your God, and you are to love him especially. Therefore how you should ask him to be delivered from your enemies, I shall (by his grace) tell you.

You have principally three enemies: the world, your flesh, and the Evil Spirit. You may flee from the world to God. But your flesh and your Enemy will go with you into the wilderness. You marvel why I say 'into the wilderness', when you dwell in a fair chapel of our Lady – blessed, worshipped and thanked may she be! Ask for no fellowship but her to talk with, I pray you; and then I say that you shall overcome your three enemies by these three virtues: that is to say, against your Enemy, ghostly obedience; against your flesh, clean [*pure*] chastity; against the world, that you do not turn to it again, but keep poverty with a good will. And then may you well say to God almighty, 'Lord, deliver me from my enemies; to thee have I fled; teach me for to do thy will, for thou art my God'.[30]

…

Three things are needful for you to keep well: one is your sight; another, your cell; the third is your silence, that is to say, hold your tongue well.

…

Your cell is the second thing that I said. And what do I call your cell, do you think, but the place or the chapel of our blessed Lady where you dwell? And know well, you have great cause to keep it well, for you need not run here and there to seek your living. God has provided for you, and therefore keep your cell, and it will keep you from sin. Be no home-runner[31] to see marvels, no gadabout from town to town, no land-loper waving in the wind like a skylark. But keep your cell, and it

30 Followed by the same quotation in Latin.

31 Presumably either someone who spends all their time away from home, or who runs from one home to another – perhaps modelled on *Rome-runner*, a derogatory term for anyone who travelled to the papacy in Rome for ecclesiastical privilege.

will keep you.[32] But now you say, perhaps, you may not keep it, for you are sent for by gentles [*members of the nobility*] in the country, whom you dare not displease. I answer and say thus: tell them that you have forsaken the world, and therefore – except in time of very great need, such as at the time of a death or such another great need – you may not let up your devotion. And when you do help them, look that you do it truly for the love of God, and take nothing except for your costs.

And when you sit on your own in the wilderness and are irked or weary, say this to our Lady as St Godric (that holy hermit) said: 'St Mary, maiden and mother of Jesus Christ of Nazareth, hold and help your Hugh; take and lead [him] safe with you into your kingdom'.[33] (Or say, 'into the kingdom of God': both are good. He said 'help your Godric', but you may say 'your Hugh', for your name is Hugh.) And I counsel you, love well St Hugh, of our order of Carthusian monks.[34] But now you say, I trow [*believe*], you must come forth to hear mass. That is full well seeming [*entirely appropriate*], unless you have masses sung within your chapel. But when you have heard mass, then flee home, unless you have a full good cause, as you say in this verse: *ad te confugi* – 'To thee, Lord, I have fled' [Ps. 142:9] – wholly, both body and soul, as thou art my all. For if you flee with your body and not with your heart from the world, then you are a false hypocrite, as scripture says: *Simulatores et callidi provocant iram Dei* – that is thus in English: 'False, wily dissemblers provoke the ire of God' [Job 36:13]. Therefore, in your [hour of] need against such temptations, say this verse, *Deliver me from my enemies, etc.*

56. Food, drink and clothing, from the *Rule of Celestine*

We encountered the *Rule of Celestine* in the previous section [**46**]. In character, it stands somewhere between the rudimentary lists of duties like the *Rule of St Linus* [**53**] and the more spiritually oriented *Cambridge Rule* [**54**], with which it shares a few passages. It deals

32 The phrasing and the thought are strongly reminiscent of the sayings of the Desert Fathers, though this is not an exact quotation.

33 In the original this is given in Latin, and then in English translation. Godric (c. 1070–1170) was a seafarer and adventurer who later became a hermit and settled at Finchale (Co. Durham). Four Middle English hymns were recorded by his biographer, Reginald of Durham, of which this is the first and the best-known. The music also survives.

34 St Hugh of Lincoln (1140?–1200), prior of the Carthusian house of Witham (Somerset) and subsequently bishop of Lincoln, was canonised in 1220.

mostly in externals and practicalities, and reveals many details of the expected daily life of a fairly ordinary hermit. The discretion allowed the hermit in the matter of a hairshirt (the wearing of which is required by the *Rule of St Linus* [**53**]) is humane. It is envisaged that, though his life is to be a simple one, he might have books, and that he might go on pilgrimage, including overseas (compare [**43**]). And we might note that, somewhat counter-intuitively, the hermit is counselled against spending too much time on his own.[35]

Translated from the Latin, chapters 5–6, 8–9, edited by Oliger 'Regulae tres', pp. 313–15.

How he should receive the things of this world
A hermit, who is a true poor man for Christ, should desire nothing, have nothing, nor ask for anything in God's name, unless it is strictly necessary for sustaining his body. He should not carry silver or gold or money with him when he is on the road, except for three purposes: that is, for mending his cell, or building a new one, or for mending essential clothes or books, or for carrying out other work. For example, if people give alms to him rather than the needy, he should receive them in God's name and give them to poor people whose need is greater; he should distribute them to the poor at the earliest opportunity, and not hold on to them any longer.

Keeping supplies in his cell
A poor hermit who lives in a borough, town or city, or near to one, where he can readily beg for his daily food every day, should distribute what is left of his food (if there is any) to Christ's poor people before the sun goes down. But if he lives a long way from the said places, in a township in the country or in a deserted place, one or two miles distant from other people, then he should get supplies for exactly one week, that is from Sunday to Sunday, or from another day until the same day the next week; and if he has any left, he should give it to the poor without delay, unless he can legitimately be excused before God because of some definite reason, that is if he is ill or weak, or is caring for someone who is ill, or he is at home doing some spiritual or bodily work pleasing to God.

...

35 On this, see further my 'Vae Soli! Solitaries and pastoral care' in *Texts and Traditions of Medieval Pastoral Care* edited by Cate Gunn and Catherine Innes-Parker (Woodbridge: York Medieval Press, 2009), pp. 11–28.

His clothing

He should wear such clothes as are determined by the bishop in whose diocese he resides or his patron (if [the latter] is a prelate of the Church, and possesses discernment), so long as his clothes are humble, that is not too fancy nor too wretched – according to these words of St Bernard, where he says (in the person of the Lord), 'I have loved poverty, but never filth'.[36] And so that he should not give people of religion cause to speak ill of him, he should above all take care not to have a habit that is entirely the same as that of any religious order. He should not wear linen or linsey-wolsey [*linen mix*] or soft clothes against his flesh, either night or day, but clothes that are made of wool, and humble, as aforesaid, such as can be found in the area where he lives. And if, out of devotion, he wants to wear a hairshirt against his flesh, that is certainly permitted, except when he is engaged in contemplative prayer, when the biting of the worms that come out of the hairshirt might hinder him from his contemplation, and thus make him think more about the miseries of his flesh than the contemplation of his spirit. And so we leave the question of a hairshirt to his conscience.

His shoes

He should not wear shoes or clogs that are too fancy, but such as he can get hold of for the love of God; or he should go barefoot, if he is able to do that without injury to his body; but he should do everything with moderation. 'Woe to him that is alone!' [Eccles. 4:10].[37] But he is not alone if 'he dwelleth in love', because he 'dwelleth in God, and God in him' [1 John 4:16], and therefore with him. He should never go out alone, if he can readily have a companion or servant with him. And he should not travel around the country too much – but he should send his servant (if he can get one) as a messenger to do the things he needs doing – so that he doesn't derive too much bodily enjoyment from illicit wandering about, and thus (God forbid) lose his prayer and devotion through neglect. If he should have to travel overseas or on a distant pilgrimage, he can do that, with his patron's licence (if he is readily able to speak with him). He shouldn't occupy himself with gadding about or wandering[38] around the country, but he should beg simply for his food and clothing in God's name.

36 Quotation from the *Life* of Bernard by Geoffrey of Clairvaux, Book 3 chapter 2 (*PL* 185, 306).

37 A verse traditionally used to warn against the dangers of the solitary life, in which excesses and errors can go unchecked.

38 The MS here has 'adulation', which makes little sense; I have emended in the light of the Middle English texts.

VII: RENEGADES, CHARISMATICS AND CHARLATANS

Introduction

Solitaries dwelt on the margins of the religious establishment. Their liminal status was the source of much of their cultural power. Their position outside the structures of temporal society made them a valuable reference point for ordinary Christians, whilst giving them a vantage point from which to turn a disinterested eye on the social and religious structure and, where necessary, to speak truth to power.[1] Alongside the desert saints Anthony and Paul the First Hermit, eremitic discourse appealed to outspoken biblical models: the prophet Elijah and John the Baptist, the solitary voice crying in the wilderness. In the reign of King John, the hermits Robert of Knaresborough and Peter of Wakefield both confronted the king. Robert lived to enjoy royal patronage, but Peter (as readers of Shakespeare's *King John* will know) was, like John the Baptist, not so fortunate.[2] Where there was disillusion with the established religious orders, the hermit – who seemed to represent the highest religious ideals without being bound to the tired and corrupt institutions that claimed to be the guardians of those ideals – could become a magnet for popular enthusiasm [**59**]. But he had to be careful not to encroach on the rights of the clergy [**62**], or to stray into error or heresy.

The principal challenge to orthodoxy in late medieval England was of course the Wycliffite heresy, or Lollardy. Solitaries and Lollards on the face of it make unlikely bedfellows. Wyclif was outspoken in his rejection of the established religious orders, or 'private religions': among the propositions declared to be erroneous at the Blackfriars council of 1382 was the stark statement 'that the religious living in private

1 I explore these issues in 'O Sely Ankir' in *Anchorites in Their Communities*, edited by Cate Gunn and Liz Herbert McAvoy (Cambridge: D.S. Brewer, 2017), pp. 13–34. The classic study is Henry Mayr-Harting, 'Functions of a Twelfth-century Recluse', *History* 60 (1975): 337–52. See also Christopher Holdsworth, 'Hermits and the Power of the Frontier', *Reading Medieval Studies* 16 (1990): 55–76.

2 'O Sely Ankir', pp. 27–9. For some examples from the Reformation period, see [**66**], [**68**].

religions are not of the Christian religion'.[3] Whilst hermits and anchorites might have escaped Wyclif's critique of the lavish endowments of the friars and monastic orders, these most private of private religions certainly shared in his strictures against the elaborate, non-biblical forms and structures that separated the 'religious' from ordinary good Christian people. On the other hand, these were men and women of strong religious commitment, and (one must assume) a deep sense of engagement with questions of faith, who nevertheless had not found what they were looking for in the established forms of living that the mainstream institutional church offered them. So perhaps it is not entirely surprising that one of the early preachers of Wycliffite heresy in Leicester should have been the hermit William Swinderby [**60**]. A few years later, in 1389, Matilda (or Maud) the anchoress at the church of St Peter in the same town was found to be 'infected … with the pestiferous contagion' of Lollardy. Though initially defiant, she eventually submitted and recanted her erroneous opinions, to be re-enclosed in her cell.[4] Whether another Lollard anchoress, Amy Palmer of Northampton, did likewise may be doubtful: at her last appearance in the record [**61**] she denounced the bishop of Lincoln as Antichrist and scornfully refused to answer the charges against her. Palmer was a contemporary of Julian of Norwich, just as Richard Rolle was a contemporary of the charismatic Yorkshire preacher Henry Staunton [**59**]. It is easy to think of the heretic and the mystic as opposites, but these examples suggest that it may also be worth considering what they might have in common.

If hermits' liminal position brought with it a certain cultural prestige and spiritual energy, it also placed them on the fringes of English society, where they might rub shoulders with some shady characters. Indeed, especially before the attempts at regulating the vocation in the fifteenth century, there was no easy way to distinguish the true hermit from the false; and, among the latter, the hermit's robe could be an excuse for a life of idleness [**63**], or cover for something more sinister. In the late fourteenth century, Henry Hermyte of South Stoneham (Hants.) was 'a common disturber of the peace, highwayman … and harbourer of felons' (cf. [**64**]), though he did receive a royal pardon.[5] In

3 Henry Gee and William John Hardy, eds, *Documents Illustrative of English Church History* (London: Macmillan, 1896), p. 110.

4 John Foxe, *The Unabridged Acts and Monuments Online* or *TAMO* (1576 edition) (Sheffield: HRI Online Publications, 2011), book 5, p. 513.

5 *Cal. Pat. Rolls 1381–1385*, p. 238.

1517, Henry VIII was sent intelligence about a planned French offensive that had come from 'a French spy, a man of low stature, with a red beard and a grey hermit's habit'. The following year, Thomas Dacre, Henry's leading magnate in the Scottish borders, and full of schemes to destabilise the region to English advantage, wrote to Wolsey recommending that, if he will send him 'a wise yeoman in hermit's weed, … he will see more waste done by such means than if the King had laid a garrison of 3,000 men there'.[6]

57. A pious Oxfordshire hermit

Thomas Gascoigne (1404–58) was an Oxford theologian, and sometime chancellor of the University.[7] His wide-ranging collection of preaching materials, the *Dictionarium Theologicum*, is famous for its story of Geoffrey Chaucer lying on his deathbed and repenting of the sinful poetry he had written, and could not now unwrite. (Gascoigne places the story in his section on repentance that comes too late; his other example under this head is Judas Iscariot.) It also includes this snippet recording the piety of an otherwise unknown hermit at Newbridge, a crossing of the Thames near Standlake, some 10 miles west of Oxford.[8] The hermitage was still standing in the seventeenth century when the Oxford antiquarian Anthony Wood investigated it (by this date the building had been turned into an inn). Wood found that, by the 1460s, the bridge had fallen into serious disrepair, until 'the hermit at length, called Thomas Brigges, being moved with a good intent obtained a license to require the goodwill and favour of passengers that came that way and of other neighbouring villages towards the reparation of it againe'.[9]

Translated from the Latin, *Loci e Libro veritatum: Passages selected from Gascoigne's theological dictionary illustrating the condition of church and state, 1403–1458*, edited by James E. Thorold Rogers (Oxford: Clarendon Press, 1881), pp. 105–6.

6 *Letters and Papers, Henry VIII*, Vol. 2 part 2, pp. 889, 1306.

7 For Gascoigne, see the life by Christina von Nolcken in *ODNB*.

8 For more on the Newbridge hermitage, see my 'The Hermits and Anchorites of Oxfordshire', *Oxoniensia* 63 (1998): 51–77, p. 70.

9 *Survey of the Antiquities of the City of Oxford … by Anthony Wood, Vol. 2: Churches and Religious Houses* edited by Andrew Clark, Oxford Historical Society 17 (1890), p. 499.

The good man William of Cornwall, sometime hermit at Newbridge, used to say, when he was stirred or tempted to sin:

> O sin! What a great price I should have to pay for you, if I should receive you, and consent to you. For you, o sin, if I consent to you, I should have to pay and to suffer the loss of God's grace and of everlasting glory, and many punishments I shall have to suffer for you. And so, o sin, I will not pay so many and so much for the sake of having you. For so many evils and pains I should have to pay for you, sin, and so many evils I should have to suffer for you, if I should consent to you. And so, o sin, I won't have you or purchase you at so great and so dear a price.

That good man William of Newbridge said this around the year of our Lord 1434.

58. Pilgrims flock to the hermit of Losfield

The hermit of Newbridge impressed Thomas Gascoigne, but we do not know what kind of popular audience he might have found. About a century earlier, the hermit of Losfield, in Windsor Forest (in the parish of Clewer, Berks.), seems to have attracted quite a following, though in his case we do not know whether this was due to his teachings, his personal sanctity or the virtues of the holy well located near his chapel. He certainly had a powerful patron. Bernard Brocas was a soldier who fought at the Battle of Crécy (1346), entered the service of Henry duke of Lancaster, and was later a courtier of Edward III. He was lord of the manor of Clewer Brocas until his death in 1395.[10] His support must have been instrumental in gaining this generous papal indulgence for visitors to his chapel. The hermitage is last recorded in the early sixteenth century. A succession of later houses has been built on the site on St Leonard's Hill, which is now part of the Legoland theme park. For another hermitage popular with pilgrims, see [**39**].

Summaries of the Latin originals: (i) is quoted with slight modifications from W.H. Bliss, ed., *Calendar of Papal Registers Relating to Great Britain and Ireland. Petitions to the Pope: Vol. 1: 1342–1419* (London: HMSO, 1896), p. 270; and (ii) from W.H. Bliss and C. Johnson, eds, *Calendar of Papal Registers Relating to Great Britain and Ireland: Vol. 3: 1342–1362* (London: HMSO, 1897), p. 572.

10 See his life by Henry Summerson in *ODNB*.

(i) [Petition of] Bernard de Broquasio (Brocas), knight of Henry, duke of Lancaster

Whereas William the hermit, chaplain of St. Leonard, Loffold, in Windsor forest, lives a solitary life, and serves God alone, and whereas a multitude of people flock to the chapel, the pope is prayed to grant an indulgence to those who visit the said chapel yearly at Whitsuntide and the Assumption, and give alms to the fabric.

Granted for one year and forty days. Avignon, 4 Kal. Feb. [29 Jan. 1355].

(ii) Avignon, 4 Kal. Feb. [29 Jan.] 1355.

Relaxation of a year and forty days enjoined penance to penitents visiting the chapel of St Leonard in Loffeld in Windsor forest, on the feasts of Pentecost, the Assumption of the Blessed Virgin [15 Aug.] and St Leonard [6 Nov.].

59. Henry de Staunton, hermit-preacher

Renegade, charismatic or charlatan? Henry de Staunton (or Stanton) seems to have embodied elements of all three. This Yorkshire contemporary of Richard Rolle was evidently a preacher of some magnetism, whose ideas struck a popular chord, however socially divisive they may have proved. He perhaps fits the model of the anti-establishment hermit-preacher (like John the Baptist, a voice crying in the wilderness) that Rolle, too, often cultivates. But Staunton clearly crossed a line, and the official Church, in the person of Archbishop William Melton, stepped in. It is understandable that Melton chose not to give recognition or further publicity to Staunton's teachings by recording them in his register – but frustrating for those of us left intrigued as to what they might have contained.

Translated from the Latin in *The Register of William Melton, Archbishop of York 1317–1340: Volume III*, edited by Rosalind M.T. Hill, Canterbury & York Society 76 (1988), pp. 131–2.

A letter forbidding anyone from listening to the preaching of Brother Henry de Staunton, hermit

William etc. to our Dean of the Christianity of York,[11] etc.

11 The official responsible for the church courts in the city of York.

The office of a prelate (who is duty bound carefully to ensure that by banishment of heretical depravity from the bounds of the Church the Catholic faith may prosper and have continual increase) cannot allow dark clouds to obscure the usual splendour of that faith, through the rash and wrongful actions of foolish people who, relying on their own prudence, fall into various errors, nor that unsound doctrine corrupt the hearts of the faithful.

A very trustworthy report has now repeatedly come to our attention that brother Henry de Stanton, a hermit and (so he claims) a priest, though instructed only in the basics, insisting more than is appropriate on the literal sense 'that killeth',[12] and usurping the office of a preacher, though he has no such commission, has taught and most boldly publicly preached within our city of York articles touching on the Catholic faith, containing a number of errors which redound greatly to the injury of God's name and the contempt of the Christian faith. From this sacrilegious and perverse teaching, instigated by the Sower of Evil Works,[13] a certain sect has arisen of people professing pious motives; dissension and division have sprung up between clergy and laity; strife, insults, quarrels, riots, plots and conventicles have been occurring against the law, while encouragement and occasion are given to married people wrongfully to leave their partners.

We, therefore, wishing to know if the things alleged to us had any truth, have caused the said hermit to be challenged with the said erroneous articles (which for good reason we do not reveal), for him to explain them, with theologians and others learned in the law in attendance, and we have given a full hearing to his defence of himself before those people in our presence. Although he did his best to defend several of the said articles put to him, which he affirmed to contain true Catholic belief, since there were still many people to indict and accuse him on articles that they contradicted, and moreover they were determined to prove him to be in the wrong, at last when he could not reply to the reasons advanced against him, he confessed himself to have been in error, by humbly asking for pardon to be granted him. We ourselves, having heard his arguments with the said experts on these matters, have had a learned discussion of the said erroneous articles, and have examined the said hermit on his literacy – that is, whether he is suitable to preach the word of God in public.

12 Cf. 2 Cor. 3:6, 'For the letter killeth, but the spirit quickeneth' – a popular proof-text for advocates of the advanced allegorical reading of scripture.

13 That is, the devil.

As a result of the foregoing discussion and examination of these matters, we have found the points preached by him to be not sound but dangerous doctrine, containing much contrary to the truth, and that he himself is far from suitable to teach the people under our jurisdiction or to perform the office of a preacher; and that his naivety (while it could invite either the hope of immunity or severity of punishment) on past evidence could in course of time easily let loose contagion; on that account – notwithstanding that, as we have learned from favourable and trustworthy testimony, the sincerity of his penitence and the merits of his life in other respects speak abundantly in his favour – we have, as seemed necessary, banned him from the office of preaching, hearing confessions (except of people at the point of death), and of absolving and enjoining healthful penance.

And therefore, in our desire that the ways of truth should be made known to the faithful, and no entry permitted to the errors of heretical depravity, lest they should lead to the subversion of morals, strongly requiring you in virtue of your obedience, we order that, standing before the people in every church of our city of York, during the rites of the mass, publicly revealing and explaining the foregoing with great eloquence in the vulgar and maternal tongue to each and every one of our subjects, you should on our behalf strictly forbid them (or see to it that they are forbidden) to attend to the preaching of the said brother Henry, if they should hear him preaching; nor to follow him in future as if he were a teacher or preacher of the truth since, by reason of the aforesaid process, we have removed the capacity to preach from him; nor to confess their sins to him, since he is unable to give absolution; nor to ⌜hear⌝ or pay attention to him in such things, on pain of the greater excommunication, which we mean to pronounce against any who disregard or disobey ⌜this prohibition⌝, on this coming Sunday and the ⌜Sunday⌝ following, and on the intervening feast days.

And you shall let us know clearly and plainly what you have done about the foregoing by the feast of the Assumption of the Blessed Virgin Mary ⌜15 Aug.⌝, by letters patent containing an account of such actions. Farewell.

Given at Cawood,[14] nones of August ⌜5 Aug.⌝ AD 1334 and the 17th year of our pontificate.

14 Near Selby (N. Yorks.), principal residence of the archbishops of York.

60. The Lollard hermit, William Swinderby

One of the first places where the heretical ideas of John Wyclif took root, outside the University of Oxford where he had originally advanced them, was Leicester; and one of the key figures in their early dissemination was the charismatic hermit-preacher William Swinderby. He is first recorded there in 1382, the year that twenty-four propositions from Wyclif's writings were declared heretical, and several of the opinions attributed to him echo those propositions quite precisely. This account of Swinderby's activities in Leicester comes from the chronicle of Henry Knighton, a canon of the abbey there, and an important (if hostile) source for the early history of Wycliffism. After Swinderby had been forced to leave Coventry, Knighton has nothing more to say about him, but in other sources he turns up again in the early 1390s in the Welsh borders, where his preaching had once again brought him to the authorities' attention. He was again condemned as a heretic, and is last heard of in 1392, as a fugitive somewhere in Wales.[15]

Excerpts from *Knighton's Chronicle 1337–1396*, edited and translated by G.H. Martin (Oxford: Clarendon Press, 1995), extract from pp. 307–25. English text. By permission of Oxford University Press.

In those days also there was a priest in Leicester, William Swinderby, who was popularly known as William the hermit, because he had long followed the life of a hermit there. Where he came from, or what his origins were no one knew, but it was a remarkable business, because he proved to be of inconstant life and morals, having tried many styles of life, and he fidgeted from one to another, never finding one satisfactory to himself. On first coming to the town he lived ordinarily, mixing amongst other people. Then he began to preach, and began by denouncing the shortcomings of women, and their pride.

He greatly despised women's adornments, and he disdained their pride and their general behaviour, and detested their lewdness. And even when they behaved decently, he nevertheless treated the subject most unsuitably, for he had no notion of moderation, whether in preaching or in anything else. So much so in fact, that the women of the town, both the good and grave sort, and others, were moved to wrath by the

15 For what is known of Swinderby's life and career, see the entry by Anne Hudson in *ODNB*. The standard history of the Wycliffite movement is Anne Hudson's *The Premature Reformation: Wycliffite texts and Lollard history* (Oxford: Clarendon Press, 1988).

violence of his preaching and his denunciations, and they proposed to gather stones, and stone him out of the town.

Seeing, therefore, that such preaching did him no good, and far from gaining approval excited great discord, he abandoned the subject, and turned to address his sermons to merchants and the rich, often asserting that no one could enjoy riches in this world, and an abundance of material things, and still hope to enter the kingdom of heaven. And he so dwelt on the topic that some worthy men of the town, but for the workings of divine mercy, would have fallen into the error of despair.

Then he wished to exchange the common life for the solitary life, because again his preaching brought him no praise, and he asked the Duke [*sc.* John of Gaunt] for the hermitage in the woods, and lived there for a time, sometimes running into the town, and sometimes into the country. And when pious people in Leicester, believing in his sanctity, tried to send food to him, as was their wont, he would pretend to austerity, as though content with his lot in the world, and would refuse and return those offerings and gifts, and say that the little allowance which the Duke made to him sufficed for his needs.

For the lord Duke was glad to provide for him. But when he had spent some time there, and began to find that he had not bread enough in his wallet, his enthusiasm for such a life cooled from day to day, and he became disgusted with it, and yet could not for shame return to the town which he had left. …

[*Having tired of the hermit's vocation, Swinderby seeks 'a more seemly way of life' at Leicester Abbey, but before long he is on the move again, joining a Wycliffite group at the chapel of St John Baptist by the leper hospital in Leicester.*]

… The said William Swinderby, seeing that his usual style of preaching earned small thanks from the people, neither pleasing the laity nor secular clergy nor drawing many into his affinity, turned his preaching against the liberties of the Church, and the clergy, and he sought as much as he could, or could contrive, to denigrate churchmen and their reputation. …

[*The document then lists the 'Opinions of William the hermit'. They centre on the Wycliffite contention that a priest is a priest by virtue of his standing before God (and in the eyes of Wycliffites) rather than his ordination by a bishop; and that tithes should be withheld from any priests whose way of life should not match up to the ideal of priesthood.*]

... Preaching those and other errors and heresies, some of which will appear below, he attracted the approval of the crowd, and he so far gained their esteem that they said that no-one had ever been seen or heard to teach the truth like him, and he was revered by them as though he had been another god.

When such reports came to the ears of John Buckingham, the bishop of Lincoln, he immediately sent word suspending him from preaching in the said chapel, or in any other church or churchyard in the diocese. And he forbade the populace to listen to any such preaching, or to further it under pain of the greater excommunication, all which the bishop sent in letters, with instructions to publish them in various other churches.

However, there was a pair of millstones for sale, standing in the street outside the chapel, and William made his pulpit there, between the stones, and assembled the people, and preached there many times in defiance of the bishop, saying that he could and would preach in the king's highway, in spite of the bishop, for as long as he had the goodwill of the public.

Then would you have seen crowds of people from all parts, both from the town and the country, not only in greater numbers than usual, but even twice as many as when they had been free to listen to him, hastening to hear him preaching after that prohibition and sentence of excommunication, which had been pronounced both in the abbey and in many other churches. ...

[*Swinderby is summoned before the bishop and convicted of heresy. Gaunt intervenes on his behalf, and Swinderby is given the opportunity to renounce his errors. The document sets out the procedure to be followed, and the form of words Swinderby is to use in making his recantation. His heresies and errors are listed: again, they focus on the distinction between true and false priests.*]

... Those things done, the aforesaid William the hermit stayed in the said chapel in Leicester, sad and mournful, because those who, in the times when things went well with him, had seemed to be his friends, now left him desolate, neither visiting nor consoling him, nor making their customary gifts to him. For once he had ceased from preaching as he used to do, the people's clamour and enthusiasm for him began to cool, and from day to day they became colder towards him, and so he began to weary of his life.

Therefore within a short time he turned about, and fled covertly to the town of Coventry, where for a while he was held in greater honour by the laity than he had been before, preaching for about a year, and teaching as he had previously, and converting many to his execrable beliefs, until news of his fame and his evil seductions came to the notice of the bishop and clergy, and then he was driven forth from the diocese with ridicule and the greatest shame.

61. Amy Palmer, Lollard anchoress

The early 1390s saw an outbreak of Lollardy in Northampton. Although the then mayor was held to be a sympathiser, the centre of activity seems to have been the cell of the anchoress Amy (*Amia*) Palmer,[16] reputed as the principal *receptrix lollardorum* in the town, and clearly identified by the authorities as the ringleader of a network of heretics there. She and her circle denounced vicious priests, images and pilgrimage, and clerical property; they further claimed that any layperson could function as a priest, and that Christian worship was better undertaken privately ('in bedrooms or in the fields') rather than ostentatiously in a physical church building.[17] Some time after he had imprisoned her, the bishop was instructed to deliver Palmer to London, but (as so often with medieval sources) we do not know what became of her.

Translated from the Latin in *Royal Writs Addressed to John Buckingham, Bishop of Lincoln 1363–1398* edited by A.K. McHardy, Canterbury & York Society 86 (1997), no. 446 (pp. 140–1).

Return to chancery of writ of *venire faciatis*,[18] dated 26 March 1394

John [Buckingham] bishop of Lincoln to Richard II. We have recently received your writ by force of which we send to your royal majesty and your council in your chancery Amy Palmer, detained in our custody at Banbury, and earnestly setting forth the reason for the arrest of the same Amy and her detention in our aforesaid custody, as the terms of the aforesaid writ demand and require.

16 Earlier sources call her Anna, under which name she is included in the entry 'Lollard women' by Norman P. Tanner in *ODNB*.

17 The list of errors (not included here) is printed and discussed by A.K. McHardy, 'Bishop Buckingham and the Lollards of Lincoln Diocese' in *Schism, Heresy and Religious Protest* edited by Derek Baker, Studies in Church History 9 (1972), pp. 131–45. In contrast to most such documents of later date, there is no mention of the group's understanding of eucharistic doctrine, nor their attitude to the other sacraments.

18 *Venire faciatis ad respondendum*: essentially, a summons.

As thus: by popular noise and report it was recently brought to our notice that certain children of darkness, then dwelling in our vill or town of Northampton in our diocese, had been publicly holding errors, heresies, and other outrages repugnant to the Catholic faith and the determinations of holy Mother Church, and taught them to the people of the same town, in public streets and houses, both secretly and openly, as if damnably to pervert them for the greater part from the Catholic faith; whereupon, in order that the draft of their pestiferous poison should not spread further and infect the souls of Christ's faithful, and make them deviate from the paths of truth and orthodox faith by false words and feigned simplicity, we sent then by our letters patent in the first place our commissaries and then in the second place our venerable brother Sir William, by God's grace bishop 'Pisenensis',[19] our suffragan to the aforesaid town for the reformation of the aforementioned and the execution of our commands then to be carried out against certain persons in this regard, but these same commissaries of ours found themselves in so much danger there, in carrying out our commands in this manner, that with great difficulty for the saving of their lives they fled to the vestry of the church of All Saints in the aforesaid town.

On this account, and that their blood should not be required of our hands at the Last Judgement, we came down in person to the aforesaid town of Northampton to see whether the open clamour might be confirmed, and there, in the church of All Saints, the Thursday, Friday and Saturday before the feast of the Exaltation of the Holy Cross [14 Sept.] last past, made diligent general enquiry through the better and more worthy men of the aforesaid town and the surrounding region, by which enquiry we discovered that the aforementioned Amy Palmer, then an anchorite and enclosed in a certain house adjoining the church of St Peter in the aforesaid town, was the foremost harbourer of Lollards [*receptrix lollardorum*] in her house by night, and especially Thomas Patteshull, John Chory, Simon Colyn, John Wolf, John Wheelwright, chaplain, and Thomas Wheelwright, chaplain, the principal Lollards then dwelling in the aforesaid town; and that in her house they secretly held conventicles and illicit gatherings, and that the same Amy Palmer and the aforementioned Thomas Patteshull,

19 William Egmund (alias Ouneby), a regular suffragan in Lincoln and elsewhere. He is more often styled *prissinensis* though, as often with the names of suffragans' sees, it is not entirely clear where this bishopric was, or was imagined to be. See David M. Smith, 'Suffragan Bishops in the Medieval Diocese of Lincoln', *Lincolnshire History and Archaeology* 17 (1982): 17–27, pp. 20, 25.

John, Simon, John, John and Thomas openly and publicly held and taught the articles annexed to the present document. And after that the same Amy having been moreover detected in incontinence by our aforesaid enquiry, we ordered and caused her to be called to judgement before us to respond to the aforesaid articles and to the following articles annexed to the present document, but the same Amy appearing in person before us in judgement openly and publicly before a large multitude declared us to be the Antichrist and our clerks to be disciples of Antichrist, and the articles that follow having been recited one-by-one in the vernacular to the same Amy by our chancellor, the same Amy contumaciously and with a scornful expression said that she would not respond to those same articles, except for the accusation of incontinence, which she denied.

In consideration of the foregoing, holding the same Amy to be strongly suspected of heresies, errors and Lollard depravity, and due to her manifest contumacy displayed before us, and in order that she should not infect others of Christ's faithful, we ordered her, on account of the foregoing, to be imprisoned, and caused her to be detained in our prison at Banbury until such time as the same Amy should declare herself to be ready to return to the bosom of holy Mother Church.

Concerning all and everything of this, we send by the present document to your royal excellency our letters close sealed with our seal.

Lincoln, 27 April 1394.[20]

[*A list of articles or heretical propositions was appended.*]

62. A hermit of Cripplegate punished for making false claims

A hermit, as we have seen, could attract a following by his charismatic preaching, or by indulgences attached to his hermitage. But the former might be suspect (as Staunton's [**59**] and Swinderby's [**60**] were), and claims of the latter could be bogus. The authorities would be especially quick to act where parochial rights were being infringed. When, in 1311, the hermit of Cripplegate (London), Thomas de Byreford,[21] was found to have been hearing confessions, administering the sacraments, preaching, advertising indulgences, parading images of the saints

20 The register here has 1393, which is an error.

21 Although he was resident in the same district of London, there is no suggestion that Byreford occupied the royally endowed hermitage of St James, Cripplegate [**40**].

through the streets, receiving offerings and burying the dead, all without licence, the bishop responded in the strongest terms.

Translated from the Latin entry in *Registrum Radulphi Baldock, Gilberti Segrave, Ricardi Newport et Stephani Gravesend, Episcoporum Londoniensium, A.D. 1306–1338* edited by R.C. Fowler, Canterbury & York Society 7 (1911), pp. 141–2.

Against a hermit of Cripplegate

Ralph by [divine] permission etc. to the official of the archdeacon of London, greetings etc.

Whereas, a legal prosecution having lately been brought against Thomas de Byreford, who styles himself chaplain and hermit in the parish of St Olave in Mugwell by Cripplegate, he has made a judicial confession and been convicted (or held to be convicted) of the outrages detailed below – that is,

> that he has heard the confessions of our subjects and imposed penances on them, administered sacraments and sacramentals,[22] and publicly preached the same (in his own manner) and admitted these same subjects together with various others to the aforesaid [sacraments etc.] without any sufficient authority whatsoever, without having sought our consent or that of the rectors or others with cure of souls under us, and in doing so he has scorned the power of the keys,[23] and not feared miserably to endanger the souls of unfortunate people in the ways described above;
>
> and that the same Thomas has had it preached and advertised that those who visit his hermitage will be granted an indulgence of fifty days, when there is nothing to suggest that there is the slightest truth in such a grant;
>
> and that on St Loy's [Eligius, 25 June], St Dunstan's [19 May] and other saints' days, he would solemnly carry, or have carried, images of St Loy, St Dunstan, and other saints, around the public streets and profane places, attracting our subjects by giving money to them in order that, scorning their own mother churches, they might follow his processions and visit his hermitage, and thus withdraw their alms from their mother churches and offer them there instead;

22 Observances (such as the sprinkling of holy water) which may be categorised alongside, but are not in themselves numbered among, the seven sacraments.

23 The apostolic privilege of earthly jurisdiction first conferred by Christ on St Peter (Matt. 16:13), and by extension now inhering in the pope and the Catholic hierarchy.

> and that on the feast of the Purification of the Blessed Mary [2 Feb.] he gathered the people together, providing each one of them with candles and with money as a fee, and they, abandoning their own churches, paraded all around the public streets and profane places in his procession;
>
> and that he gave burial in his hermitage to a certain prior Theford, sometime monk of [Saffron] Walden, and that ten others were buried there, when he can have had no confidence concerning his right of such burials or choice of burials there –

and whereas for his part he advanced nothing reasonable in justification of his foregoing actions or any one of them, our commissaries and auditors general[24] by due process in this matter have by way of their sentence and determination pronounced the aforesaid Thomas the hermit to be guilty and in breach of the law in each and every one of the foregoing [articles], declaring that on account of the extreme temerity of his transgressions he should be punished according to canon law, and legally restrained so that he ceases from these transgressions in the future, with the penalty to be imposed upon him reserved to us and to those same auditors, according as it appears to us plainly from what has transpired before the said commissaries and the report they have made of it to us.

And so by strict command we entrust to you our order that you should warn and effectively coerce the said Thomas the hermit that he should make reparation for the foregoing transgressions to our church and the neighbouring parish churches and to other parties injured by the foregoing within fifteen days from the same warning as he is obliged to do; and issue a public injunction in each church in the vicinity of the said hermitage, and other places that seem expedient to you, to him and to each and every one of our subjects, that this T[homas] henceforth should not of his own temerity preach to our subjects, or accept them for confession or penitence, or sacraments or sacramentals, without particular licence from us or one of our parish priests, or attract or otherwise induce them away from their own churches to attend his hermitage for divine services or to make or go on processions with him, or to choose to be buried there; and that our subjects should not presume, against the precepts of canon law, to attend his preaching, or make their confessions, or unwisely receive their penance, sacraments or sacramentals from him, or go on his processions, or leave their own churches to attend his aforesaid hermitage for divine service.

24 The bishop's legal officers.

And if he or they refuse to submit to your warning as described above, then you shall cause this T[homas] and others who do not submit – whom, the canonical warnings having been given, we hereby excommunicate with immediate effect – to be publicly and solemnly denounced each day and in the most appropriate places as excommunicate.

You should be sure to give us an account of what you have done in this matter, together with the names of any who do not submit to the foregoing or to any article of the foregoing, along with the contents of these letters, before the feast of St Peter Ad Vincula [1 Aug.].

Given at Stepney,[25] 8 id. July [8 July], in the year of our Lord 1311.

63. A fraudulent hermit

Here is an early fifteenth-century example of the kind of 'lewd hermit' that William Langland [**36**] inveighs against: the able-bodied layabout who uses the hermit's habit as a cover for idleness and unprincipled scrounging. The man's extravagant claims for his pilgrimages, though not unheard-of for a hermit (see [**43**]), would have drawn attention to him, and raised the stakes in his fraud. The pillory was a punishment that aimed above all at public humiliation, although the time the criminal spent thus exposed was also painful and (where offended parties took the opportunity to seek revenge, or simply where mob mentality took over) could be dangerous; fatalities were not unknown. The whetstone also imposed on our false hermit was a symbol reserved especially for frauds and liars.[26]

Quoted from *Memorials of London and London Life in the 13th, 14th and 15th Centuries* edited by H.T. Riley (London: Corporation of London, 1868), p. 584.

Punishment of the Pillory and Whetstone, for pretending to be a Hermit

On the 20th day of July, in the 13th year etc. [1412], William Blakeney, shuttlemaker,[27] who pretended to be a hermit, was brought unto the

25 The manor of Stepney was one of the bishop of London's principal residences in the Middle Ages.

26 See C. David Benson, 'Piers Plowman as Poetic Pillory: The Pillory and the Cross' in *Medieval Literature and Historical Inquiry: Essays in honor of Derek Pearsall* edited by David Aers (Cambridge: D.S. Brewer, 2000), pp. 31–54.

27 A shuttle is the boat-shaped wooden instrument used in weaving to carry the thread of the weft.

Guildhall, before Robert Chichele, Mayor, the Aldermen, and Sheriffs, for that, whereas he was able to work for his food and raiment, he, the same William, went about there, barefooted and with long hair, under the guise of sanctity, and pretended to be a hermit, saying that he was such, and that he had made pilgrimage to Jerusalem, Rome, Venice, and the city of Seville, in Spain; and under colour of such falsehood he had and received many good things from divers persons, to the defrauding, and in manifest deceit, of all the people.

And he was asked how he would acquit himself thereof. Whereupon, he acknowledged that for the last six years he had lived by such lies, falsities, and deceits, so invented by him, to the defrauding of the people, under the colour of such feigned sanctity; and that he never was in the parts aforesaid; which was also found out by the Court. And therefore etc. it was adjudged that the said William should be put upon the pillory for three market-days, there to remain for one hour each day, the reason for the same being there proclaimed; and he was to have, in the meantime, a whetstone hung from his neck. And precept was given to the Sheriffs to do execution thereof.

64. Hermit, con-man and thief

Edward the Hermit was an alias of Robert Berkworth or Bekworth. In April 1402, he was accused of being a member of a gang of 'ambushers of highways', who had robbed two men of £10 on the road between London and Tottenham.[28] Presumably his hermit's garb had been a key component of the scam described in this incident that took place a few weeks earlier in East Sussex. We do not know the outcome of these investigations, or what became of the accused.

Quoted from the translation of the Latin in Musson, *Crime, Law and Society*, p. 98, with a few additions.

Inquisition held before Thomas Camoys, knight, Henry Huse, knight, John Tremayn, John Tauke, John Preston and Robert Oxenbridge justices of the peace of the lord king in the county of Sussex at Eastbourne on Wednesday in the week of Pentecost in the third year of the reign of King Henry IV [17 May 1402] on the oath of [*twelve named jurors*].

28 *Crime, Law and Society in the Later Middle Ages* edited by Anthony Musson with Edward Powell (Manchester: Manchester University Press, 2009), p. 94.

Who said on oath that Edward the Hermit plotting how he could rob Johanna lately wife of John Coggere by pretending to be a prophet on Friday the feast of St Matthias in the third year of the reign of King Henry IV [24 Feb. 1402] feloniously broke and entered the close and house of the same Johanna at Mayfield [East Sussex] speaking to the same Johanna these words: 'Unless divine grace and my intervention help you the whole house and all your goods and chattels will be consumed by fire and you will be blind before the third day of this coming May.'[29] The said Johanna fearing the said words asked him to help her in this matter. And the said Edward told the same Johanna, 'Collect all your goods and chattels before me as I am able to conjure away all malign spirits.' So Johanna by his command collected all her goods and chattels and thus by the said false machinations the said Johanna the day, year and place aforesaid was feloniously robbed of a bowl (worth 20s), six silver spoons (worth 12s), six gold rings (worth 20s), three pairs of beads of jet and amber with a silver gilt crucifix (worth 12s), two gowns with silver fastenings (worth 10s) and 6s in cash of the same Johanna found there and he is a common thief.

65. A hermitage of ill-repute in Chester

According to a medieval legend, Harold II did not die at Hastings; instead the last Anglo-Saxon king retired to live as a hermit in the chapel of St James, Chester.[30] More certainly, in the mid-fourteenth century John Spicer built himself a hermitage by the bridge over the River Dee in the town where (like the hermits in [**37**]) he worked on the road and collected pavage towards his support.[31] A century later, the hermitage seems to have fallen into less worthy hands.

(i) is translated from the Latin entry in the Chester sheriffs' book, Cheshire Archives and Local Studies ZSB 1, fol. 122r; (ii) is translated from the Latin of TNA CHES 2/129, m.1.

29 May 3 was one of the *dies mali*, or unlucky days, and so a plausible date for the coming catastrophe (my note).

30 The legend is recorded as current in the fourteenth century by the historian Ralph Higden: see *Polychronicon Ranulphi Higden monachi Cestrensis: Vol. 7* edited by Joseph Rawson Lumby, Rolls Series (London: Longman & Co., 1879), p. 245.

31 'Religious Houses: Introduction' in *A History of the County of Chester: Vol. 3* edited by B.E. Harris (London: Oxford University Press for the Institute of Historical Research, 1980), p. 127. The hermitage, much modified, and now a private house, is still extant: see https://historicengland.org.uk/listing/the-list/list-entry/1375947.

(i) *Item* the aforesaid jury on the Monday after the Translation of St Benedict in the 30th year of King Henry VI [17 July 1452] at Chester said that John Benet, hermit of St James, Chester, is a receiver of common criminals and maintains such miscreants in his lodgings etc., and that he keeps a common brothel within his aforesaid dwelling etc.; by continuation of[32] the aforesaid trespass up until the day of the taking of this inquiry, [against] the order made and proclaimed in the said city, etc.

(ii) Commission to enquire into the regimen, governance and conversation [*behaviour*] of a certain hermit in the hermitage of St James beyond the bridge in the city of Chester

The King [Henry VI] etc. to the mayor and sheriffs of the city of Chester, greetings.

Whereas by our letters patent we have recently ordained and constituted [by a bill in the English Exchequer][33] Ieuan ap Bleth ap Carewet to be the hermit in the hermitage of St James beyond the bridge in the aforesaid city which is of our foundation; furthermore, being moved by certain causes, and wishing to be notified and certified in all respects concerning the regimen, conversation and governance of the same hermit, we command you that you should carefully make enquiry, both by the oath of worthy and lawful men of your same bailiwick, and by all other ways and means which you may best know or be able to undertake, by which we may best have notice of the regimen, governance and conversation of the same hermit,

And without delay send the inquisition made clearly and openly in this way, to us in our Exchequer of Chester under your seals and the seals of those by whom it was done, along with this writ. Witness myself at Chester, the 16th day of February in the 34th year of our reign [1456].

32 A legal phrase used in cases of repeated trespass.

33 This phrase inserted above the line. The palatinate of Chester had its own Court of Exchequer.

VIII: DISSOLUTION

Introduction

In the mid-1520s Henry VIII began his attempts to have his marriage to Katherine of Aragon annulled, and set off the chain of events that would lead to his divorce and the English church's break with Rome. Around the same time, Elizabeth Barton, the 'Holy Maid of Kent', was beginning her visionary career. Her early trances and prophecies took place at the chapel of our Lady, Court at Street, in Aldington (Kent) and as increasing numbers of visitors (and income) were attracted to the chapel it was provided with a hermit-chaplain named William. Though Barton subsequently became a nun of Canterbury the hermit remained one of her confidants. Barton's notoriety increased in 1532 when she prophesied that, if Henry's divorce went ahead, he would die a villain's death. She was arrested in 1533 and she and five associates (but not William the hermit) were executed for treason in 1534.[1]

Another solitary was caught up in the affair. The Dominican Christopher Warener was an anchorite at Canterbury, and in 1533 was accused of having received Barton and one of her supporters at his reclusory. This he did not deny; as he says in his letter to Thomas Cromwell, he could hardly refuse to see them, since 'I am a prisoner'. But he never spoke with them 'in this cause they are troubled for', never saw Barton in a trance, and 'Against the King I never heard her say anything, except that and [*if*] the marriage went forward she thought it would turn to great trouble'. He signs off by suggesting reproachfully to Cromwell that 'You may learn more of the truth by the people of the world. It is to me a great hindrance of my contemplation that I should have in Almighty God.'[2]

Around the same time the Norwich anchoress Katherine Manne found herself dangerously close to the centre of doctrinal and political controversy [**73**]. But for most solitaries the events of the early 1530s will

1 For Elizabeth Barton, see the entry by Diane Watt in *ODNB*, and her *Secretaries of God: Women prophets in late medieval and early modern England* (Cambridge: D.S. Brewer, 1997), chapter 3.

2 *Letters and Papers, Henry VIII*, Vol. 6, p. 537.

have passed by without significant disturbance to their established way of life. As we have already seen, hermits and anchorites were still being professed [**6**], [**52d**] and they could still enjoy respect and financial support from the rest of society, up to and including the king himself [**44**], [**45**]. Indeed, the solitary lives in England were not actually abolished during the Reformation. Neither of the acts of parliament that accomplished Henry VIII's dissolution of the monasteries mentioned hermits or anchorites by name, though it is doubtful that their omission can have reflected any positive desire to see the vocations continue. The Dissolution occupied Henry VIII and his chief minister, Thomas Cromwell, for much of the second half of the 1530s. The process began with a valuation of monastic property in 1534–5, and in 1536 the smaller monasteries were dissolved by act of parliament. It is not clear whether Henry meant from the first to extinguish monastic life in England altogether, but by the late 1530s this was clearly the intention. The dissolution of the larger houses was achieved by a series of 'voluntary' surrenders, extracted from monastic superiors by a combination of blackmail, intimidation, and bowing to the inevitable. Cromwell appointed local commissioners to tour their districts receiving signed documents of surrender and compiling inventories of assets. In a few cases Cromwell's agents came across solitaries and, as we will see below, they did not always know what to do with them [**67a**].

Henry's Dissolution is sometimes characterised as an opportunistic landgrab, and in this respect contrasted with the reforms of the committed protestant Edward VI. The 1547 Chantries Act opened with a clear statement of its doctrinal basis, declaring that

> a great part of the superstition and errors in the Christian religion hath been brought into the minds and estimation of men by reason of the ignorance of their very true and perfect salvation through the death of Jesus Christ and by devising and phantasying vain opinions of purgatory and masses satisfactory to be done for them which be departed, the which doctrine and vain opinion by nothing more is maintained and upholden than by the abuse of trentals, chauntries and other provisions made for the continuance of the said blindness and ignorance.[3]

Once again, there is no mention of hermits or anchorites, but the act's effect was to close down over two thousand chapels, most of them founded as chantry chapels, but including a significant number of rural

3 The Chantries Act is included in *English Historical Documents V: 1485–1588* edited by C.H. Williams (London: Eyre & Spottiswoode, 1967), pp. 775–7.

chapels of ease and those other miscellaneous small chapels that had dotted the late medieval landscape. They were the sort of places where one might expect to find a hermit,[4] but in the decade since the dissolution of the monasteries there had doubtless been some significant attrition, and the records of the chantry commissioners make melancholy reading [**69**]. Whatever the precise legal situation, it had become clear enough that solitaries would have no place in the new religious dispensation. Here and there, taking on perhaps the eremitic persona of the 'voice crying in the wilderness', they became the source or focus for expressions of dissent [**66**], [**68**], but for the most part, it seems, they just fizzled out.

So what happened to solitaries in the wake of the dissolutions? Those who had been formally removed from their cells or chapels at least had the compensation of a pension, which they could put towards their support in secular life [**67**]. But those who had survived the process of dissolution faced a dilemma. Should they attempt to continue with their chosen form of life, or bow to the pressures of the time, and leave of their own volition? For hermits, the jibe had always been that their manner of living was almost indistinguishable from normal secular life [**36**], and those who were prepared to keep their heads down could sometimes melt back into quiet obscurity [**71**].[5] Anchorites, with their vocation of total dependence, faced a more pressing decision. Even if they decided to continue, would popular support still be forthcoming? In Norwich, where some of the nuns of Carrow Priory retired to a private house in the city in order to continue a version of community life together, at least two former anchoresses likewise maintained some sort of religious vocation for a decade after the dissolution [**72**], [**73**]. But the majority, whether reluctantly or with quiet relief, must simply have returned, like Thomas Parkinson [**74**], to secular life.

Although, during her brief reign (1553–58), the Roman Catholic Mary Tudor restored a handful of the monasteries, no attempt was made to resurrect the solitary lives in England. Parkinson's account of his attempt to return to his former life in the 1550s [**74**] is a sorry tale in which official enthusiasm for a rekindled solitary vocation is conspicuous by its absence. The Protestant martyrologist John Foxe

4 For detailed discussion of another example, see my 'Canons and Hermits: The chapel of St Simon and St Jude, Coverdale', *Yorkshire Archaeological Journal* 76 (2004): 153–69.

5 See also [**45**], where a hermit was able to continue his service to the community after the dissolution much as he had done before it.

includes Parkinson's example in order to illustrate the 'great and terrible scourge of persecution' under Mary. No rank of society was exempt, he says: 'In so much that, coming to the lowest of all, a poor hermit – there being only one then as I think in the whole realm – could not come into their hands without open penance and other molestations, as in the story here following to the reader may appear.' But in truth Parkinson seems to have suffered at the hands of both Catholic and Protestant authorities, in a narrative that elicits, more than any anti-papal outrage, sympathy for the unfortunate and often apparently bewildered hermit. Instead, by the second half of the century, hermits and anchorites had already taken their place among the curiosities of a bygone age. Henceforward they would feature not in the historical record but in the pages of the new breed of English antiquarians [**75**], [**76**], the mistily imagined Middle Ages of the poets (from Spenser's *Faerie Queene*, by way of Milton's *Il Penseroso*, to the novels of Walter Scott), or the Gothic fancies of eighteenth-century landscape gardening.[6]

66. A supporter of Queen Katherine

In 1535, the year after the execution of the Maid of Kent, and two years on from the royal divorce, a Bristol hermit visited Katherine of Aragon at Kimbolton castle in Lincolnshire, where she was kept following the divorce. He returned pronouncing her still morally the queen of England (if that is what his phrase 'Queen of Fortune' may be taken to mean) and suggesting that she enjoyed a level of popular support that could see the king overthrown. The statements are at least as treasonable as Elizabeth Barton's but, though when last we hear of him he is in gaol, we do not know the hermit's ultimate fate.

(i) is modernised from the English of TNA SP 1/93, fol. 12r; (ii) is modernised from the English of TNA SP 1/95, fol. 151r.[7]

(i) Depositions before Roger Coke, mayor of Bristol
The 2nd day of June in the 27th year of King Henry VIII [1535]

6 Gordon Campbell, *The Hermit in the Garden: From imperial Rome to ornamental gnome* (Oxford: Oxford University Press, 2013).

7 There are summaries of the two documents in *Letters and Papers, Henry VIII*, Vol. 8, p. 308, and *Letters and Papers, Henry VIII*, Vol. 9, p. 48.

Henry Roche, leather-worker[8] of Bristol, of 40 years or thereabouts, sworn and examined with his right hand touched [*placed*] upon the holy Evangelists of God, said and deposed before Roger Coke, mayor of the aforesaid Bristol, John Shipman, John Hinton, Richard Abyngdon, Clement Bays and William Chipman, late mayors of the same town, at the mayor's court or place of the common audience of the same town, that he was personally present at the house of William Jonys, leather-worker, set [*situated*] in Lewins Mead[9] of the aforesaid Bristol, about the hour of one o'clock in the afternoon of the same day, where and when one Hugh Lathbury, hermit, in the presence as well of this deponent as of Thomas Stokbridge and the same William Jonys, that he, the same hermit, was lately in Lincolnshire with Katheryn the Queen of Fortune, and that she would make 10 men against the king's one.

The aforenamed Thomas Stokbridge and William Jonys deposeth in everything as the same Henry Roche hath said and deposed etc.

Moreover, the said Lathbury being present the day and year above-written before the said mayor and the other late mayors above-said at the mayor's court above-specified, said that he was late with Katheryn, late Queen of Fortune, and further said that he trusteth that she shall be hereafter queen again.

(ii) Roger Coke, mayor of Bristol, to Thomas Cromwell

Right honourable: pleaseth your discreet worship to be advertised that one Henry Roche, named in a schedule herein enclosed concerning his deposition, and others as in the same schedule more plainly is contained, came before me Roger Coke, mayor of this the king's town of Bristol and other late mayors of the same town; which deposed in everything [*in every respect*] as is comprised within the said schedule. And furthermore, one Hugh Lathbury, hermit, named in the said schedule, said before me and other late mayors aforementioned in everything as by the same schedule appeareth. Whereupon I, the said mayor, have commanded the said Lathbury unto the king's castle of Newgate in Bristol aforesaid,[10] there to remain under sure and safe

8 Roche is described as a *whitawer*. The editors of the *State Papers* interpreted this as 'widower', but the word designates people involved in the production of whitleather, a soft, pale-coloured leather.

9 An area of Bristol just outside the medieval city walls.

10 Newgate, part of the castle, served as Bristol's gaol up until the early nineteenth century.

custody until the king's most high pleasure and yours shall be known in this behalf [*in this regard*]. And the Blessed Trinity preserve your honourable worship to your heart's desire, for which I and all this town are bound to pray.

From Bristol, the 3rd day of June.

-- Which letter I sent unto your honourable worship accordingly, but for as much as by chance the same letter came not unto your hands (as I have perceived), therefore now I send unto your said worship the tenor of the said letter newly written, beseeching your said worship to have at me no displeasure in this behalf, for I am and always have been ready to observe the king's high commandment and yours, and that knoweth God – who ever preserve your said honourable worship.

From Bristol aforesaid, the 23rd day of August.

By me, Roger Coke, mayor.

67. The dissolution of the monasteries

Cromwell's correspondents in these two letters were leading figures in the process of dissolution. Their job was to visit all the religious houses remaining in the areas assigned to them, and to receive their documents of 'release' or surrender. A priority was to survey the houses' fixed and movable property, and to estimate its value; they were also on the look-out for any recent attempts to cash in on property or to sequester it out of the king's reach.

67a. The fate of an Oxford anchorite

John London was Warden of New College, Oxford, and (though in other matters of religion he was broadly conservative) became the government's principal agent in the dissolution of the monasteries in Oxford, Reading, and the neighbouring counties of Warwickshire and Northamptonshire.

Excerpted and modernised from the English original in Henry Ellis, ed., *Original Letters illustrative of English History, including numerous royal letters, from autographs in the British Museum … and one or two other collections*, 3rd ser. (4 vols, London: Richard Bentley, 1846),vol. 3, pp. 214–220 (corrected against the manuscript, TNA SP 1/134, fol. 114r). Calendared in *Letters and Papers, Henry VIII*, vol. 13 part 1, pp. 499–500.

(i) [Dr London to Cromwell, 1538]
In my most humble manner I have me commended unto your good lordship with my assured prayer and service during my life. It may like you to be advertised that Mr Mayor, the master, aldermen and I have been, according to the king's grace's commission, at all the places of the friars in Oxford, and for as much as we be in doubt of many things, we thought good to know your lordship's pleasure ere we went any further; and I shall express in order what hitherto we have done.

At Mr Pye's coming home, Mr Mayor and Mr Fryer were at London, and for as much as we doubted of their speedy coming home, and Mr Pye and I were credibly informed that it was time to be doing among the friars, we went to every place of them and took such a view and stay among them as the time would permit, till Mr Mayor came home with Mr Fryer. And first went to the White Friars. There they have lately sold to the abbot of Eynsham an annuity of £3, which came out of the same house of Eynsham, and received but £40 for it, which they have divided among them, and were ready to sell another annuity of £4, paid to them by the abbot of Westminster. They have but little ground belonging to them, yet they have let it out for 30 years, and had bargained for [*agreed the sale of*] such elms as grow about the house, and some were delivered. We have stayed the rest. Two shrewd husbands [*crafty managers*], priors there, have sold in manner all their jewels and plate; such as is left is comprised in a bill. They have nice[11] ornaments, as copes and vestments. All the goods of the house beside is not worth £5. The prior has been abroad since before Whitsuntide and will be home this week, as they say. In the mean time all thing is made safe there. …

The Blackfriars have to the rear likewise diverse land well-wooded, and contain in length a great ground. Their choir was lately new built and covered with lead. It is likewise a big house and all covered with slate save for the choir. They have a nice store of plate and jewels, and especially there is a good chalice of gold set with stones, and is better than 100 marks; and there is also a good cross, with other things contained in the bill. Their ornaments are old and of small value. They have a very fair conduit,[12] and it runs fresh. There are only 10 friars, being priests, beside the anker [*anchorite*] who is a well-disposed man, and have 50 marks yearly of the king's coffers. …

11 The word used is *pretty*, which in the sixteenth century had a similarly wide range of broadly positive meanings as *nice* does today.

12 That is, a water supply.

Item: as we have sent up all the names of such as have made submission, if your lordship will accept it, then that with speed we may have their capacities,[13] for the longer they tarry the more they will waste.

Item: to have your pleasure how you will have the goods kept when they have their capacities.

Item: to know your pleasure concerning the anker [*anchorite*] of that house come into the king's hands, whether he shall remain there or not. He built the house out of the ground and would fain end his life there if it be the king's grace's pleasure and your lordship's.

Item: what rewards every friar shall have with them at their departing.

Item: whether we shall require of my lord of Eynsham such muniments [*documentation*] as he had of the White Friars concerning the said annuity of £3.

Our Lord save your good lordship with increase of much honour.

Oxford, 8 July.

Your most bound orator [*obliged petitioner*], John London.

(ii) Postscript

On 31 Aug. 1538, Dr London reported that all members of the Oxford Blackfriars had surrendered their habits and asked for capacities, and enclosed a list of their names. The anchorite is included in the list, and named as William Dingle.[14]

67b. A troublesome anchoress at Worcester

Richard Ingworth had been prior provincial of the Dominican order in England before he was appointed suffragan bishop of Dover in 1537. He took the leading role in the dissolution of the houses of friars, including those of his own order, and also of the monasteries in the West of England.

Excerpted and modernised from the English original in Ellis, *Original Letters*, vol. 3, pp. 189–92. Calendared in *Letters and Papers, Henry VIII*, vol. 13 part 2, p. 16.

13 A 'capacity' was a licence to take up a new career as a secular priest.

14 See *Letters and Papers, Henry VIII*, Vol. 13, part 2, p. 92.

[Richard bishop of Dover to Cromwell, 1538]

My singular good lord, may it please your good lordship that since I last wrote to you from Gloucester I have received into the king's hands two convents of Worcester and one in Bridgenorth, and one in Atherstone, and now I am in Lichfield. Of the release of the two convents in Worcester, my lord [bishop] of Worcester had it to bring to your lordship. The copies of the inventory, I send to you here. The release of Bridgenorth I send here to your lordship, and the copy of the inventory.

Diverse of the friars are very loth to forsake their houses, and yet they be not able to live, for I think, for the more part of them, if all their debts should be paid, all that is in their houses is not able to do it.

I am now in Lichfield, which is in that taking, and yet loth to give up.

Blackfriars in Worcester is a proper house without any lead, and may dispend by year in rotten houses above 20 nobles by year, but all is in decay. There was an ancress, with whom I had not a little business to have her grant to come out, but out she is. …

The copy of this inventory I send, meekly beseeching your lordship to be so good lord to me to send to these friars their warrants to change their habits by this bringer. […] I ever your orator.

Your beadsman [*petitioner*] and servant

Richard [bishop] of Dover

68. An outspoken hermit of Chesterfield

Elizabeth Barton and the Bristol hermit Hugh Lathbury [**66**] spoke out over the king's divorce. In this document from 1538, things have moved on rapidly and the opposition to Henry has taken on a more clearly confessional aspect. This Chesterfield hermit rages against the royal supremacy, the dissolution of the monasteries and Protestant iconoclasm. Not surprisingly, the local justice sent him to Cromwell, who interrogated him and returned him to Derbyshire for trial. We do not know the outcome, but Cromwell's chillingly cordial covering letter leaves little room for doubt as to his expectation.

Modernised from the English originals transcribed by Heather Wolfe, 'Interrogating a Hermit', *The Collation*, 20 October 2011: http://collation.folger.edu/2011/10/interrogating-a-hermit (accessed 21 July 2015).[15]

15 (i) is also calendared in *Letters and Papers, Henry VIII*, vol. 13, part 1, p. 501. Ludlam is noted by Eamon Duffy, *The Stripping of the Altars: Traditional religion in England*

(i) Godfrey Foljambe[16] to Thomas Cromwell, 1538
Honourable and my good lord, I recommend myself unto your good lordship.

And so it is that, my lord bishop of Chester's suffragan and the chancellor of Lichfield being at Chesterfield the fifth day of July last past, one William Ludlam, hermit of St Thomas's chapel at the aforesaid Chesterfield, there spoke in a ranting manner ⌜*after a rage fashion*⌝ these words as follow:

> First he said, 'I was at Rome with Doctor Carne and Doctor Benet[17] being messengers for the king in his matter, and because the pope (now called the bishop of Rome) would not consent to the marriage of the king he was put out of his authority.'
>
> *Item* he said: 'If a man will pluck down or tear the king's arms he shall be hanged, drawn and quartered. What shall he do then that does pluck down churches and images, being but a mortal man as we be?'

with many other raging words, in the presence of Richard Martyn, registrar to the bishop of Chester; John Dyott, notary; Robert Sanforde and Thomas Tyder, servants of the chancellor of the aforesaid bishop; and Richard Rawson, servant of the aforesaid bishop; and Edward Crosse, servant to my lord suffragan; and George Asshe, Alan Crosselande, Hugh Cluworth, John Wodwarde, Richard Janson, John Worth and Ralph Assh of the town of Chesterfield.

And the bailiff of the said town under my lord steward[18] brought the said hermit unto me to be examined because I was the nearest justice, and so I examined him on the said words that were in the indenture that the said bailiff brought with him, and he denied every word and said he never spoke any of them. And then I caused the ⌜men⌝[19] of

1400–1580 (2nd ed., New Haven, CT: Yale University Press, 2005), p. 406. For comparable words against the king and his policies, see David Cressy, *Dangerous Talk: Scandalous, seditious and treasonable speech in pre-modern England* (Oxford: Oxford University Press, 2010), esp. chapter 3.

16 The Foljambes of Walton Hall were significant landowners in and around Chesterfield.

17 Edward Carne and William Benet spent the early 1530s in Rome engaged in arguments over the king's divorce from Katherine of Aragon.

18 George Talbot, 4th earl of Shrewsbury, lord steward of England, and lord of Chesterfield.

19 The letter is damaged here. Wolfe conjectures 'mayor', but given what follows 'men' seems more likely.

Chesterfield herebefore written to come before me, and I examined every one of them by himself, and they said he spoke the words before rehearsed, and many more, in a ranting manner, as in the said indenture is specified. And then I sent unto my lord steward to know his pleasure because it was within his town, and he was agreed (and so were we all) that his lordship should send his bailiff of Chesterfield, and I one of my servants, and the alderman of Chesterfield and his brethren should send a man, for them to bring the said hermit unto your lordship to do with him as it shall please the king's grace and his noble counsel.

And thus I beseech the Holy Trinity send your lordship good health and long life with much honour [to] long endure.

At Walton in Derbyshire, the 9th day of July.

Yours, Godfrey Foljambe, knight.

(ii) Cromwell to Shrewsbury
To my very good lord the earl of Shrewsbury, lord steward to the king's Majesty.

After my right hearty commendations to your lordship. I have by this bearer, your servant, bailiff of Chesterfield, received your letters and the bill therein enclosed concerning the hermit. The which, being by me examined, answered that he could not tell whether he ever spoke the same traitorous words or not. Therefore I have caused an indictment to be drawn up, which your lordship shall receive herewith; and also I have thought it appropriate to return the said hermit unto you there again, to be tried before the justices of assize and, to the example of all other, to be punished according to right and the king's laws.

I thank ever more your lordship for your good zeal, diligence and dexterity in repressing and apprehending such pernicious and detestable felons, and thereof I shall not fail to make true report to his highness who, I am assure[d], shall take the same in most thankful part.

Thus I beseech our holy Creator to send you prosperity and long life.

From Chelsea, this 13th of July.[20]

Your lordship's assured,

Thomas Cromwell.

20 Notwithstanding Cromwell's best wishes, Shrewsbury died 26 July 1538.

69. The dissolution of the chantries

The process of dissolving the chantries was accomplished during 1548. A selection of local men and officials of the Court of Augmentations were commissioned to enquire into the history and purpose of all the chantries and similar foundations in their county, and to produce an inventory of their endowments and possessions. They sent questionnaires to the various parishes, and compiled the responses into a 'chantry certificate', which was returned to the Court of Augmentations.[21] Some were thriving establishments, some had fallen into disrepair, and some (even if not founded for that purpose) now housed a hermit.

69a. A deserted hermitage

The parish of Batheaston with St Catherine's lies by the River Avon near the city of Bath, and was centred on a grange and monastic retreat belonging to Bath Abbey. Horteley was probably the kind of isolated rural chapel that was often looked after by a hermit. (The present Hartley Farmhouse may mark its location.)

Modernised from the English in *The Survey and Rental of the Chantries, Colleges and Free Chapels ... in the County of Somerset* edited by Emanuel Green, Somerset Record Society 2 (1888), pp. 151–2.

Batheaston [Somerset] with the chapel of [St] Catherine annexed

The chapel situate in Horteley [Hartley] within the said parish

The rent of the same chapel wherein a hermit sometime dwelled and now in the occupying of William Lewys, ... 2s 8d.

The same William Lewys hath occupied the said chapel or hermitage by the space of 12 years last past without anything paying therefore.

69b. A deserted reclusory

The church of St Mary and St Cuthbert in the town of Chester-le-Street has a long and illustrious history. In the ninth and tenth centuries it was home to the relics of St Cuthbert and the see of the bishop of Lindisfarne. (Both relocated to Durham in 995.) An anchorite is recorded here first in the late fourteenth century. The 'anker's house' (though remodelled) is still extant and open to visitors: www.mary

21 A good account of the process of dissolution is given by C.J. Kitching in *London and Middlesex Chantry Certificate 1548*, London Record Society 16 (1980).

andcuthbert.org.uk/parish-church-/ankers-house/ (accessed 22 June 2018).

Modernised from the English with added Latin in *The injunctions and other ecclesiastical proceedings of Richard Barnes, Bishop of Durham from 1575 to 1587* edited by James Raine, Surtees Society 22 (1850), appendix vi, p. lxiv.

Chester in the Street [Co. Durham]

…

The Anker's house. Incumbent none. Lead in covering the said house about 14 square yards of webs [*lead sheeting*], *in weight*, according to the rate aforesaid, 1 quarter [of a ton].

69c. The former hermit of Tadcaster

Tadcaster is a market town about half-way between Leeds and York. In February 1548 the commissioners reported chantries of St John Baptist, St Nicholas, and St Katherine, in the parish church; there were a further three chantries in the chapel of ease at Hazlewood Castle three miles away. All these chantries were still active, though the chantry priest of St John in the parish church was unlearned and suffering from gout. They also noted the hermitage, where the situation was altogether more pathetic.

Quoted from the translation in *The Certificates of the Commissioners Appointed to Survey the Chantries, Guilds, Hospitals, etc. in the County of York*, Vol. 2 edited by William Page, Surtees Society 92 (1892), p. 375.

Tadcaster [N. Yorks.]

There is a chapel in the said parish, covered with stone, which in time past has been a hermitage, wherein a poor impotent man, sometime the hermit thereof, dwells, not able to pay the rent. Which chapel with its appurtenances is worth a yearly rent of 6s 8d, as it appears by the rental.

70. From hermit to parish priest

Around 1533 the hermit John Steward witnessed the will of William Tailer, chantry priest in the church of Our Lady, Sandwich (Kent). That he was styled Sir (*Dom*) John suggests that (somewhat unusually for a hermit) he too was ordained. Tailer was succeeded in the chantry by a certain John Deyos, but when he in turn died in 1539 he was succeeded by the one-time hermit John Steward. The chantry was closed down in 1548 but, though the commissioners were rather faint in their praise of his qualities, Steward was able to continue a clerical career. Pensioned in June 1548, he became rector of Ham in 1550, was vicar of St Mary's by 1555, and became rector of Old Romney in 1560. He was dead by 1565.[22]

William Tailer's will (i) is modernised from the English (and the brief note of probate at the end translated from the Latin) in Kent Archives and Local History Service DCb/PRC17/20/30; the entry from the chantry certificate (ii) is modernised from the English in *Kent Chantries*, edited by Arthur Hussey, Kent Archaeological Society 12 (1936), pp. 261–2.

(i) Will of William Tailer

In the name of God, Amen. I Sir William Tailer, chantry priest of the church of our Lady in Sandwich, being in good mind and perfect memory, make my testament and last will in this manner.

First I bequeath my soul into the hands of almighty God and to our blessed Lady St Mary, and my body to be buried within our Lady's chapel within the aforesaid church of our Lady. *Item* I bequeath 4 marks for a vestment to be made for the altar of the said chapel. *Item* to Sir John Castelyn of Chilham I bequeath my best gown. *Item* I bequeath to Agnes Tayler of the parish of St Peter in Canterbury for her keeping of me in my sickness 6s 8d. *Item* I bequeath to Robert my child and to Hubbard at Master Hungerford's 13s 4d. *Item* I give to Sir John the hermit my third gown. *Item* I give to Sir John Crofte, parish priest, my second gown. *Item* I give to William Spert(?) my scholar one of my short gowns. *Item* I give to Robert my child a featherbed, a bolster, a carpet, a coverlet and a pair of sheets. *Item* I give to the aforesaid Agnes Tayler my red mantle.

Also I make, ordain and constitute executors of this my present testament Thomas Manhode the elder and Robert Tayler.

The above-written testament was proved on the 27th October AD 1533 by the oath of Sir John Meryman, vicar there, and Sir John Steward, hermit, witnesses. And it was approved etc. And the burden of ⌜executing⌝ the same was committed to the aforesaid Thomas Manhode the executor named above, he having first been sworn in form of law.

22 For details of John Steward's later career, see *The Clergy of the Church of England Database* (www.theclergydatabase.org.uk).

(ii) Chantry Certificate, 1548
The parish of our Lady in the town of Sandwich

The chantry called Cundy's Chantry within the said parish church of our Lady in Sandwich, founded by one John Cundy with the intent that one priest should celebrate divine service there, and pray for the souls of the said John Cundy, his father and his mother, and all Christian souls for ever.

The yearly value of the lands and possessions of the same chantry: £9 7s 4d, of which

in 'rent resolute'[23] 11s 2½d.

perpetual tenth 18s 9d.

and so there remains clear to the chantry priest yearly £7 17s 4½d.

John Steward is now incumbent and chantry priest there, of the age of 40 years, indifferently learned and of honest qualities and behaviour [*conversation*], and [he] has not any other living besides the same chantry.

There is a vicar already endowed within the parish church there, and there is 280 housling people [*communicants*] within the same parish.

71. John Glass, hermit of Hensington

The manor of Hensington near Woodstock, a few miles north of Oxford, had been granted to the Knights Templar in the twelfth century. The crusading order had rich holdings in Oxfordshire. After the suppression of the Templars in 1312 their property passed to the Knights Hospitaller, who held it until the Dissolution. In 1546 Hensington was sold to a pair of speculators, Robert Tyrwhitt and Thomas Kydall. Among the Hospitallers' long-standing tenants in Hensington had been a hermit, John Glass. He outlasted his landlords, still occupying his chapel and garden at the time of the sale, though, perhaps prudently, he was no longer styling himself 'hermit'.[24]

23 That is, Crown rents from lands formerly in the possession of now dissolved religious bodies.

24 For the manor of Hensington, see *A History of the County of Oxford: Volume 12, Wootton Hundred (South) Including Woodstock*, edited by Alan Crossley (London: Oxford University Press for the Institute of Historical Research, 1990), pp. 20–2. For Glass, see also my 'The Hermits and Anchorites of Oxfordshire', *Oxoniensia* 63 (1998): 51–77, p. 67.

(i) is translated from a Latin rental of Templar lands at Sandford and Littlemore belonging to the preceptory of Sandford, dated 14 February 1512: Corpus Christi College, Oxford, MS 320, fol. 24r. (ii) is quoted from Edward Marshall, *The early history of Woodstock manor and its environs, in Bladon, Hensington, New Woodstock, Blenheim: with later notices* (Oxford: James Parker & Co., 1873), pp. 43–4.

(i) Rental [1512]
Balscote within the parish of Wroxton

...

Hensington

Customary lands there

First, John Glase, hermit, holds of the lord a chapel of St John and a garden with its appurtenances, and a stone quarry for *le Walling*, for an annual rent of 3s 4d. And the quarry is presently leased to John Bagott with the consent of the said hermit.

(ii) Particulars of sale to Sir Robert Tyrwhitt and Thomas Kiddall, 1546
Parcel of the lands and possessions of the late Priory or Hospital of St John of Jerusalem in England.

...

The Manor of Hensyngton, lying in the parishes of Bladon and Shipton-on-Cherwell in the county of Oxon., parcel of the late Preceptory of Sampfford, in the same county is worth in:–

Rent of a certain chapel of St John, and of a garden with its appurtenances therein demised to John Glasse by copy of Court Rolls: Rendering therefrom yearly … 2s 0d.

72. Will of Thomas Waterman, 1546

Thomas Waterman had been rector of All Saints Ber Street in Norwich since 1530.[25] The last rector to have been presented by the living's medieval patron, the Benedictine priory of Carrow, he was clearly an adherent of the old religion. He left his soul not only to God but to the Virgin

25 Francis Blomefield, *An essay towards a topographical history of Norfolk* (4 vols, London: W. Miller, 1805), Vol. 4, pp. 130–1.

Mary as well, and made ample provision for masses for his soul – though he recognised that the political changes going on around him might prevent them from being said. His beneficiaries included Cicely Suffield, the former prioress of Carrow. After the priory's dissolution in 1536, she shared a house in St Peter Hungate with three of her former nuns, including Agnes Swanton, formerly the sacrist, and Joan Bond, both of whom were also remembered by Waterman.[26] He also made bequests to two former anchoresses: Margaret Kydman, last in a long line of anchorites attached to Carrow Priory,[27] and the unnamed occupant of the cell at St Julian's Conisford where, half a century earlier, the mystic Julian of Norwich had lived. His description of the latter anchorite, which refers to her chastity and locates her still at St Julian's, suggests that (like the former Carrow nuns) she was doing her best to maintain her vows and form of living, despite the Dissolution. The anchoress at St Julian's Conisford in 1524 was Agnes Edryge,[28] but whether she is the same woman remembered by Waterman is unknown.[29]

Modernised from the English in Norfolk Record Office, Norwich Consistory Court Will Register Wymer, 75–7.

In the name of God. Amen. The 21 day of July in the year of our Lord God 1546 I, Thomas Waterman, priest and parson of the church of All Saints in Ber Street and of the chapel of St Katherine in Norwich, being whole of mind and good remembrance (thanks be to God) ordain and make this my present testament and last will in this manner and form following.

First, I bequeath my soul to God Almighty and to our Blessed Lady and to all the company of heaven; and my body to be buried in the church of All Saints aforesaid, before the going up to the spindle-beam[30] in the south side of the church aforesaid.

26 For the post-Dissolution community around Cicely Suffield, see Marilyn Oliva, *The Convent and the Community in Late Medieval England: Female monasteries in the diocese of Norwich, 1350–1540* (Woodbridge: Boydell Press, 1998), p. 202.

27 For Margaret Kydman, see Norman P. Tanner, *The Church in Late Medieval Norwich: 1370–1532* (Toronto: Pontifical Institute of Mediaeval Studies, 1984), pp. 60, 61.

28 Tanner, *Church in Late Medieval Norwich*, p. 200.

29 John Swayn left 12d to the anchoress of St Julian's in 1547: see F.I. Dunn, 'Hermits, Anchorites and Recluses: A study with reference to medieval Norwich' in *Julian and Her Norwich: Commemorative essays and handbook to the exhibition 'Revelations of Divine Love'* edited by Frank Dale Sayer (Norwich: Celebration Committee, 1973), pp. 18–26, p. 25.

30 Axle-tree, or cross.

In property I bequeath to the same church of All Saints my vestments with the alb and all that belongs thereto, & my book of Gradual psalms. Also I bequeath to the same church 2 altar cloths. Also I bequeath to Margery Trump my niece my tenement lying in All Saints aforesaid ... [*details of its location and descent, here omitted*] ... *Item* I bequeath to the said Margery my old chest with a tapestry cloth. *Item* I bequeath to the same Margery my covering of red cloth with all my pewter and brass and three candlesticks with a basin of pewter and my counterpane that stand in the chamber, and all the kerchiefs that were her mother's. ... [*more detail on the tenement*] ... *Item* I bequeath to Mrs[31] Cicely Suffelde one of my silver spoons. *Item* to Mrs Joan Bonde one silver spoon. *Item* to Agnes Swanton one silver spoon. *Item* I give to Parnell the wife of Thomas Davys of the same parish of All Saints one silver spoon. *Item* to Margery Trump my niece one silver spoon. *Item* to Sir Thomas Warner priest one silver spoon.

Item I give and bequeath to 20 curates, parsons, vicars and priests of the parishes in Norwich, to every[one] of them 6d, so [*provided*] that they will say *Dirige* and mass for me and my friends (as far as they may).

Item I bequeath to the chaste woman in St Julian's, sometime anchoress, 3s 4d. *Item* I bequeath to every householder dwelling within the said parish of All Saints, poor and rich, 8d. *Item* to the prisoners in the castle within Norwich 2s. *Item* to the prisoners in the guildhall in Norwich 16d. *Item* to every leper house belonging to the same city of Norwich, 6d. *Item* I will that there shall be dealt to the poor folk dwelling in the same parish at the feast of the birth of Christ next ensuing after my decease, one hundred faggots of wood, and so forth yearly at the same feast in like manner, the space of 3 years after, one hundred [faggots of] wood. *Item* I bequeath to the church of the Trinity in Norwich 16d.

Item I bequeath to Joan Bonde my kinswoman my best featherbed with a pair of my best sheets and my fustian blanket with 3 pillows and the transom[32] and one of my furred gowns. *Item* I bequeath to Sir Thomas Warner my gown of worsted and my clavichords. *Item* I give to Thomas Bonde of Gelston[33] my featherbed with the new ticking and the covering of tapestry work and a pair of sheets with a bolster and a pillow. *Item* I give to Thomas Bond's wife a gown. *Item* I give to my niece Margery the hangings of my house that were her mother's. ... [*further injunctions to executors*] ...

31 The title 'Mrs' is an indication of respect, not of marital status.

32 ?A bolster; or part of a bedstead answering the same purpose (*OED*).

33 Geldeston (Norfolk)

Item I will have dealt for me to the poor people at the day of my burial 40s in halfpenny bread. *Item* I give to Mrs Kydman sometime anchoress of Carrow 6s 8d. *Item* I bequeath to Mrs Cicely Suffelde a ring of gold with the five wounds. *Item* I give to Joan Bonde a gold ring with a diamond. *Item* I give to Joan Bonde, Margery Trump and to Thomas Bond's wife of Gelston, to every[one] of them, a cushion of tapestry work.

The residue of my goods not disposed I put them to the good disposition of my executors to do for me to the pleasure of God and comfort of my soul. ... [*appoints Thomas Warner, Thomas Davys and others his executors*].

The will was proved at Norwich 17 October 1547.

73. Katherine Manne, anchoress at Norwich

The Norwich anchoress Katherine Manne was more closely involved in the events of the English Reformation than any of the other individuals recorded in this section. She was a friend of the Cambridge evangelical Thomas Bilney, who was burnt as a relapsed heretic in 1531. He 'converted' her (as he did the Marian martyr Hugh Latimer), and gave her copies of early Protestant books. She was also the friend of a friend of the Catholic martyrs Thomas More and John Fisher. The Carthusian monk John Bouge wrote a supportive and affectionate letter to her in the aftermath of their execution for refusing to submit to the Act of Supremacy, offering some (partly coded) advice on how to avoid their fate. Just what Manne's doctrinal position was – or Bouge's, or even, to some extent, Bilney's – remains obscure; more than anything, their example shows the range and fluidity of positions possible in the early 1530s, before the Reformation battle-lines were firmly drawn. The anchoress survived the ensuing turmoil, and it was not until 1548, after the dissolution of the chantries [**69**], that she was removed from her cell. Even then, she was not summarily expelled, but bought out by the corporation of Norwich, which continued to recognise her as an independent woman or *femme sole* for the remainder of her life.[34]

34 For a full analysis of Manne and her milieu, see Mary C. Erler, *Women, Reading, and Piety in Late Medieval England* (Cambridge: Cambridge University Press, 2002), pp. 100–6. She is last recorded in 1555. A blocked squint in the north wall of Blackfriars Hall (formerly the chancel of the Dominican friary church) is likely to have been connected with her cell.

(i) is modernised from the English of John Foxe's *The Unabridged Acts and Monuments Online* or *TAMO* (1563 edition) (Sheffield: HRI Online Publications, 2011), Vol. 3, p. 534, from www.johnfoxe.org. (ii) is modernised from the English printed as an appendix to Vol. 4 of the edition of Foxe by George Townsend (8 vols, London: Seeley, Burnside & Seeley, 1843–49). The appendix is entitled 'Documents relating to Thomas Bilney, martyr'; its pages are unnumbered. (iii) is modernised from the English printed by James Gairdner, 'A Letter concerning Bishop Fisher and Sir Thomas More', *English Historical Review* 7 (1892): 712–15.[35] Latin quotations in the letter are translated and italicised. The entries in (iv) are modernised from the English texts in Dunn, 'Hermits, Anchorites and Recluses', pp. 25–6, except the entry dated 11 May, which is Norfolk Record Office, NCR Case 16c/2, fol. 244v.

(i) From Foxe's account of Thomas Bilney

At last Mr Bilney, taking his leave, in Trinity Hall [Cambridge] at 10 o'clock at night, of some of his friends, said he would 'go to Jerusalem' and so to see them no more.[36] And immediately he departed to Norfolk, and there preached first privately in households, to confirm the brothers and sisters, and also to confirm the anchoress, whom he converted to Christ. Then he preached openly in the fields, confessing his fact [*crime*] and preaching openly that thing which before he had abjured to be a very truth, and bade all men beware by him and never to trust to their fleshly friends in causes of religion.

And so setting forward in his journey towards the celestial Jerusalem he departed from thence to the anchoress in Norwich and there gave her a New Testament of Tyndale's translation and *The Obedience of a Christian Man*.[37] And forthwith he was apprehended and carried to prison, there to remain till the blind bishop Nix[38] sent for a writ to burn him.

(ii) Bilney's exoneration of Manne, according to Edward Rede, mayor of Norwich

These are the words opened and declared by Thomas Bilney at the place of his execution, called the Lollards' Pit without Bishopsgate of

35 Also in Elizabeth M. Nugent, ed., *The Thought and Culture of the English Renaissance: An anthology of Tudor prose, 1481–1555* (London: Cambridge University Press, 1956), pp. 547–9.

36 The allusion of course is to Christ's last journey to Jerusalem for the events of his Passion.

37 William Tyndale's translation of the New Testament was printed at Worms in 1526, and his polemical *Obedience of a Christian Man* at Antwerp, 1528.

38 Richard Nix, bishop of Norwich 1501–35, and a vigorous persecutor of heretics.

the city of Norwich, to the people gathered and present to see the same execution, as to the knowledge and remembrance of Edward Rede of Norwich, and as far as he could bear away: 'Good Christian people, I hear [people] say that the three orders of friars be put in blame for my death and that they should be the occasion thereof, and that the alms of the people are withdrawn from them because of my trouble. I exhort and pray you to be good to them and to extend your charitable alms to them, for it is not they that put me to death. And whereas that the lady anchoress of the Blackfriars is put in great trouble and surmised that she should be an heretic, and that I should teach and instruct her with heresies as well by books as otherwise, good Christian people here I take my death upon it that I do know her but for a full good and virtuous woman. I beseech God to preserve her in her goodness. And I know none heresy in her nor I never taught her heresy. I would to God there were many more so good living in virtue as she is, both men and women.'

(iii) A letter sent to Dame Katheryn Manne by Sir John Bouge
To my good lady and madam Dame Kateryn Man, from your lover and friend and father, Sir John Bouge. He dwells in the Charterhouse of Axholme beyond Hull.

Jesus, Mary. In the year of our Saviour 1535.

O devout madam and dear daughter in our Lord God. In the spirit of meekness and of all humility I have me commended unto you.

The cause of my writing to you at this time: one is to thank you for your token you sent by Sir Richard Huson – but I would have been more glad if you had sent me a little bill of 3 lines scribbled with your own hand, how and in what case you stand in, in this time of tribulation and calamity of this wretched world. The second cause of my writing is to thank you that you are at a due and true concordance [*reconciliation*] with my lover and old friend Sir R. Hewson – witness the gospel *Blessed are the peacemakers* [Matt. 5:9] – wherefore I have exhorted him, and now you, on both your parts, that there be perseverance and due continuance in the same. For if any person intend to please God in a good beginning, and if he ceases and is not perseverant unto the end, his body may have pleasure for a little while, but his soul shall be tormented in pains infernal. And to this holy purpose says St Augustine, 'Every man and woman as they are found at the hour of death when they depart out of this world, so they shall be rewarded in that state, either into pain or into glory.' [*Bouge then quotes in Latin the two passages attributed to Augustine on which the foregoing is based.*] These are great terrible sentences to be had in memory, in so much that holy St Jerome says, 'In all my actions, where that I eat or drink, or pray, or study, or in any other holy pastime, ever more my mind is on 4 things: first, that my days are short; 2nd, death draws near; the 3rd, my end is doubtable [*to be feared*] and doubtful; the 4th, my departing [will be] painful and my reward pain or joy.'

Now moreover another lesson is to you to be noted, and it is this: how to order yourself in this time of this great schism in the Church of God; how to honour our Lord God most principal to his pleasure, and what person next in degree. Of this matter I will not greatly entreat because I showed my good godson Sir Thomas Halle, well and properly learned, desiring to keep in mind these 2 articles: the first is the due understanding of this article *I believe in the holy Catholic church*; the 2nd, the 4th commandment, which is *Honour your father and mother, and honour your parents.* In these with their appurtenances I advise you, good daughter, soberly, devoutly and discreetly, pray to almighty God for grace and believe you to [*put your faith in*] discreet and taught fathers, as Mr Dr Boknam and Mr D. Warner my good friends and masters, for to answer in these foresaid articles.[39] It is my study night and day. If any man will reason with you 'What name of person take you next almighty God?', say no more but *I believe in the holy Catholic church.* I pray Jesus help and our Lady to worship all things that are admitted by our mother Holy Church, except other devout doctors passing my learning, *for the disciple is not greater than his master.* As a prisoner arraigned at the bar there, standing betwixt 2 judges having 2 naked swords, one of death of body for a little while, but the other is of life and death in pain everlasting. And this was the answer Mr More, knight, [gave] to Mr Cromwell when he came from the Tower toward his place of execution, this was his answer: 'I had rather put my life of body to suffer pain for a little season than my silly [*poor, humble*] soul to perish for ever, etc.'

[*Bouge recounts anecdotes concerning Thomas More and also John Fisher, executed with More earlier that year.*]

The residue of my purpose I shall write, partly in Sir Hewson's letter and a part in my godson's letter. And thus fare you well and pray for

39 William Buckenham and William Warner were Cambridge theologians with Norwich connections, who managed to tread the fine line between intellectual exploration and heterodoxy. Warner had been a close friend of Bilney.

us, me and my brethren, for as yet we live in fear and dread. There are but two ways: one for pleasure of body, and that is the common way of great peril, but the other for soul – that is the point.

(iv) Norwich civic records
Mayor's Court, 28 March 1548

This day it is agreed that Mistress Kathrine late anchoress etc. shall receive and have of the City during her life for her interest in the house late granted to her in the Blackfriars, 20s by year.

The 'Assembly' (or town council), 11 May 1548

A meeting held there on the Friday after the feast of the Lord's Ascension in the second year of the reign of King Edward VI.

...

Item It is agreed that Kateryn Man, late recluse in the house of the late Black Friars, shall have and receive of the goods of the community yearly by the hand of the Chamberlain and during her natural life, 20s. And the first payment thereof to be given at the feast of the Annunciation of our blessed Lady [25 March] last past, according to a grant thereof made to her by Mr Mayor and the aldermen the 28th day of March last past, the same Kateryn relinquishing to the community all such right as she had in the anchoress's house with its appurtenances.

Ibid., 28 March 1550

A meeting held there on the Friday after the feast of the Annunciation of the Blessed Virgin Mary in the fourth year of King Edward VI.

...

Item It is agreed and granted that Katheryn Manne, single woman, shall have free liberty to occupy within this city, so long as she shall keep her shop and be sole and unmarried.

74. Thomas Parkinson, England's last anchorite

John Foxe (1516/7–87) published the first edition of his *Actes and Monuments of these latter and perillous dayes, touching matters of the Church* in 1563. The work's full title gives an indication of its scope and tone: it 'comprehended and described the great persecutions & horrible troubles, that have been wrought and practised by the Romish prelates, specially in this realm of England and Scotland, from the year of our Lord a thousand, unto the time now present'. Despite its massive size (about 1800 pages in the first edition) the book was popular, and three further, enlarged, editions appeared in Foxe's lifetime. Despite its obvious bias, it is an important historical source for late medieval Lollardy and the reign of Queen Mary (1553–58). See also [**73**]. Though included in the first printing of *Acts and Monuments*, the story of Thomas Parkinson was omitted from subsequent editions.

Modernised from Foxe's English, in *The Acts and Monuments Online* (1563 edition), Vol. 5, pp. 1761–2.

The examination and trouble of Thomas Parkinson, a silly [*humble, pitiable*] poor hermit, driven to open penance by the papists

In the last year of Queen Mary, 1558, Thomas Parkinson, of the diocese of Coventry and Lichfield, being a member of the order of anchorites, was brought before Dr Draycot[40] on suspicion of having a wife. He was examined as follows.

Being asked what age he now is, he says that next Whitsuntide he shall be 70 years old, and was born and christened in a town called Bedale in Yorkshire, and was the son of one Thomas Parkinson, bailiff of Thirsk, in the same county of York. And when he was 12 years old he was set to the tailor's craft as an apprentice. After that, before he was 20 years old, he took for his wife one Agnes, the daughter of Hugh Hallywell, dwelling in the Liberty of Ripon, being a maid of 24 years, and was married to her in Thirsk by one Sir William Day, then curate there.

And within two years of their marriage, his wife was delivered of a male child which, though it moved and lived while it was in her body, as she and others felt, nevertheless after the birth it was dead, so that it could not be christened, with the result that the midwife and other women with her buried the said child (as they said) in the fields; but whereabouts the accused cannot tell.[41] And less than three weeks later, it chanced that a raven had got the said child out of the ground, and torn the clothes from around the said child, and had begun to rip up the said child to feed upon it, and had brought it into a tree near the

40 Anthony Draycot, chancellor of the diocese, and one of the villains of Foxe's book.

41 Unbaptised infants could not be buried in consecrated ground, though belief and practice on this point was subject to some fluidity during the Reformation period. See Madeleine Gray, 'Ritual Space and Ritual Burial in the Early Modern Christian Tradition' in *Faith of Our Fathers* edited by Joan Allen and Richard C. Allen (Newcastle-upon-Tyne: Cambridge Scholars Press, 2009), pp. 11–25.

cemetery of Thirsk church, on a Saturday, a little before Evensong. And when the people and the aforementioned priest saw the same child, they contrived to drive away the raven and to get the child from it. Then, reasoning amongst themselves whose child it should be, they judged that it was the accused's child, that was stillborn and buried in the fields. And the said William Day came to the accused's house and asked him for his child, and the accused revealed that the women had buried it in the fields; and the priest also examined the women on this point and found it to be true. And then he revealed to the accused the raven's bringing of the child. Whereupon the accused and his wife were straightaway stricken with repentance to God, and they each vowed thenceforth to live chaste and solitary lives. And as a result the accused, when he was but 22 or 23 years old, was professed in the order of St Francis at Richmond, five miles from Middleham, and was a hermit or penitentiary at Thirsk, and kept the chapel of St Giles at the end of the town of Thirsk. And his wife also was a sister of the Franciscan order, and obtained the place of a beadswoman [*almswoman*] at Northallerton by the help of Sir James Strangways, knight.

And after the accused had kept the order of St Francis two or three years, he determined to live a more hard and strict life, and to be an anchorite, and to seclude himself from the company of the world. And to that end he was first enclosed in a little house in the church porch at Thirsk, where he lived by the help of good people for two years, before he was professed. And when it was perceived that he liked that kind of life, and could endure the same, a chapel and a place was provided for him at Mount Grace, above the Charterhouse,[42] by Queen Katherine [of Aragon], and he was professed into that house by one Doctor Mackerel, then suffragan to Cardinal Wolsey.[43] And the suffragan had £5 from the accused's friends, for his profession. And the accused remained for 12 years and more in that house. And his wife would sometimes take one of his sisters and come over and see how the accused did, but she died 6 or 7 years before the accused came out of his house.

And after this came Dr Lee, and he pulled the accused out of his house, and the monks also out of the Charterhouse,[44] with the result that the accused was forced to venture forth to get his livelihood from good

42 See [**55**].

43 Matthew Mackerel, abbot of Barlings and titular bishop of Chalcedon. He was executed for his part in the 'Pilgrimage of Grace' in 1537.

44 Thomas Legh was one of the 'visitors' of monasteries in the province of York during the dissolution. Mount Grace surrendered in 1539.

people and, when he could get any work to get a penny, to take it. None the less, he kept his habit still. Then he went to London, and stayed there amongst his friends that had provided for him at Mount Grace. And thence he went to Lincolnshire, thinking to have the anchorite's house at Stamford, but it was not to be at that time. He was counselled by Sir John Harrington, then sheriff, to change his habit from the grey which he wore at that time to black, and so wandered from place to place in a black habit like a priest.

And at length, about 9 years past, he came into Shropshire, to Bridgnorth, and there by chance fell into acquaintance with one Elizabeth, who was the wife of one William Romney, a tinker, who died there. And because he had in these days both punishment and trouble for declaring himself a professed man to the order of authority, and it had been clearly shown him that it was against God's commandment that any man should make any such vow, he therefore, partly persuaded of that point and crediting the same, was the more readily moved to desire the said Elizabeth Romney to be his wife. And she agreeing to that, they were married together about 6 years past, in the chapel within the castle of Bridgnorth, by one Sir William Malpas, that is now dead. And so they dwelled together in the lower town of Bridgnorth, the accused practising the tailor's craft, and travelled forth into the country to get his living and his wife's, and sometimes did not come home for a whole month. Being asked what moved him to marry, he said that he was foully troubled with vermin, and had no help with washing and tending, as was necessary, nor did he have any house to be in. And thus he complained to this woman, and she being troubled (as she said) with certain unruly children of hers, and able to get no peace from them, was content to go with the accused and be his wife. Being asked whether he knew her carnally, as men do their wives, he utterly denies the same, and says that that was neither of their intention.

Being asked how he chanced to come to this town, he says that, now since the Queen's reign, he was moved in his conscience to observe his former profession, and to hire this house here at Stow, where an anchorite had been before.[45] He contrived to let my Lady Gifford[46] know of his intent, not declaring in any way that he was married. And the said Lady Gifford wrote to Sir T[homas] Fitzherbert to move the

45 Stowe, just to the north of Lichfield, whose founder St Chad reputedly used to retire to a chapel here as a hermit in the seventh century.

46 Ursula Throckmorton, wife of Sir Thomas Giffard of Chillington Hall (Staffs.), and thus a member of two of the most prominent Catholic families in the region.

lord bishop in his favour. And so the said Sir Thomas did, and got my lord ⌜bishop⌝'s favour in that respect. Being asked if my lord ⌜bishop⌝ did newly profess him into his religious order, he says 'no', but he did put him into the house, and restored him to his former religious order and profession. Being asked where his wife was when he came hither to be enclosed, he said she was at Bridgnorth, and knew nothing of his intention to return to his religious order. In fact he told her that he meant to go to Lichfield.

And then about last Whitsuntide she came here to search for the accused. And he said that it was agreed between him and her that she should go to Worcester and be an anchoress there, but that she fell sick and was not able to go. Again, being asked when she was last with him, he said that she was with him on Palm Sunday last, and had nothing to do or say to him but to ask him how he did. They asked moreover what moved her to come to town that day. And she said to them that she came for her clothes, that were in the town here. Furthermore, they asked him whether he revealed to Sir Thomas Fitzherbert that he was married. He said 'no', but that he told him that he had a sister, who was a poor woman who was desirous that she should be in attendance on him. And this was the said Elizabeth that he married at Bridgnorth.

For this cause the papists, suspecting the poor hermit to have a wife (as indeed he did), after other molestations enjoined him as penance for this to go before the cross barefoot and barelegged in the cathedral church of Lichfield, with a taper in his hand and I don't know what else. And at Easter they cast him into a close cell, there to remain until he heard more of the bishop's pleasure.

75. Leland's *Itinerary*

One response to the many and rapid changes of the sixteenth century was an attempt to take stock of the English landscape and its history, as a means of asserting and securing English identity: in the words of one of the project's most celebrated exponents, William Camden, 'to restore antiquity to Britain, and Britain to its antiquity' (*Britannia*, first published 1586). One of the earliest of the antiquarians was John Leland (c. 1503–52).[47] He was an important humanist scholar and Latin poet, but he is remembered above all for his efforts during the 1530s to

47 For Leland, see the entry by James P. Carley in *ODNB*.

visit, in the years prior to their dissolution, the English monasteries, and to record the books held in their libraries; and for his journeys around England and Wales, during which he gathered materials for a topographical history of the country. Leland did not complete his ambitious project, and his notes were not published during his lifetime, but they were very influential (Camden, for example, made extensive use of them), and they remain one of our most valuable sources for a medieval world that was vanishing, in some cases having been swept away, but whose memory yet remained.

The Itinerary of John Leland in or about the Years 1535–1543, edited by Lucy Toulmin Smith (5 vols, London: George Bell and Sons, 1907–10), Vol. 1, pp. 27, 154, 6, 84; Vol. 5, p. 38; Vol. 4, p. 62; Vol. 2, pp. 45–6. Leland writes in English, with a sprinkling of Latin: the English is modernised, and the Latin translated and printed in italic.

(i) Ancaster (Lincs.)
Ancaster stands on Watling [Street] as in the high way to Lincoln. It is now but a very poor street, having a small church. An old man told me that it was sometime called Oncaster or Onkaster, but he showed me no reason why. But in times past it has been a celebrate[d] town, but not walled as far as I could perceive. The building of it lay in length by south and north. In [the] south end of it be often-times found in ploughing great square stones of old buildings and Roman coins of brass and silver. In the west end of it, where now meadows be, are found in ditching great vaults. The area where the castle stood is large, and the ditches of it appear, and in some places the foundation of the wall. In the highest ground of the area is now an old chapel dedicated to St Mary, and there is a hermit.

(ii) Sherborne (Dorset)
There was a chapel of St Michael in the town now clean down. There was a chapel of Thomas Becket on the green in Sherborne: it stands, but [is] uncelebrated. There was a hermitage of St John by the mill, now down. There was a hospital begun by devotion of good people in Sherborne in the 4th year of Henry VI, and the king is taken for the founder of it. It stands yet. There is a chapel in St Mary's churchyard. One Dogget, a canon of Salisbury, made it of late days.

(iii) Thrapston (Northants.)
At the very end of Thrapston Bridge stand ruins of a very large hermitage and principally well builded, but of late discovered and sup-

pressed. And hard by is the town of Islip on Avon as upon the farther bank. And about a mile further (but not on the bank of the Avon) is Drayton village and castle, the prettiest place in those quarters.

(iv) Bridge Hewick (N. Yorks.)
There is a fair chapel of freestone on the farther bank of [the River] Ure, at the very end of Hewick bridge, made by a hermit that was a mason. It is not full finished.

(v) Wakefield (W. Yorks.)
Wakefield upon Calder is a very quick [*lively*] market town, and moderately large; well-served of flesh and fish, both from the sea and the rivers, whereof divers be thereabout at hand; so that all vittles are a very good bargain there. A right honest man shall fare well for twopence a meal. In the town is but one chief church. There is a chapel beside where was wont to be *an anchorite in the midst of the town, and sure enough*[48] *she became pregnant.* There is also a chapel of our Lady on Calder Bridge wont to be celebrated *by pilgrims.*

(vi) Richborough (Kent)
The site of the old town or castle is wonderful fair upon a hill. The walls, the which remain there yet, be in compass almost as much as the Tower of London. They have been very high, thick, strong and well embattled. The matter of them is flint, marvellous and long bricks both white and red, after the Britons' fashion. The cement was made of sea-sand and small pebbles. There is a great likelihood that the goodly hill about the castle, and especially towards Sandwich, has been well inhabited. Corn grows on the hill in marvellous plenty, and in going to plough there hath [time] out of mind [been] found, and now is, more antiquities of Roman money than in any place else of England. ... Within the castle is a little parish church of St Augustine, and a hermitage. I had antiquities of the hermit, the which is an industrious man. Not far from the hermitage is a cave where men have sought and dug for treasure. I saw it by candle within, and there were coins. It was so strait [*narrow*] that I had no mind to creep far in. In the north side of the castle is a head in the wall, now sore defaced with weather. They call it Queen Bertha's Head. Near to that place hard by the wall was a pot of Roman money found.

48 Leland introduces this scandalous information (which he puts safely into Latin) with the conjunction *unde*, which generally indicates some kind of loose causal connection, and is often translated 'wherefore'.

(vii) Guy's Cliffe (Warwicks.)[49]

There is a right goodly chapel of St Mary Magdalene upon the river Avon, *on the right bank* scant a mile above Warwick. This place of some is called Gibcliff, of some Guy's Cliff. And old fame remains with the people there that Guy earl of Warwick in King Athelstan's days had a great devotion to this place, and made an oratory there. Some add to it that, after he had done great victories in outward parts, and had been so long absent that he was thought to have been dead, he came and lived in this place like a hermit, unknown to his wife Felicia, until at the point of his death he showed what he was.[50] Men show a cave there in a rock hard on Avon's bank, where they say that he used to sleep. Men also yet show fair springs in a fair bright meadow by there, where they say that Earl Guy was wont to drink. This place had, before the time of Richard earl of Warwick, only a small chapel and a cottage wherein a hermit dwelled.

Earl Richard, bearing a great devotion to the place, made there a goodly new chapel, dedicated to St Mary Magdalene, and founded two chantry priests there to serve God. He set up there an image of Earl Guy great like a giant, and enclosed the silver wells in the meadow with pure white, sleek stone like marble, and there set up a pretty[51] house open like a cage covered, only to keep comers thither from the rain. He also made there a pretty house of stone for the chantry priests by the chapel. The lands that he gave to it lie about the house. It is a place of pleasure, a house meet for the muses. There is silence, a pretty wood, *grottos in the living rock*, the river rolling with a pretty noise over the stones.

76. Redstone Hermitage, Astley

The cave-hermitage at Astley (Worcs.) was sited above an important crossing of the River Severn, on one of the principal routes

49 For the chapel here, and its refoundation by Richard earl of Warwick, see [**26**].

50 Guy was one of the best-known heroes of medieval England. See *Guy of Warwick: icon and ancestor* edited by Alison Wiggins and Rosalind Field (Woodbridge: D.S. Brewer, 2007), and for the Anglo-Norman romance, *Boeve de Haumtone; and, Gui de Warewic: Two Anglo-Norman romances*, trans. Judith Weiss (Tempe, AZ: Arizona Center for Medieval and Renaissance Studies, 2008).

51 A much-used adjective in sixteenth-century English, with a range of meanings: here, perhaps, 'ingenious'; in subsequent sentences, something closer to the modern sense of 'attractive', 'charming'.

between England and Wales. Its strategic importance lies behind the comments of Bishop Hugh Latimer, who wrote in 1538 to Thomas Cromwell, 'Hereby is an hermitage in a rock by Severn, able to lodge 500 men, and as ready for thieves and traitors as true men. I would not have hermits masters of such dens, but rather that some faithful man had it'.[52] It was visited in the early years of the seventeenth century by Thomas Habington (1560–1647). Habington was a courtier and a Catholic and (perhaps inevitably) in the mid-1580s he became associated with a plot against Elizabeth I. He spent six years as a prisoner in the Tower of London following its discovery, while his elder brother was executed for his part. On his release he went to live at his house at Hindlip in Worcestershire, which became a centre for local recusant activity. Though probably innocent, Habington was implicated in the Gunpowder Plot of 1605. He was spared, but spent the remaining forty years of his life in retirement at Hindlip, researching and writing a compendious history of Worcestershire that remains one of the most important sources for the history and topography of the county.[53]

(i) is modernised from Thomas Habington's *A Survey of Worcestershire*, edited by John Amphlett, 2 vols, Worcestershire Historical Society 1–2 (1895–99), Vol. 2, pp. 17–18. (ii) The photograph is copyright Andy Gayne, and used with his permission.

(i) Where Astley at its border with Areley [Kings] joins the Severn there is a great and high rock so near the river that the over-swelling water beats sometimes on it. Here has been, in forepast days, hewn out of the stone a hermitage consisting of a chapel and other rooms, the altars and all formed out of the rock – yea, the chimney rising steeple-height through the stone vents the smoke to the over-topping hill. There is an easy ascent made to this place, which mounts up to avoid the dangerous streams, and a descent also on the other side. Over the altar is painted an archbishop saying mass before all the instruments of our Saviour's passion, and above certain lines now dashed out, declaring (I think) some indulgence to such as frequented here with devotion, which caused me to suppose it was dedicated to St Thomas of Canterbury. But this I refer to a farther enquiry. Other things which

52 *Letters & Papers, Henry VIII*, Vol. 13, part 2, p. 186. For the hermitage's medieval history, see 'Parishes: Astley', in *The Victoria History of the County of Worcester: Vol. 4* edited by William Page (London: The St Catherine Press, 1924), pp. 230–7.

53 See his life by A.J. Loomie in *ODNB*.

I received from uncertain rumours I will rather conceal than hazard myself to father an untruth.

I heard from a gentleman born in this parish who, numbering many years long since, died: that many who trafficked on this river gave as they passed by in their barges somewhat of their commodities in charity to this hermit. And to show how much great princes have valued this place, there appear on the very front of the hermitage the arms of England, between Beauchamp, earl of Warwick, with his crosses croslets[54] on the right hand, and Mortimer, with an escutcheon ermine quartered (as far as I can guess) with a cross on the left. And how long Beauchamps and Mortimers have vanished away, let antiquaries judge; but these monuments of honour are here so worn as they are instantly perishing, wherefore with others so fadeth this world's glory. I will preserve, therefore, within these paper walls what that strong rock cannot keep.

(ii)

54 A cross crosslet in heraldry is a cross, each of whose arms is itself crossed. The arms of the fourteenth-century earl Thomas Beauchamp may be seen at http://commons.wikimedia.org/wiki/File:Thomas_de_Beauchamp_Arms.svg.

BIBLIOGRAPHY

Manuscripts

Cambridge: Corpus Christi College, MS 79
St John's College, SJCA/D91/13; SJCA/D91/20; SJCA/D91/21
Cambridge University Library, MS Mm.3.21
Chester: Cheshire Archives and Local Studies ZSB 1
Chippenham: Wiltshire & Swindon History Centre, Episcopal Registers, 'Register of John Chaundler'
Durham: Durham University Library, Durham Cathedral Archive, Reg. Lang
Exeter: Devon Record Office, Exeter diocesan records, Chanter Catalogue 8
Hertford: Hertfordshire Archives and Local Studies, 1AR
Lewes: East Sussex Record Office, RYE/60/5; RYE/147/1
Lincoln: Lincolnshire Archives Office, Episcopal Register 3; Formulary 2
London: Lambeth Palace Library, LPL 1
Metropolitan Archives, COL/CA/01/01/005
The National Archives, TNA C1/142/40; TNA C66/89; TNA C66/94; TNA CHES 2/129; TNA DL 27/119; TNA SC 8/25/1232; TNA SC 8/150/7470; TNA SP 1/93; TNA SP 1/95; TNA SP 1/134
Maidstone: Kent Archives and Local History Service, DCb/PRC17/20/30; PRC 17/9/150
Northallerton: North Yorkshire County Record Office, ZDV I 80
Norwich: Norfolk Record Office, NCR Case 16c/2; Norwich Consistory Court Will Register Wymer
Oxford: Bodleian Library, MS Tanner 176
Corpus Christi College, MS 320
St John's College, MS 94
Taunton: Somerset Record Office, D/D/B. Reg. 1
Worcester: Worcestershire Record Office, x716.093/BA2648/Parcel 1(i)
York: Borthwick Institute for Archives, York Abp Reg 16

Printed sources

Aelred of Rievaulx. *De Institutione Inclusarum. Two English Versions*. Ed. John Ayto and Alexandra Barratt. Early English Text Society, original series 287 (1984).

Allen, H.E. *Writings Ascribed to Richard Rolle Hermit of Hampole and Materials for His Biography*. New York, 1927.

Alexander, James W. *Ranulf of Chester, a Relic of the Conquest.* Athens: University of Georgia Press, 1983.

André, J. Lewis. 'Compton Church.' *Surrey Archaeological Collections* 12 (1895): 1–19.

Anon. *Collegium divi Johannis Evangelistae 1511–1911.* Cambridge: Cambridge University Press, 1911.

Anon. 'The Last Ancress of Whalley.' *Historic Society of Lancashire and Cheshire* 64 (1912): 268–72.

Anson, Peter F. *The Call of the Desert: The solitary life in the Christian church.* London: SPCK, 1964.

Baker, T.F.T., ed. *A History of the County of Middlesex: Vol. 6: Friern Barnet, Finchley, Hornsey with Highgate.* London: Oxford University Press for the Institute of Historical Research, 1980.

Bannister, Arthur Thomas, ed. *The Register of Charles Bothe, Bishop of Hereford (1516–1535).* Cantilupe Society. Hereford: Wilson and Phillips, 1921.

Barnum, P.H., ed. *Dives and Pauper,* vol. 1, part 2. Early English Text Society, original series 280 (1980).

Barratt, Alexandra. 'Creating an Anchorhold.' In *Medieval Christianity in Practice,* edited by Miri Rubin, pp. 311–17. Princeton: Princeton University Press, 2009.

Barron, Caroline M. *London in the Later Middle Ages: Government and people 1200–1500.* Oxford: Oxford University Press, 2010.

Bartlett, Anne Clark, and Bestul, Thomas H., eds. *Cultures of Piety: Medieval English devotional literature in translation.* Ithaca: Cornell University Press, 1999.

Bell, Maurice, ed. *Wulfric of Haselbury [by] John, Abbot of Ford.* Somerset Record Society 47 (1933).

Benedict of Nursia. *The Rule of Saint Benedict in Latin and in English with Notes.* Edited and translated by Timothy Fry OSB. Collegeville: The Liturgical Press, 1981.

Benson, C. David. 'Piers Plowman as Poetic Pillory: The pillory and the cross.' In *Medieval Literature and Historical Inquiry: Essays in honor of Derek Pearsall* edited by David Aers, pp. 31–54. Cambridge: D.S. Brewer, 2000.

Binski, Paul, and Zutshi, Patrick. *Western Illuminated Manuscripts: A catalogue of the collection in Cambridge university library.* Cambridge: Cambridge University Press, 2011.

Bliss, W.H., ed. *Calendar of Papal Registers Relating to Great Britain and Ireland: Petitions to the Pope: Vol. 1: 1342–1419.* London: HMSO, 1896.

Bliss, W.H., and Johnson, C., eds. *Calendar of Papal Registers Relating to Great Britain and Ireland. Vol. 3: 1342–1362.* London: HMSO, 1897.

Bliss, W.H., and Twemlow, J.A., eds. *Calendar of Papal Registers Relating to Great Britain and Ireland: Vol. 5: 1398–1404.* London: HMSO, 1904.

Blomefield, Francis. *An essay towards a topographical history of Norfolk. containing a description of the towns, villages, and hamlets …* 4 vols. London: W. Miller, 1805.

Bottomley, Frank, trans. 'Office for the Benediction of Hermits (16th century).' Available from www.hermitary.com/articles/benediction.html.

Brigg, William, ed. *The Herts Genealogist and Antiquary*. 3 vols. Harpenden: William Brigg, 1895–99.

Brocklesbury, R., ed. *The Register of William Melton, Archbishop of York, 1317–1340*. Vol. 4. Canterbury & York Society 85 (1997).

Brown, William, ed. *Register of William Wickwane, Lord Archbishop of York 1279–85*. Surtees Society 114 (1907).

Brownbill, John, ed. *The Ledger Book of Vale Royal Abbey*. Record Society of Lancashire and Cheshire 68 (1914).

Calendar of Close Rolls, Edward I: Volume 1, 1272–1279. Edited by H.C. Maxwell Lyte. London: HMSO, 1900.

Campbell, Gordon. *The Hermit in the Garden: From imperial Rome to ornamental gnome*. Oxford: Oxford University Press, 2013.

Chaucer, Geoffrey. *The Riverside Chaucer*. Edited by Larry D. Benson. 3rd edition, Boston: Houghton Mifflin, 1987.

Clark, Andrew, ed. *Survey of the Antiquities of the City of Oxford … by Anthony Wood: Vol. 2: Churches and Religious Houses*. Oxford Historical Society 17 (1890).

Clay, Rotha Mary. 'Further Studies on Medieval Recluses.' *The Journal of the British Archaeological Association* 3rd series, 16 (1953): 74–86.

——, 'Some Northern Anchorites.' *Archaeologica Aeliana* 4th series, 33 (1955): 202–17.

Colegate, Isabel. *A Pelican in the Wilderness: Hermits, solitaries and recluses*. London: HarperCollins, 2002.

Cox, J. Charles. *Notes on the Churches of Derbyshire*. 4 vols. Chesterfield: W. Edmunds, 1875–79.

Cressy, David. *Dangerous Talk: Scandalous, seditious and treasonable speech in pre-modern England*. Oxford: Oxford University Press, 2010.

Crossley, Alan, ed. *A History of the County of Oxford: Vol. 12, Wootton Hundred (South) Including Woodstock*. Oxford: Oxford University Press for the Institute of Historical Research, 1990.

Cullum, P.H. 'Vowesses and Female Lay Piety in the Province of York, 1300–1530.' *Northern History* 32 (1996): 21–41.

Darwin, Francis D. *The English Mediaeval Recluse*. London: SPCK, 1944.

Davis, Virginia. 'The Rule of St Paul the First Hermit in England in the Later Middle Ages.' In *Monks, Hermits and the Ascetic Tradition* edited by W.J. Sheils, pp. 203–14. Studies in Church History 22. London: Wiley-Blackwell, 1985.

Dean, James M. *Six Ecclesiastical Satires*. Kalamazoo: Medieval Institute Publications, 1991.

De Boer, George. *A History of the Spurn Lighthouses*. York: East Yorkshire Local History Society, 1968.

Deedes, Cecil, ed. *The Episcopal Register of Robert Rede, ordinis predicatorum, Lord Bishop of Chichester, 1397–1415: Part I*. Sussex Record Society 8 (1908).

Dodd, J. Phillip. 'The Anchoress of Frodsham 1240–1280.' *Cheshire History* 8 (1981): 30–51.

Dowding, Clare M. '"Item receyvyd of ye Anker": The relationships between a parish and its anchorites as seen through the churchwardens' accounts.' In *Anchorites in Their Communities* edited by Cate Gunn and Liz Herbert McAvoy, pp. 117–30. Cambridge: D.S. Brewer, 2017.

Duffy, Eamon. *The Stripping of the Altars: Traditional religion in England 1400–1580.* 2nd ed. New Haven, CT: Yale University Press, 2005.

Dugdale, William, Dodsworth, Roger, Stevens, John, Caley, John, Ellis, Sir Henry, Bandinel, Bulkeley, and Taylor, Richard C. *Monasticon Anglicanum.* 6 vols in 8. London: Longman, Hurst, Rees, Orme & Brown, 1817–30.

Duncan, Leland L., ed. *Testamenta Cantiana.* London: Mitchell Hughes and Clarke, 1906.

Dunkin, John. *The History and Antiquities of Dartford.* London: privately printed, 1844.

Dunn, F.I. 'Hermits, Anchorites and Recluses: A study with reference to medieval Norwich.' In *Julian and Her Norwich: Commemorative Essays and Handbook to the Exhibition 'Revelations of Divine Love'* edited by Frank Dale Sayer, pp. 18–26. Norwich: Celebration Committee, 1973.

Dunning, R.W., ed. *A History of the County of Somerset: Vol. 3.* London: Oxford University Press for the Institute of Historical Research, 1974.

Dunstan, G.R., ed. *The Register of Edmund Lacy, Bishop of Exeter, 1420–1455: Registrum Commune,* 5 vols. Canterbury & York Society 60–3, 66 (1963–71).

Ellis, Henry, ed. *Original Letters illustrative of English History, including numerous royal letters, from autographs in the British Museum … and one or two other collections,* 3rd series. 4 vols. London: Richard Bentley, 1846.

Elton, G.R. *Policy and Police: The enforcement of the Reformation in the age of Thomas Cromwell.* Cambridge: Cambridge University Press, 1972.

Erler, Mary C. 'Margery Kempe's White Clothes.' *Medium Aevum* 62 (1993): 78–83.

——, *Women, Reading, and Piety in Late Medieval England.* Cambridge: Cambridge University Press, 2002.

——, '"A Revelation of Purgatory" (1422): Reform and the politics of female visions.' *Viator* 38 (2007): 321–83.

——, *Reading and Writing During the Dissolution: Monks, friars, and nuns 1530-1558.* Cambridge: Cambridge University Press, 2013.

Farrer, William, and Brownbill, J., eds. *The Victoria History of the County of Lancaster.* Vol. 4. London: Constable and Company Limited, 1911.

Fowler, R.C., ed. *Registrum Radulphi Baldock, Gilberti Segrave, Ricardi Newport et Stephani Gravesend, Episcoporum Londoniensium, A.D. 1306–1338.* Canterbury & York Society 7 (1911).

Foxe, John. *The Unabridged Acts and Monuments Online* or *TAMO.* Sheffield: HRI Online Publications, 2011. Available from: www.johnfoxe.org.

Friedberg, Emile, ed. *Corpus iuris canonici.* 2 vols. Leipzig: Tauchnitz, 1879–81.

Gairdner, James. 'A Letter Concerning Bishop Fisher and Sir Thomas More.' *English Historical Review* 7 (1892): 712–15.

Gee, Henry, and William John Hardy, eds. *Documents illustrative of English church history.* London: Macmillan, 1896.

Gilchrist, Roberta. *Contemplation and Action: The other monasticism.* London: Leicester University Press, 1995.
Gillespie, Vincent. '*Lukynge in haly bukes*: *Lectio* in some late medieval spiritual miscellanies.' *Analecta Cartusiana* 106 (1984): 1–27.
Gillespie, Vincent, and Kantik Ghosh, eds. *After Arundel: Religious writing in fifteenth-century England.* Turnhout: Brepols, 2011.
Godfrey, Walter H. 'Church of St. Anne, Lewes: An anchorite's cell and other discoveries.' *Sussex Archaeological Collections* 69 (1928): 159–69.
Goldberg, P.J.P., ed. *Women in England c. 1275–1525: Documentary sources.* Manchester: Manchester University Press, 1995.
Gransden, Antonia. 'The Reply of a Fourteenth-century Abbot of Bury St. Edmunds to a Man's Petition to Be a Recluse.' *English Historical Review* 75 (1960): 464–7.
——, *A History of the Abbey of Bury St Edmunds, 1257–1301.* Woodbridge: The Boydell Press, 2015.
Gray, Madeleine. 'Ritual Space and Ritual Burial in the Early Modern Christian Tradition.' In *Faith of Our Fathers* edited by Joan Allen and Richard C. Allen, pp. 11–25. Newcastle-upon-Tyne: Cambridge Scholars Press, 2009.
Green, Emanuel, ed. *The Survey and Rental of the Chantries, Colleges and Free Chapels … in the County of Somerset.* Somerset Record Society 2 (1888).
Grossus, Geoffrey. *The Life of Blessed Bernard of Tiron.* Translated by Ruth Harwood Cline. Washington, DC: The Catholic University of America Press, 2009.
Gunn, Cate. 'Was There an Anchoress at Colne Priory?' *Transactions of the Essex Society for Archaeology and History* 4/2 (2011–13): 117–23.
Habington, Thomas. *A Survey of Worcestershire.* 2 vols. Edited by John Amphlett. Worcestershire Historical Society 1–2 (1895–99).
Hanna, Ralph. 'Will's Work.' In *Written Work: Langland, labor, and authorship* edited by Steven Justice and Kathryn Kerby-Fulton, pp. 23–66. Philadelphia: University of Pennsylvania Press, 1997.
——, *A Descriptive Catalogue of the Western Medieval Manuscripts of St John's College, Oxford.* Oxford: Oxford University Press, 2002.
——, *English Manuscripts of Richard Rolle: A descriptive catalogue.* Exeter: University of Exeter Press, 2010.
Hardy, T.D., ed. *Rotuli litterarum clausarum in Turri londinensi asservati.* 2 vols. London: Eyre & Spottiswoode, 1833, 1844.
Harley, Marta Powell. *A Revelation of Purgatory by an Unknown, Fifteenth-century Woman Visionary.* Lewiston, NY: Edwin Mellen Press, 1985.
Harmless, William. *Desert Christians: An introduction to the literature of early monasticism.* Oxford: Oxford University Press, 2004.
Harris, B.E., ed. *A History of the County of Chester: Vol. 3.* London: Oxford University Press for the Institute of Historical Research, 1980.
Hill, Rosalind M.T., ed. *The Register of William Melton, Archbishop of York 1317–1340.* Vol. III. Canterbury & York Society 76 (1988).
Hingeston-Randolph, F.C., ed. *The Register of Edmund Stafford, 1395–1419, an index and abstract of its contents.* London: Bell, 1886.

Hobhouse, E., ed. *Calendar of the register of John De Drokensford, Bishop of Bath and Wells, A.D. 1309–1329.* Somerset Record Society 1 (1887).

Holder, Nick. *The Friaries of Medieval London: From foundation to dissolution.* Woodbridge: Boydell Press, 2017.

Holdsworth, Christopher. 'Hermits and the Power of the Frontier.' *Reading Medieval Studies* 16 (1990): 55–76.

Horstman, Carl. *Yorkshire Writers: Richard Rolle of Hampole, an English Father of the Church, and His Followers.* 2 vols. London: Swan Sonnenschein & Co., 1895–6.

Hudson, Anne. *The Premature Reformation: Wycliffite texts and Lollard history.* Oxford: Clarendon Press, 1988.

Hughes, J.B., ed. *The Register of Walter Langton, Bishop of Coventry and Lichfield: Vol. 2: 1296–1321.* Canterbury & York Society 97 (2007).

Hughes-Edwards, Mari. 'Hedgehog Skins and Hairshirts: The changing role of asceticism in the anchoritic ideal.' *Mystics Quarterly* 28 (2002): 6–26.

——, *Reading Medieval Anchoritism: Ideology and spiritual practices.* Cardiff: University of Wales Press, 2012.

——, 'Solitude and Sociability: The world of the medieval anchorite.' *Historic Churches* magazine, 2012. Available from: www.buildingconservation.com/articles/anchorites/anchorites.htm.

Hussey, Arthur, ed. *Kent Chantries.* Kent Archaeological Society 12 (1936).

Innes-Parker, Catherine. 'Medieval Widowhood and Textual Guidance: The Corpus revisions of *Ancrene Wisse* and the de Braose anchoresses.' *Florilegium* 28 (2011): 95–124.

Jones, E.A. 'Langland and Hermits.' *Yearbook of Langland Studies* 11 (1997): 67–86.

——, 'The Hermits and Anchorites of Oxfordshire.' *Oxoniensia* 63 (1998): 51–77.

——, 'A New Look into the *Speculum Inclusorum.*' In *The Medieval Mystical Tradition: England, Ireland and Wales* edited by Marion Glasscoe, pp. 123–45. (Exeter Symposium VI) Cambridge: D.S. Brewer, 1999.

——, 'Canons and Hermits: The chapel of St Simon and St Jude, Coverdale.' *Yorkshire Archaeological Journal* 76 (2004): 153–69.

——, 'Christina of Markyate and the *Hermits and Anchorites of England.*' In *Christina of Markyate: A twelfth-century holy woman* edited by Samuel Fanous and Henrietta Leyser, pp. 229–53. London: Routledge, 2004.

——, 'Hermits and Anchorites in Historical Context.' In *Teaching Anchorites and Mystics* edited by Roger Ellis, Dee Dyas and Valerie Edden, pp. 3–18. Cambridge: D.S. Brewer, 2005.

——, 'A Mystic by Any Other Name: Julian(?) of Norwich.' *Mystics Quarterly* 33/3–4 (2007): 1–17.

——, 'Anchoritic Aspects of Julian of Norwich.' In *A Companion to Julian of Norwich* edited by Liz Herbert McAvoy, pp. 75–87. Woodbridge: Boydell & Brewer, 2008.

——, 'Ceremonies of Enclosure: Rite, Rhetoric and Reality.' In *Rhetoric of the Anchorhold: space, place and body within the discourses of enclosure* edited by Liz Herbert McAvoy, pp. 34–49. Cardiff: University of Wales Press, 2008.

——, 'Vae Soli! Solitaries and Pastoral Care.' In *Texts and Traditions of Medieval Pastoral Care* edited by Cate Gunn and Catherine Innes-Parker, pp. 11–28. Woodbridge: York Medieval Press, 2009.

——, 'Rites of Enclosure: The English *Ordines* for the enclosing of anchorites, s. xii–s. xvi.' *Traditio* 67 (2012): 145–234.

——, 'Hidden Lives: Methodological reflections on a new database of the hermits and anchorites of medieval England.' *Medieval Prosopography* 28 (2013): 17–34.

——, *Speculum Inclusorum / A Mirror for Recluses: A late-medieval guide for anchorites and its Middle English translation.* Liverpool: Liverpool University Press, 2013.

——, '*A Mirror for Recluses*: A new manuscript, new information and some new hypotheses', *The Library* 7/15 (2014): 424–31.

——, 'O Sely Ankir.' In *Anchorites in Their Communities* edited by Cate Gunn and Liz Herbert McAvoy, pp. 13–34. Cambridge: D.S. Brewer, 2017.

Jones, Michael K., and Underwood, Malcolm G. *The King's Mother.* Cambridge: Cambridge University Press, 1992.

Kempe, Margery. *The Book of Margery Kempe.* Translated by B.A. Windeatt. Harmondsworth: Penguin, 1985.

Kerling, Nellie J.M., ed. *Cartulary of St. Bartholomew's Hospital, Founded 1123: A calendar.* London: St Bartholomew's Hospital, 1973.

Kerry, Charles. 'Hermits, Fords, and Bridge Chapels.' *Journal of the Derbyshire Archaeological and Natural History Society* 14 (1892): 54–71.

Kirby, Joan, ed. *The York Sede Vacante Register 1423–1426: A calendar.* York: Borthwick Publications, 2009.

Kitching, C.J., ed. *London and Middlesex Chantry Certificate 1548.* London Record Society 16 (1980).

Lander, Jeremy. 'The Sacristy, the Church of St. Mary & All Saints, Willingham, Cambridgeshire: The case for an anchorhold' (2005), www.oldwillingham.com/History/SMAS/Lander/Lander.htm (accessed 21 June 2018).

Langland, William. *The Vision of Piers Plowman.* Edited by A.V.C. Schmidt. London: J.M. Dent, 1995.

——, *Piers Plowman. The C-Text.* Edited by Derek Pearsall. Exeter: University of Exeter Press, 1994.

Leland, John. *The Itinerary of John Leland in or about the Years 1535–1543.* Edited by Lucy Toulmin Smith. 5 vols. London: George Bell and Sons, 1907–10.

Leyser, Henrietta. *Hermits and the New Monasticism.* London: Macmillan Press, 1984.

Licence, Tom. *Hermits & Recluses in English Society 950–1200.* Oxford: Oxford University Press, 2011.

Lumby, Joseph Rawson, ed. *Polychronicon Ranulphi Higden monachi Cestrensis.* Vol. 7. Rolls Series. London: Longman & Co., 1879.

Lyndwood, William. *Provinciale, seu Constitutiones Angliae.* 1679. Reprint, Farnborough: Gregg, 1968.

McAvoy, Liz Herbert. *Medieval Anchoritisms: Gender, space and the solitary life.* Woodbridge: D.S. Brewer, 2011.

——, 'Gender, Rhetoric and Space in the *Speculum Inclusorum, Letter to a Bury Recluse* and the Strange Case of Christina Carpenter.' In *Rhetoric of the Anchorhold: Space, place and body within the discourses of enclosure* edited by Liz Herbert McAvoy, pp. 111–26. Cardiff: University of Wales Press, 2008.

——, ed. *Rhetoric of the Anchorhold: Space, place and body within the discourses of enclosure.* Cardiff: University of Wales Press, 2008.

——, ed. *Anchoritic Traditions of Medieval Europe.* Woodbridge: The Boydell Press, 2010.

——, trans. *A Revelation of Purgatory.* Cambridge: D.S. Brewer, 2017.

McCann, Alison. 'The Chapel of St. Cyriac, Chichester.' *Sussex Archaeological Collections* 113 (1975): 197–9.

McHardy, A.K. 'Bishop Buckingham and the Lollards of Lincoln Diocese.' In *Schism, Heresy and Religious Protest* edited by Derek Baker, pp. 131–45. Studies in Church History 9. Cambridge: Cambridge University Press, 1972.

——, ed. *Royal Writs Addressed to John Buckingham, Bishop of Lincoln 1363–1398.* Canterbury & York Society 86 (1997).

Malden, H.E. *The Victoria History of the County of Surrey: Vol. 3.* London: Constable and Company Limited, 1911.

Marshall, Edward. *The early history of Woodstock manor and its environs, in Bladon, Hensington, New Woodstock, Blenheim: with later notices.* Oxford: James Parker & Co., 1873.

Martin, G.H., ed. *Knighton's Chronicle 1337–1396.* Oxford: Clarendon Press, 1995.

Maxwell-Lyte, H.C. and Dawes, M.C.B., eds. *The Register of Thomas Bekynton, Bishop of Bath and Wells, 1443–1465.* 2 vols. Somerset Record Society 49–50 (1934–5).

Mayhew, Graham. *Tudor Rye.* Falmer: Centre for Continuing Education, University of Sussex, 1987.

Mayr-Harting, Henry. 'Functions of a Twelfth-century Recluse.' *History* 60 (1975): 337–52.

Middleton, Anne. 'Acts of Vagrancy: The C version "autobiography" and the statute of 1388.' In *Written Work: Langland, labor, and authorship* edited by Steven Justice and Kathryn Kerby-Fulton, pp. 208–317. Philadelphia: University of Pennsylvania Press, 1997.

Morris, Colin. *The Sepulchre of Christ and the Medieval West: From the beginning to 1600.* Oxford: Oxford University Press, 2008.

Musson, Anthony, with Edward Powell, trans. and ed. *Crime, Law and Society in the Later Middle Ages.* Manchester: Manchester University Press, 2009.

Nicolas, Nicholas Harris, ed. *The Privy Purse Expences of King Henry the Eighth, from November MDXXIX, to December MDXXXII.* London: W. Pickering, 1827.

Nugent, Elizabeth M., ed. *The Thought and Culture of the English Renaissance: An anthology of Tudor prose, 1481–1555*. London: Cambridge University Press, 1956.

O'Clabaigh, Colman. 'Anchorites in Late Medieval Ireland.' In *Anchoritic Traditions of Medieval Europe* edited by Liz Herbert McAvoy, pp. 153–77. Woodbridge: The Boydell Press, 2010.

Oliger, Livarius. 'Regulae tres reclusorum et eremitarum Angliae saec. XIII–XIV.' *Antonianum* 3 (1928): 151–90; 299–320.

——, 'Regula Reclusorum Angliae et Quaestiones tres de Vita solitaria saec. XIII–XIV.' *Antonianum* 9 (1934): 37–84; 243–68.

Oliva, Marilyn. *The Convent and the Community in Late Medieval England: Female monasteries in the diocese of Norwich, 1350–1540*. Woodbridge: Boydell Press, 1998.

Orme, Nicholas. 'Church and Chapel in Medieval England'. *Transactions of the Royal Historical Society* 6 (1996): 75–102.

Page, William, ed. *The Certificates of the Commissioners appointed to survey the Chantries, Guilds, Hospitals, etc. in the County of York*. Vol. 2. Surtees Society 92 (1892).

——, *A History of the County of Hertford*. Vol. 2. London: Archibald Constable and Company Limited, 1908.

——, *The Victoria History of the County of London: Vol. One: Including London within the Bars, Westminster and Southwark*. London: The University of London, 1909.

——, *The Victoria History of the County of Worcester*. Vol. 4. London: The St Catherine Press, 1924.

Pezzini, Domenico. 'An Edition of Three Late Middle English Versions of a Fourteenth-Century Regula Heremitarum.' *Leeds Studies in English* 40 (2009): 65–104.

Power, Eileen. *Medieval English Nunneries, c. 1275 to 1535*. Cambridge: Cambridge University Press, 1922.

Powicke, F.M. and Cheney, C.R., eds. *Councils and Synods with Other Documents Relating to the English Church*. 2 vols. Oxford: Clarendon Press, 1964.

Raine, James, ed. *The injunctions and other ecclesiastical proceedings of Richard Barnes, Bishop of Durham from 1575 to 1587*. Surtees Society 22 (1850).

——, *Testamenta Eboracensia: A selection of wills from the registry of York*. Vol. 3. Surtees Society 45 (1865).

Rice, Nicole. *Lay Piety and Religious Discipline in Middle English Literature*. Cambridge: Cambridge University Press, 2008.

Riddy, Felicity. 'Julian of Norwich and Self-Textualization.' In *Editing Women* edited by Ann M. Hutchison, pp. 101–24. Cardiff: University of Wales Press, 1998.

Riley, H.T. *Memorials of London and London Life in the 13th, 14th and 15th Centuries*. London: Corporation of London, 1868.

Roach, J.P.C., ed. *A History of the County of Cambridge and the Isle of Ely: Vol. 3: The City and University of Cambridge*. London: Oxford University Press for the Institute of Historical Research, 1959.

Robertson, Elizabeth. 'An Anchorhold of Her Own: Female anchoritic literature in thirteenth century England.' In *Equally in God's Image: Women in the Middle Ages* edited by Julia Bolton Holloway, Constance S. Wright and Joan Bechtold, pp. 170–83. New York: P. Lang, 1990.

Rogers, James E. Thorold, ed. *Loci e Libro veritatum: Passages selected from Gascoigne's theological dictionary illustrating the condition of church and state, 1403–1458.* Oxford: Clarendon Press, 1881.

Rolle, Richard. 'The Form of Living.' In *English Writings of Richard Rolle, Hermit of Hampole* edited by H.E. Allen. Oxford: Clarendon Press, 1931.

Ross, Charles, ed. *The Rous Roll: With an historical introduction on John Rous and the Warwick Roll by Charles Ross.* Gloucester: A. Sutton, 1980.

Rotuli Parliamentorum: ut et petitiones et placita in parliamento Tempore Henrici R. V. London: HMSO, 1777.

Rubin, Miri. 'An English Anchorite: The making, unmaking and remaking of Christine Carpenter.' In *Pragmatic Utopias: Ideals and communities, 1200–1630* edited by Rosemary Horrox and Sarah Rees Jones, pp. 204–23. Cambridge: Cambridge University Press, 2001.

Rymer, Thomas. *Foedera.* 10 vols. The Hague: Joannes Neulme, 1739–45.

Sansterre, Jean-Marie. 'Le monachisme bénédictin d'Italie et les bénédictins italiens en France face au renouveau de l'érémitisme à la fin du Xe et au XIe siècle.' In *Ermites de France et d'Italie (XIe–XVe siècle)* edited by André Vauchez, pp. 29–46. Rome: École française de Rome, 2003.

Scott, Kathleen L. *A Survey of Manuscripts Illuminated in the British Isles: Vol .6: Later Gothic manuscripts 1390–1490.* 2 vols. London: Harvey Miller, 1996.

Shalev, Zur. 'Christian Pilgrimage and Ritual Measurement in Jerusalem.' La misura, *Micrologus* 19 (2011): 131–50.

Sharpe, Reginald R., ed. *Calendar of Letter-Books of the City of London: A, 1275–1298.* London: HMSO, 1899.

Sheehan, Michael M. 'The Formation and Stability of Marriage in Fourteenth-century England: Evidence of an Ely register'. *Mediaeval Studies* 33 (1971): 228–63.

Silver, Ray. 'The Anchorite's Cell at Kingston Buci.' *Sussex County Magazine* 1 (1927): 144.

Sinclair, Alexandra, ed. *The Beauchamp Pageant.* Donington: Richard III and Yorkist History Trust in association with Paul Watkins, 2003.

Smith, David M. 'Suffragan Bishops in the Medieval Diocese of Lincoln.' *Lincolnshire History and Archaeology* 17 (1982): 17–27.

Statutes of the Realm. 11 vols. London: Dawsons of Pall Mall, 1810–28.

Stephens, W.B., ed. *A History of the County of Warwick: Vol. 8: The city of Coventry and borough of Warwick.* London: Oxford University Press for the Institute of Historical Research, 1969.

Stewart-Brown, R., ed. *Cheshire in the Pipe Rolls, 1158–1301.* Lancashire and Cheshire Record Society 92 (1938).

Storey, Anthony. *Mount Grace Lady Chapel: An historical enquiry.* Beverley: Highgate Publications, 2001.

Storey, R.L., ed. *The Register of Thomas Langley, Bishop of Durham 1406–1437*. Vol. 4. Surtees Society 170 (1961).

Swanson, R.N., ed. *A Calendar of the Register of Richard Scrope, Archbishop of York, 1398–1405*, Part 1, Borthwick Texts and Calendars 8. York: Borthwick Institute of Historical Research, 1981.

Tanner, Norman P. *The Church in Late Medieval Norwich: 1370–1532*. Toronto: Pontifical Institute of Mediaeval Studies, 1984.

Townsend, George. *The Acts and Monuments of John Foxe, with a Life of the Martyrologist, and Vindication of his Work*. 8 vols. London: Seeley, Burnside & Seeley, 1843–49.

Turner, Edward. 'Domus Anachoritae, Aldrington.' *Sussex Archaeological Collections* 12 (1860): 117–39.

Twemlow, J.A., ed. *Calendar of Entries in the Papal Registers Relating to Great Britain and Ireland: Vol. 12: 1458–1471*. London: HMSO, 1933.

Van Engen, John. 'Multiple Options: The world of the fifteenth-century church.' *Church History* 77 (2008): 257–84.

Watson, Nicholas. *Richard Rolle and the Invention of Authority*. Cambridge: Cambridge University Press, 1991.

Watson, Nicholas, and Jenkins, Jacqueline, eds. *The Writings of Julian of Norwich: A vision showed to a devout woman and a revelation of love*. Turnhout: Brepols, 2006.

Watt, Diane. *Secretaries of God: Women prophets in late medieval and early modern England*. Cambridge: D.S. Brewer, 1997.

Weaver, F.W., ed. *Somerset Medieval Wills: Second series: 1501–1530, with some Somerset wills preserved at Lambeth*. Somerset Record Society 19 (1903).

Weiss, Judith, trans. *Boeve de Haumtone and Gui de Warewic: Two Anglo-Norman romances*. Tempe: Arizona Center for Medieval and Renaissance Studies, 2008.

Wesker, Arnold. *Arnold Wesker's Historical Plays*. London: Oberon Books, 2012.

Westlake, H.F. *St. Margaret's Westminster: The church of the House of Commons*. London: Smith, Elder & Co., 1914.

Whitaker, Thomas D. *An History of the original Parish of Whalley and Honor of Clitheroe ... To which is subjoined an account of the Parish of Cartmell ...* 4th edition. 2 vols. London: George Routledge & Sons, 1872–76.

Wiggins, Alison and Field Rosalind, eds. *Guy of Warwick: Icon and ancestor*. Woodbridge: D.S. Brewer, 2007.

Williams, C.H., ed. *English Historical Documents: Vol. V: 1485–1588*. London: Eyre & Spottiswoode, 1967.

Wilson, H.A. *The Pontifical of Magdalen College, with an Appendix of Extracts from Other English Mss. of the Twelfth Century*. Henry Bradshaw Society 39 (1910).

Windeatt, Barry, ed. *English Mystics of the Middle Ages*. Cambridge: Cambridge University Press, 1994.

Wolfe, Heather. 'Interrogating a Hermit', *The Collation*, 20 October 2011. http://collation.folger.edu/2011/10/interrogating-a-hermit. Accessed 21 July 2015.

INDEX

The index includes names of all hermits and anchorites, and their patrons, and those places associated directly with them. Hermits are designated by (H) after their name, anchorites by (A). Solitaries identified in the sources only by their first name are listed under their place of residence, with cross-references. Saints (e.g. Godric, Wulfric) are indexed under their first names, as is Julian of Norwich (following common usage). Place-names are further identified by their historical counties. Where the same subject appears in two or more successive sources this can produce overlapping index entries (thus, for example, wills 46, 60–1, 61–3, etc.). The index was compiled with the assistance of Katie Ashcroft-Jones.

Milton Keynes UK
Ingram Content Group UK Ltd.
UKHW040730150823
426904UK00001B/96

9 781526 127235